Contents

EDITOR'S PREFACE

The re-issue of a series of books after fifteen years' exploitation of its field invites justification and prompts reflection. The justification – other than what lies in the qualities of the books themselves – is simply that no comparable series has appeared to replace it. Our purpose was to sum up what had so far been achieved in the rather new study of 'war and society' and to make it available as an attractive accompaniment to the Fontana and other general series on the history of Europe and its empires. That we were right to sense a need for such enlargement of view on the military side, has been amply confirmed by the army of historians and history-minded social scientists who have continued active in the field, and whose relevant contributions will be duly noted in our revised reading lists. Some of them, especially in the United States, march under the banner of 'the new military history'; which however boils down to much the same thing as was meant by the 'war and society' pioneers, a generation ago. The more recent writers evidently having shared with the earlier ones the aim of distinguishing their historical operations from those of the 'old' military history, it seems worth while to reconsider what I wrote about the series' purposes and principles, fifteen years or so ago.

The 'war and society' movement took shape in the 1960s, to make good what had come to be felt as something missing in the traditional style of histories of wars and warfare. Although the latter had paid much attention to what armed forces did to one another in war, they normally showed little interest in how those armed forces related to the societies from which they were drawn and in what war itself – the experience of it while it was going on, the perhaps huge net effect of it once it was over – did to the societies which engaged in it. The years 1935–1945 were crucial to the new perception. Each of the Second World War's major participants experienced social mobilization on a scale of totality historically unprecedented. Even before it was over, official histories of it were being planned to do justice to everything that happened away from the firing lines as well as on them; and those who survived it tended to feel sure that it must have caused great social changes. Particular inquiries into this latter possibility were what brought to the forefront of the movement the historian who more than anyone else launched 'war and society' as a viable and (to the limited extent that any area of historical studies can be so) self-sufficient branch of historical studies. Arthur Marwick effected this notable step forward when his history department at the Open University produced in 1973 its famous third-year course 'War and Society', in which pretty well every apposite part of the field came into view. About five thousand students took this course during its six years' lifetime, the teaching units expressly produced for it acquired a wide circulation, and some of them remain among the best things so far written. (Nor is that the end of the story; over six thousand students have, by the time of writing, taken its successor 'War, Peace and Social Change'.)

This new approach to war history's popularity was no doubt partly because it offered to those who disliked war (numerous indeed after the Second World War, and subsequently under the shadow of nuclear weapons) a way of studying war without what seemed to them its rebarbative and retrogressive aspects. From certain morally committed standpoints the new approach might appear to be positively progressive. After all, it was happening during the same years as the movement within the social sciences to learn more about the causes of war – and thus a hoped-for preventability of war – than had been made apparent in the well-established genres of political and diplomatic history. From the traditional point of view, these were the very novelties and connections which invited criticism. Practitioners of military history proper, continuing to work within the parameters of the tradition, pointed out that the new fashion, too enthusiastically followed, failed to do justice to certain inescapable historical facts: for instance, that war was about the use of force, that force normally made itself felt as armed violence, and that books about war without the battles which usually brought it to a close were not to be taken seriously. That such books, ignoring what they did not like to recognize, did surface on the further edges of the field, cannot be denied. Our series, however, seeks to avoid such imbalance. Far from rejecting, we gladly acknowledge the parallel labours of those (one of the most distinguished of them, a contributor to this series) who prefer still to be known by the honourable title of military historian. Their campaigns and commanders, their armies and battles and the ways in which they were fought are all to be found here, in proportionate relation to the societies which supported them and which would in the natural course of events be affected by them. All that is missing is, inevitably, space to dwell as much on any of the many relevant aspects as keen inquirers may wish; and for them, our up-dated reading lists will show the way forward.

There are some passions for military history and war studies which the 'war and society' approach will never satisfy. Believing that the place of war in the world is best studied with as much detachment and objectivity as can be managed, it avoids the nationalistic and hyper-patriotic attitudes which were the norm in military history writing (one might just as well say, in national history writing) before the early twentieth century, and which continue to colour many of its popular productions. Nor can 'war and society' history appeal to men who find excitement and stimulus in tales of violence and in the contemplation of instruments of violence: all those guns and knives, etc. which fill a certain class of magazines and picture books, and which (along perhaps with innocent interests in military uniforms and model soldiers) are evidently what many 'militaria' fans alone are interested in. In the face of those interests, and in obvious contrast with them, our war and society approach is no doubt better suited to the interests of the peace-minded than the military enthusiast. There is no reason why it should not prove interesting to military persons – indeed, one volume in the series has seemed interesting enough to the Spanish Ministry of Defence to have been translated into their language – but it will not long hold the attention of the militaristic.

The attractiveness of the kind of war studies which this series has helped to popularize is no doubt partly because it matches the very common civilian feeling that war and soldiering – ancient, admirable and 'normal' though they may seem to be – are worth more critical inquiry than military men and their numerous admirers used to seem to like, and the not uncommon realization by thoughtful people that war and peace, after all, are two sides of the same medal. Ideal as a title would be 'peace, war and society'. That alone comprehends the two poles of moral and historical interest between which 'war and society' studies oscillate. Why do wars happen at all?, is a question much more likely to be in the mind of a historian now than it was before the Second World War. Like the post-war boom in 'conflict analysis and peace research', it is related to the preoccupations of the generation born under that shadow of the mushroom-shaped cloud.

But it is nothing new, that the more reflective of our humankind should ponder upon the idea of war itself. War and the imagination of it are the ultimate link between armed forces and society. Human society, politically organized, becomes a State; and States have traditionally distinguished themselves from other States, to put it bluntly, by their abilities to defend their borders and, should they be of the expanding sort, to extend them. Whether there is something congenital in the natures of men (I say 'men' deliberately, because women may be different) and States which impels them towards competitiveness and conflict, is an enormous field of inquiry which has for long engaged the attention of some of the most thoughtful and caring of our kind. The idea of war may, to many living now, have become repulsive, unnatural and essentially destructive. The historian has to note that this marks a big change from the past. War appeared in quite a different light through the greater part of history. It was the normal accompaniment of State-making and almost inevitably the means by which States gathered empires around them. Societies which benefited from these processes thought nothing wrong in them; societies which lost out, bemoaned only the failure of their fights to defend themselves. Win or lose, the literatures and traditional ethics and (if they had them) written histories of societies throughout all history before the twentieth century accepted war as a fact of international life and admired the heroes who were good at it. War may not wholly begin in the minds of men (a lot of it begins simply in material need or greed, and in the gross appetites attached thereto) but a good case can be made for saying that it begins there more than anywhere else. The idea of war therefore, the place of war in what the French and many of the rest of us call *mentalité*, is of itself a matter of giant historical importance: how at particular epochs and in particular societies the idea of war is diffused, articulated, coloured and connected. Only by way of that matrix of ideas about God and man, nature and society, can come full understanding of the causes of wars that have happened, and of the armed forces which have for the most part conducted them.

Ideas, then, we consider to matter at least as much as the social and economic history of war and of readiness for war; they form the, so to speak, cultural and material envelope within which exist the armed forces whose existence and activities lie at the centre of our common interest, and about which something more must be said. Armed forces are a very special sort of social organization. They can be more nearly 'complete societies' than any other of the 'secular' associations and interest groups which structure society within States so far as governments permit. Their internal life is by nature peculiarly structured, tough and ritualistic; their business – discipline, force, violence, war – makes them exceptionally formidable; by definition they subscribe to codes of behaviour – honour, loyalty, obedience, etc. – which emphasize their solidarity and reinforce their apparent differences from the societies beside and around them. It is not difficult to understand why so much that has been written about them (not least, by 'old' military historians) has treated them as if they were absolutely different and apart.

But of course they are by no means wholly so. Except in cases where an armed force or a coalition of armed forces succeeds in totally militarizing society, or where a 'war-minded' ideology possesses a whole society to the extent that every citizen is as much a soldier as any other, there are bound to remain differences and distinctions between armed forces on the one hand, and the societies from which they spring on the other. And yet, while there are differences and distinctions, there must also be relationships and interactions. So they can and to some extent must be studied 'on their own', because in their own right they tend to be so remarkable and influential; but in other respects their history, nature, and influence demands that they be studied in their relationship with the world they belong to. We try, within the limits of our enterprise, to acknowledge both demands.

War, to sum up, is a unique human interest and activity, with its own character, its own self-images, its own mystiques, its own forms or organization and, to crown all, a prime place in determining the standards of national societies and their political viability as States. Such is our case for picking out of the whole seamless web of history the scarlet warps of war, for putting the more social and cultural of them under a magnifying microscope, and for writing about them in a way which the general historical reader, who is not normally a 'military buff', will appreciate. This was brilliantly done in miniature by Michael Howard in his *War in European History* (1976), a few years before this series began to appear. At that time, there was not much of similarly relevant character that had to be pointed out besides his book, the pioneer classics by Alfred Vagts (*A History of Militarism, Civilian and Military*, 1937) and Preston and Wise (*Men in Arms: A History of Warfare and its Interrelationships with Western Society*, 1956), and such specialized periodicals as the American periodical *Armed Forces and Society* and the *War and Society Newsletter*, since 1975 an English-language annual supplement to the celebrated German periodical *Militärgeschichtliche Mitteilungen*, and an ideal way to scan everything that is published year by year. A good deal has come out since then (besides the Open University material already mentioned) and this general preface may appropriately close by highlighting some of the most useful items.

Conspicuous among the war-and-warfare publications of the past twenty years are some of encyclopaedic type, worth mentioning because they should be available in most libraries and because within their broad spans of coverage, particular war-and-society interests may find satisfaction. The most impressive is the improved English-language version of what was begun by the most eminent French historian in the field; it now appears as the *Dictionary of Military History and the Art of War*, edited by André Corvisier, revised and expanded by John Childs, translated by Christopher Turner (1994). Still international, but slighter and more conventional is Charles Townshend (ed.), *The Oxford Illustrated History of Warfare: the triumph of the west* (1995); of national interest merely are David Chandler (ed.), *The Oxford Illustrated History of the British Army* (1994) and John Pimlott (ed.), *The Guinness History of the British Army* (1993). Another feature of the past twenty years or so is the appearance of several periodicals dedicated to the history of war in its broader sense: probably most appropriate are the Australian *War and Society* and the British *War in History* and the *Imperial War Museum Review*.

Of the writing of long-span histories of war and/or warfare, especially by retired generals, there is no end; the only ones known to me as doing justice to the war-and-society aspects of the subject are, in their different ways, William H. McNeill, *The Pursuit of Power. Technology, Armed Forces and Society since AD 1000* (1983) and John Keegan, *A History of Warfare* (1993). Readers with an understandable curiosity as to how the outbreaks and conclusions of wars have been conditioned by the practices, customs and laws of the society of States, a.k.a. international society, within which they were all contained, will find instruction in F.H. Hinsley, *Power and the Pursuit of Peace* (1963), Kalevi J. Holsti, *Peace and War: Armed Conflicts and International Order, 1648–1989* (1991), and (though the title hardly suggests it) Martin Wight, *International Theory: The Three Traditions* (1991, ed. G. Wight and B. Porter). Two ambitious works of sociological inspiration with pockets of the suggestively relevant in them are: Michael Mann, *The Sources of Social Power* (2 v., 1986 and 1993), and David Evan Luard, *War in International Society* (1987). And it is good, at the last moment before going to press, to be able to mention Peter Paret's very instructive and finely illustrated book *Imagined Battles. Reflections of War in European Art* (1997), which begins in the Renaissance and comes right up to the present.

Geoffrey Best
Oxford, 1997

AUTHOR'S PREFACE

Teachers had no higher praise for a paladin of British history, when some of us were at school, than to call him an 'empire-builder'. It was a term suggestive of peaceful bricklayers and placid carpenters, building houses for peaceful citizens. This book, which first saw the light in 1982, was designed to make clear that empires, whatever good may have come from them in some ways, were not built in any such fashion, but, like Bismarck's Germany, with blood and iron. They were imposed by stronger on weaker peoples, often after prolonged resistance; and when the conquered strove to regain their independence, their foreign rulers often fought tooth and nail to keep them in subjection.

We are all products of a very long-drawn process in which such happenings had a prominent share. They have been part of the staple of history all over the world. Virtually all peoples with neighbours weaker than themselves have attacked and plundered, and if possible subjugated them, or sometimes wiped them out. Competition for power and wealth has been interwoven moreover with most if not all of history's other moving forces. Few deities have been offered sincerer prayers than gods of war, like the Roman Mars or the Hebrew and Christian Jehovah, the God of Battles as he was frequently addressed when Queen Victoria held 'Dominion over palm and pine'. In warlike Japan a Buddhist saint could be elevated into a war-god. Swords and guns have been among man's closest companions, though they sometimes changed sides. On Calton Hill at Edinburgh reposes a small cannon bearing a Burmese inscription and the name of 'Don Diego de Silva, Conde de Porto Alegre, 1624.' Porto Alegre is the capital of the Brazilian state of Rio Grande do Sul. This gun must have been captured by one side from the other, and then by the British. In the old armoury of the Sultans at Stamboul is a Byzantine cannon with the Greek name *Eirene*, Peace.

Europe's 19th century is known as the Age of Nationalism, but might better be called that of Imperialism. Human beings find it impossible to love all their fellow-countrymen, and seldom easy to agree with most of them, except in a conviction that they are superior to all others, and ought to be top dogs. In Britain before 1900 'Little Englander' became a term of contempt for the poor-spirited poltroon who did not long to see more lands added yearly to Britain's long list. As each country in turn was caught in the birth-pangs of industrialism, the more it needed this solace to keep it from falling apart.

Britain's defenses were on the seas, and its small army was chiefly employed in expanding and policing its empire. Its graveyards abound in memorials of deaths in exotic places far away. In the small church of St Mary-at-the-Wall in Colchester – where Boadicea once led her Britons in revolt against Roman rule – are recorded the names of Captain C.H. Newell of the East Indiaman *Alexander*, who lost his life in 1815 at the age of thirty-four in his efforts to save the ship *Bengal*, on fire off Point de Galle; an officer who died at Ootacamund in southern India in 1898, and an engineer who died at Roorkee in northern India in 1902 – in addition to a victim drowned in the wreck of *The Prince* at Balaclava in 1854. Noble and even royal blood from Europe might sometimes be shed on soil remote from home. An Archduke of Austria, brother to the emperor, was courtmartialled and shot in 1867 in Mexico, where he was trying to win a crown. The Prince-Imperial, heir to the vanished throne of Napoleon III, was killed in 1879 in Zululand while hoping to earn a martial name in service with the invading British army.

Britain's high-water mark of Kiplingite enthusiasm came about the end of the century, with the conquest of the Sudan and death of the Mahdi, followed by the much harder and less 'glorious' ordeal of the Boer War. A cascade of books celebrated this latter, works without much literary skill, Hamer remarks, and not concealing the ugly side of war, but filled with a conviction that 'the defence of the Empire is defence of God and the right'.[1] Everyone was quite able to see the faults and failings of other nations. European opinion was unanimous against Britain in this contest, and only Britain dissented from the condemnation of American aggression nearly at the same time against Spain. Occasional self-criticism could be heard at times. A pamphlet of 1877 complained that England's dealings with China showed a lack of its usual 'strict sense of justice and fairness.'[2] Some British bullyings of China were 'unchivalrous and unmanly', wrote Admiral Lord Charles Beresford, touring the Chinese ports on behalf of the Chambers of Commerce.[3] Earlier he had been a participant in the bombardment of Alexandria. Many Englishmen harboured 'a residual sense of unease about the atrocities that were being committed in Africa' by machine-guns.[4] It was not long before Englishmen themselves were being knocked over in tens of thousands by German machine-guns.

1918 was followed by a fresh distribution of spoils, chiefly colonial if only because it was hard to say what else the world had been fighting about. But pre-war illusions had lost much of their glamour, and empire was no longer so sacred a theme. At Cambridge in 1922, and then in London, a play by V.C. Clinton-Baddeley and the Canadian humourist Stephen Leacock, *Behind the Beyond*, was performed, in the style of a Victorian melodrama. It was a skit on high life, politicians, amorous intrigues, relatives in India, and a crisis over a mythical 'Kafoonistan'. In the same key was 'Lord Fluffingdon's great speech on the imperial soul', in an H.G. Wells novel.[5] Yet despite self-doubts, and heavy wartime mortality among the empire-building classes, colonies had become too much a part of European habit to be easily abandoned.

Discontent was spreading in the Third World. Secular nationalist leaders were taking the place of legendary figures of the past, prophetesses among them with a distant kinship to Joan of Arc. It was only after the West had sapped its own strength by turning its fearsome weapons against itself in the Second World War that it could be challenged successfully. All the fighting against Japan was on the sea or on colonial soil: the West bent on keeping its empires intact, Japan on extending its already wide sway. A third contestant was appearing in the form of armed colonial nationalist movements, aimed against either the old rulers or the new intruders, but either way at freedom.

In the fifteen years following the end of the war, the dismantling of the empires was substantially carried out, not without a good deal of further bloodshed. British withdrawal from India in 1947 was the decisive moment of change, though the Partition accompanying it presaged an often stormy future. Some other political settlements also made for trouble. In the twilight years of withdrawal, federations of discordant peoples, to keep them quiet, were Britain's favourite strategy. They all went more or less wrong, as Garner, the wheel-horse of the Commonwealth Office, recognizes in his book on its work.[6]

Vietnam and Algeria were the scenes of the two great rearguard actions of the old imperialism, and the former marked the direct entry of the USA. It has come to be known that President Johnson had qualms about the butchery in Vietnam, because it seemed hard on the young American conscripts he was sending into the jungle. 'What the hell is Vietnam worth to me?' he grumbled. 'What is it worth to the country?' Still, he was able to find an answer that could pass in 1964 for shrewd reasoning. 'If you start running from the communists, they may just chase you right into your own kitchen!'[7]

One effect of the carnage in both Vietnam and Algeria was to intensify the unpopularity of conscription, especially for colonial service. Symptoms of the same dislike were visible in South Africa too by the late 1980s; in 1988 it was reported that 450 young white men had refused to serve. This must have helped, along with growing Black resistance and pressure of foreign criticism and economic interests, to compel the Apartheid regime at last to capitulate.

There have been wars among the liberated countries, fought with modern weapons of destruction. Pakistan has been at war more than once with India; India has had a bout with China, China in 1979 attacked Vietnam, Iraq and Iran have come to blows. The Chinese have not easily forgotten that their country was for ages the world's 'Middle Kingdom'. Curtis has pointed to 'the historical memory and legend of a Java-based Greater Malay Empire in South East Asia', as one of the inspirations for Indonesian expansionism. Fears have been felt of both India and China becoming a menace to their small neighbours. An Indian scholar writing on the invasion of Tibet in 1904 by British and Indian forces has given it his cordial approval.[9]

In countries compelled to fight for their independence, the military had a leading place from the start. In Indonesia a clique of generals headed by Suharto came to full power after the great massacre of poor peasants and communists in 1965, when between half a million and a million are believed to have perished. If Western governments had any tears for this, they were no more than crocodile tears; during the Cold War there was always a welcome for friendly dictators, and, as in Latin America, an unlimited supply of arms to bolster their power. Suharto's army has been able to buy all it needed, and has been exceptionally ruthless in its use of them, particularly in its long-drawn conquest of the old Portuguese colony of East Timor. On 29 January 1996 three women in Britain resorted to direct action by seriously damaging a Hawker Jet plane, one of a large bevy ready for despatch to Indonesia, and intended, it could be presumed, for bombing operations in Timor. On 2 August 1996 the *Observer*, reporting the women's acquittal by a jury at Liverpool Crown Court, called on the government to take notice of this signal of public opinion. It took no notice, but the new one elected since then has shown signs of some willingness for change.

In India the British-trained army had lived alongside of a political movement under competent civil leadership; families might be represented in both. It may have proved a good thing in the long run that until near the end the number of Indian officers was carefully restricted by the British, and the many it was compelled to enroll in World War II were young and modern-minded. There has been no interference with parliamentary government from the barracks. In more backward Pakistan, where there was no equivalent political movement before the Partition, things have gone very differently, with a string of dictators from the army to veto reform. Much can be learned about the conduct of soldiers in African national life from V.A. Olorunsola.[10] African officers in Western-style uniforms have too often had a free run. The worst may have been Idi Amin of Uganda, who liked to reminisce about his doings with the British forces engaged in suppressing the 'Mau Mau' rebellion in Kenya. In Algeria when freedom at last came it was the army rather than the people that took power; and now popular discontent has erupted into blind religious fury.

A consequence of the colonial practice of recruiting soldiers from preferred areas and ethnic groups might be to give these the lead when independence came. In Pakistan the Muslim western Punjab was one such area, and it – or rather its landlord ruling class – has benefited by this. Its domination provoked the breakaway of East Bengal, now Bangla Desh, a region contrasting with it in everything except religion, as well as geographically isolated from it. Revolt in 1971 triumphed because India intervened and captured the army that was trying to suppress it by very high-handed methods. All peoples might want to break away from their Western masters, but none of them wanted to allow minorities to go their own way. Attempts to break away, not always so well justified, have been frequent. A rising in the province of Baluchistan against Pakistani rule, during 1973–77, has very much the look of an old-style colonial war.[11] Kashmir has been for Pakistan an opportunity to score off India by stirring up religious passions and harbouring guerrillas.

Free Burma was plagued from the outset by attempts at secession by the Karens and other hill peoples, robbed of their freedom by Burmese kings fond of playing empire-builder on a modest scale. This situation has helped to bring the whole country under military rule, of the usual sterile sort. Kurds have been harried by three heavily-armed states, Turkey, Persia, and Iraq. Resistance by these sturdy mountaineers has been long and resolute, but hampered by inevitable discord between factions. Another sufferer has been the southern Sudan, African and Christian but left in the lurch by the departing British, and compelled to fight for its rights under the yoke of the Muslim, Arabic north. Another grim contest has led to the breakaway of Eritrea from Ethiopia. Tibet and Sinkiang would doubtless like to quit China; in both cases religion is important.

Meanwhile the ogre of Western supremacy, expelled from so many strongholds, has been quietly reestablishing itself in new guise. The USA, never deeply committed to straightforward colonialism, has taken the lead. In place of direct control over the Third World, it and its junior partners, Britain and the rest, have resorted to a looser, less visible overlordship of finance. Their local auxiliaries have been given, or profitably sold, a sufficiency of the latest weapons, and guidance in how to use them. Pakistan's support was of vital importance for the USA's victory in the cold war, a Senator declared lately; and long after the Russian withdrawal from Afghanistan the supply of arms, by way of Pakistan, to the party of fanatical and feudal reaction has gone on.

Much progress has been made in these last decades. Nevertheless, in terms of what is legitimate in warfare and administration, there has been rapid deterioration. It began long ago, in holes and corners, and grew deviously, unrecorded. In the impeachment of Warren Hastings two centuries ago Burke accused the former governor-general of ordering or allowing the use by British officers of 'torture or cruelties' unlawful in England.[12] In 1963 when hostilities broke out at Aden between the British, intent on keeping this military base, and the National Liberation Front, Amnesty International brought charges against the authorities of resorting to torture in order to extract information. Next year the Labour Party returned to office, and the charges were brushed aside.[13] Too many of the regimes which have taken the place of Western officialdom have copied its worst doings, with additions; and too many of these have been finding their way into the civilized West itself. Already in 1968 the humane writer I.A. Richards was expressing less fear of a third World War than of this stealthy process, 'a general crumbling' of civilization.[14]

When the British empire folded its tents and departed, it seemed to have sunk into oblivion as deep as a dead whale's. One of the chief losers must have been the monarchy. Yet there has been a stirring of nostalgic remembrance, potent today when fifty years have gone by since India became independent, and few of those who lived and worked there are left. Men have succumbed readily to the fleshpots of the market and its money-grubbing, but they have always had fits of revulsion, disgust at their own servitude. Kitchener's biographer comments on how daydreams about selfless heroes guarding perilous frontiers could reassure a rootless, mercenary bourgeoisie, with no ideals of its own.[15] In 1895 a pressman who had been watching operations high up in the Himalayas closed his record with ecstatic words on this thrilling experience of life among fearless fighting-men, British and Indian, whose sole thought was of duty; life 'in a purer atmosphere', where Britain could be seen at her best, 'the pick of her sons living the larger and nobler life that men should live.'[16]

Rhapsodies have dwindled into juvenile entertainment, a Wild East merging with the Wild West. But there is a darker side, as a student of Empire has warned lately: 'a dramatic shift' away from dismissal of colonialism to a much less apologetic attitude. In some quarters it is decolonization, independence granted too tamely, that is to blame for the maladies of Africa and Asia now.[17] This may easily turn into justification of intervention, not – as in Africa in 1997 – to halt bloodshed, but for the benefit of financial predators. It is needful to remind ourselves that while part of what is good in the ex-colonial world was brought about by foreign rule, so also was a good deal of the bad.

Happily there is today, besides fantasy or self-deception, a growing perception of debts to the Third World, and interest in its past of a more realistic sort. Numbers of Indian and other historians of its own have been contributing much. In the heyday of empire there was little concern for the soldier's health, welfare, conditions of life, rewards. It may almost be said that the real empires have only begun to be discovered quite recently. One thing drawing attention has been the bizarre mentality, or psychology, of a good many empire-builders, necessary perhaps to fit them for their purposes. John Nicholson, born in Dublin and killed in the storming of Delhi during the Mutiny, as 'Nikkul Seyn' had been a cult-figure worshipped on the north-west frontier, and might himself by today's thinking be deemed a religious maniac. Imperialism, rule by strangers from across the world, was after all a strange affair, of ancient birth. Through its prism Europe has revealed a great deal of what some have believed to be its true inner self, others a painful distortion of itself.

Notes

1. W.S. Hamer, *The British Army. Civil-Military Relations 1885–1905* (Oxford, 1970), p. 214 n. 1.
2. 'Justum', *England and China* (1877), p. 1.
3. Admiral Lord Charles Beresford, *The Break-Up of China* (London, 1899), chap. 7.
4. John Ellis, *The Social History of the Machine Gun* (London, 1975), p. 106.
5. H.G. Wells, *The Autocracy of Mr Parham* (London, 1930), p. 102.
6. Joe Garner, *The Commonwealth Office, 1925–68* (London, 1978).
7. *Scotsman*, 6.10.97.
8. R. Curtis, in *New Left Review*, no. 28 (1964), p. 23.
9. Premen Addy, *Tibet on the Imperial Chessboard* (Calcutta, 1984).
10. V.A. Olorunsola, ed., *The Politics of Cultural Sub-Nationalism in Africa* (New York, 1972).
11. See Lawrence Ziring, *Pakistan. The Enigma of Political Development* (Folkstone, 1980).
12. F.G. Whelan, *Edmund Burke and India* (Pittsburgh, 1996), p. 185.
13. Robert Clough, *Labour: a party fit for imperialism* (London, 1992), pp. 111–12.
14. I.A. Richards, *Complementarities. Uncollected Essays* (Manchester, 1976), pp. 263–4.
15. Sir Philip Magnus, *Kitchener. Portrait of an Imperialist* (Harmondsworth edn, 1968), p. 528.
16. E.F. Knight, *Where Three Empires Meet* (London, 1895).
17. Frank Füredi, *The New Ideology of Imperialism* (London, 1994), p. 98.
18. Ronald Hyam, *Empire and Sexuality. The British Experience* (Manchester, 1990), p. 5, etc.

Victor Kiernan
Stow, Galashiels
OCTOBER 1997

1

EUROPE AND THE WORLD IN 1815

For centuries before Waterloo contests of dynasty against dynasty, and then nation against nation, were tempering Europe's fighting spirit, and equipping it with weapons and organization. Its supreme deity was a God of Battles, no very distant relative of Mars. Goldsmith tells of an old soldier nerving himself for an escape from a French prison with the thought that 'one Englishman is able to beat five French at any time'; his countrymen could convince themselves as easily that one of them was worth twenty Asians. Triumphs outside Europe in the later 18th century inspired soaring confidence. A patriot lauding the 'stupendous Revolution' of 1757 – the acquisition of Bengal – gave thanks to British sea-power, and exclaimed: 'There are no Limits to our Naval Power, but those by which the Creator has confined the Globe.'[1] Russia was the other nation striding towards world power, and it was in a kindred spirit that Catherine the Great's poet Derzhavin apostrophized his country –

Advance and the whole universe is thine![2]

In various theatres, the east and west Indies conspicuously, rivalries among Europeans entailed heavier fighting than almost any between them and others. Through it some new lessons were being learned in the art of war. European irregulars like the North American colonists were often quicker to pick up new methods than troops as rigidly hemmed in by conventions of European warfare as by their cumbrous uniforms. When Wolfe in Canada made use of light infantry for skirmishing in advance, he was bringing into play a tactic imparted to a Swiss officer in British service by an American ranger, and as useful against the French as against Indians.[3] The 'Royal American Rifles' added to the British army by the Red Indian wars have been called 'the first modern infantry'.[4] French officers brought skirmishing back with them from the American Revolution. A newer type of light cavalry, of which Britain after 1815 had thirteen

11

regiments, was a 'versatile element that owed its experience largely to far-ranging operations in North America, India and the Cape.'[5]

In one aspect the wars of 1793-1815 were the culmination of all Europe's previous strife over colonies, and furnished good practice for the next era, when European arms were thrust against other continents. Britain and France fought their last colonial war in Egypt, where Bonaparte led his men into the furnace of the desert as a dozen years later into the Russian snows. In 1801 he sent another army to perish in rebel Haiti; he had the poor consolation of shutting up to die in a French dungeon the most remarkable perhaps of all leaders of resistance to the white man, Toussaint l'Ouverture. Palmerston's conviction in 1806 that Napoleon was bent on gains far beyond Europe must have been shared by many in England, and have helped to keep England doggedly in the field against him. When he occupied Spain in 1808 he had his eye on the Spanish empire as well.

In British minds the conflict had an important bearing on the grand question of how far, or how fast, the subjugation of India ought to be continued. For a number of years successes there provided a salve for reverses and disappointments in Europe, and gave Wellington his military education. A change came in 1805 when Cornwallis, returning for a second term as governor-general, deplored the 'ruinous war' he found dragging on against the Marathas, and 'the almost universal frenzy ... for conquest and victory' which was reducing his government to bankruptcy.[6] There was a turn towards prudent restraint, and before long British energies, and Wellington, were fully engaged in Spain. But Captain Pasley could argue that whereas some dependencies only weakened the nation, by dispersing forces in scattered garrisons, others, and India in particular, strengthened it, by supplying resources and manpower. Confirmation came with the successful invasion of Java from India in 1811, after Napoleon annexed Holland. Meanwhile Russia went to war with Persia, and soon afterwards filled in its interval of inaction in Europe between 1807 and 1812 with another Turkish war, of which territory in Transcaucasia was one objective.

French barbarity in Haiti, reprisals by Toussaint's generals, were ominous of what the bitterness of war, aggravated by racial hatred, would often lead to. The whole quarter-century of bloodshed in Europe, with its immense destruction of life and frequent lapses into savagery, was a grim prelude to the renewed expansion which followed. Europe might well appear too exhausted for further effort, 'a worn out portion of the globe' as Byron called it in 1819.[7] Such an impression might be deepened by the break-away of nearly all the Spanish, and more peacefully the Portuguese, possessions in the New World. Yet Europe was quickly displaying a Phoenix-like vitality. Britain was the pacemaker, with imperial impulses derived from diverse strands and epochs of its evolution overlapping and combining. Industrialism fortified old economic motives. Colonial campaigns provided for some of the multitudes demobilized after Waterloo, a relief not only to them but to a government anxious about social unrest. Six years of the Peninsular War had given the better-off classes a taste for such heady excitement. An impetus peculiar to this country came from the settlements distributed about the world under its flag, including now Boers in south Africa as well as Frenchmen in Canada, all with private expansionist inclinations. Empire took on a momentum of its own. In one way or another the British temple of Janus was seldom closed, and the loud snores of the Horse Guards were echoed in cannonades across the globe, like Rip Van Winkle's ghostly game of bowls resounding in thunderclaps among the Catskill mountains.

Achievement of full paramountcy in India could seem after 1815 a matter of manifest destiny, though even one of its foremost advocates, Sir John Malcolm, felt some twinges of doubt about his people's ability to keep in being 'one of the most extraordinary empires that ever was founded in the universe.'[8] A resident of Delhi collected Napoleonic relics, and it is tempting to fancy that there was some emulation of the Corsican in the generalship Karl Marx paid tribute to, 'those *coups de main* by which the British forces in India always know how to secure their supremacy over the natives', the 'bold eccentricities' of a Napier.[9] Russia too had ambitions ready formed. Its penetration of the Caucasus had started with defensive measures against raiding hillmen. By 1800 there was a line of Cossack stations along the Kuban river, flowing west into the Black Sea, and the Terek flowing east to the Caspian. Beyond the mountains Georgia, harassed by both Turks and Persians, was not too unwilling to be attached to Russia in 1801. There was now an incentive to occupy the wild region in between.

De Musset poignantly recorded the sensations of a generation of Frenchmen growing up after 1815, born to glory and abruptly disinherited. His compatriot De Vigny was very far from the mark when he wrote that 'the spirit of conquest was fading', and a soldier must be content in future with silent fulfilment of duty instead of the lustre of the battlefields.[10] War and its thrills had become a French addiction under the old monarchy, intensified by Napoleon; the

Bourbons restored in 1815 had to find means of satisfying it, which they could hope to do only outside Europe. When De Vigny wrote in 1835 the army was already busy in Algeria. North Africa, so near at hand, beckoned to France, as later to Spain and Italy. There were vacancies in black Africa and in Asia for old Portuguese and Dutch possessions to absorb. Germany alone would find no natural sphere to stake its claim in. But all through the 19th century a good part of Europe's ingenuous youth shared Peer Gynt's fantasy image of himself, long before he set foot in Africa, as a knight in splendid armour, riding forth at the head of his retinue.

2

THE EUROPEAN ARMIES

i. Introductory

Europe's armies grew out of a feudal order of society whose aristocratic spirit long outlasted it; they preserved in simple stereotyped form the grand social division between nobility or gentry, representing *quality* (a term which in England could signify the upper classes), and plebeian mass. From the former their officer corps derived. As a means of joining together the two components, much further apart than in nearly all armies elsewhere, another, equally distinctive institution had been devised, the cadre of 'non-commissioned officers'. It gave the abler private something to aspire to, and made possible the endless drilling and supervision which gentlemen could not be expected to trouble themselves with.

This laborious process was needful to turn ordinary men into warriors. In some early stages of colonial expansion they might be conscripts, like Elizabeth's soldiers in Ireland; in the twentieth century conscripts would be employed again, and far more massively, against colonial revolt. In between, colonial fighting was left chiefly, except by Russia, to volunteer soldiers. To attract these in sufficient numbers was not easy, and there was a tendency to rely heavily on certain regions, mostly poorer than average, often peopled by national minorities like the Irish. Poverty pushed many here into emigration, of which going abroad with the army might be called one form. Industrial Britain was the first country to draw a high proportion of recruits from towns. Townsmen would be better adapted to new technical requirements, as these came in, but peasant soldiers might feel less strangeness in life in remote corners, and be better able to fend for themselves, make the most of any food they could get, and turn their hands to odd jobs, like the building work we see some of the Roman soldiers on Trajan's column engaged in, or digging and entrenching. French soldiers in Algeria impressed a

15

British observer by their faculty of turning overnight into an army of workers, busy making roads.[1]

Down to the nineteenth century European armies made lavish use of foreign mercenaries, and some of these were employed outside Europe, Swiss soldiers by the Dutch in Ceylon, Germans at the Cape. After the British seizure of Cape Colony, Germans were among those taken prisoner who were inducted into the East India Company's forces. Vestiges of old custom lingered, most prominently in France's Foreign Legion. Britain had a German Legion in the Crimean War, and after it more than two thousand Germans were shipped out to the Cape, though half of them had to be sent on before long to India, where the Mutiny had exploded. There was always a floating mass of soldiers of fortune available. When revolt broke out in western Canada in 1885 one of the corps set on foot against it, the Winnipeg Light Infantry, included 'adventurers from every point of the compass, many of whom hailed the rebellion as a great windfall': some were just back from the Sudan.[2]

Shortage of numbers, need to economize costs, climate and disease, were all arguments for use of native troops. It started as soon as white men began to find their way overseas. In the course of their clashes in India the French and British pioneered the system of 'sepoy armies', from then on an indispensable part of Europe's ability to go on conquering. Afro-Asia was taught to conquer itself for foreign pay, most of it taken out of Afro-Asian pockets. Soldiers might be recruited from the debris of defeated forces; resistance could thereby be abridged and resentment allayed. Thus the newly conquered Sikhs of the Punjab were used to good effect against the mutineers of 1857, much as the newly pacified Highlands supplied regiments after 1745 for the conquest of India and Canada. The preference was for men from 'martial races', as they came to be dubbed first in India. That human breeds are either sheep or lions, effeminate or virile, was an idea firmly implanted in the European mind by the 19th century, and easily transposed to other continents. However unscientific, it had a good deal of practical validity, as a result of local superiorities, long habituations. India proved a remarkably fertile recruiting-ground, and largely because of this, as well as of voluntary service being the rule by this time for free-born Britons, conscription was scarcely ever formally applied to subject peoples in the British empire. Other countries followed Roman example, and Napoleon's within Europe, and depended for some of their manpower on compulsion in their colonies as at home. It was in effect a version of slavery; the slave

16

soldier, it may be added, figured prominently in the indigenous military tradition of much of Afro-Asia.

On the whole the slowly evolved European military pattern proved strikingly adaptable both to colonial peoples and to the few countries which kept their independence by borrowing it in good time, as Turkey and Japan did. Asia had very few social groups fit to take command in the European style. European officers could fill the gap, and were only a degree more alien to sepoys than to most of their own rank and file. Native recruits could reach grades equivalent to NCO or slightly higher: they were even more necessary here as intermediary between upper and lower. But there were other, more impalpable attractions. Old societies, above the tribal level, offered little or nothing in the way of membership of any collective more stimulating, or more pertaining to free choice, than village or clan or caste. Entry into a powerful army, or respected regiment, even in the service of foreigners, could satisfy a craving, by conferring a share in a common purpose and spirit, heightened by martial music, banners, uniforms. *Esprit de corps* was the firmest of all guarantees of victory, until the latest technology of our own day came to obliterate everything else; and it was a flame that the old governments and armies of Asia very seldom knew how to kindle.

ii. The British army

It was significant of Britain's prime concern with empire that from 1794 to 1854 it had a single Secretary of State for War and the Colonies. Efficient management, on the other hand, was not a prime demand. Appropriately known as the Horse Guards, the Commander-in-Chief's office was the citadel of an *ancien régime*, and it was only in the late 1850s and 1860s that a reorganisation was carried out and authority firmly centralized in the hands of the Secretary of War. Even then, there was no general staff, and only a minute intelligence department. Foreigners might require such things, but they seemed superfluous to a national self-complacency coloured by the prevailing racialism. Quite late in the century one of the best army theorists wrote of 'the heritage of tactical skill which is the birthright of our race', the blend of Celt, Saxon, Norse which gave Britons their unique combination of defensive and offensive gifts. 'That a capacity for conquest is inherent in the English-speaking race', he wound up, 'it would be useless to deny.'[3] With this mystic endowment the army could have little need of the pedestrian paper-work that Prussian plodders pored over. Amateurism had a pervasive presence in many spheres of English life and government, and nowhere more than in army affairs. Each colonial campaign in turn was improvised, with available units hastily thrown together into brigades and packed off with whatever equipment might appear to be called for and could be found. From the first, moreover, the army in India was largely autonomous, and undertook, or neglected, its own planning.

Having paid £3500 for a captaincy in the King's Hussars for his son and heir, and another £1000 for accoutrements, Sir Walter Scott could not help reflecting that it was odd for anyone to give so much in return for a salary of £400 or less, and render himself liable to 'be sent to the most unhealthy climates to die of the rot, or be shot like a black-cock.'[4] Young Walter was sent to south India, and never returned. Thackeray's Lady Fanny thinks her son delicate, and 'is going to have him exchanged into a dragoon regiment, which doesn't go to that odious India'.[5] Men who could afford it often got themselves transferred into other regiments when their own were under orders for such places of exile. Having to go anywhere very far from the fleshpots of the West End, to rough it on a beefsteak and a bottle of port, as the phrase went, was not much to the dandies' taste. It was of officers of this cut that Lard Dalhousie, a Scotsman who took life seriously, was thinking at Calcutta in 1855, when he deplored their 'reluctance to serve, or readiness to escape from service in the field. Our men are not soldiers by profession, but for fun, or for fashion, or to keep them out of mischief'.[6]

After 1815, however, many anxious parents who wanted their sons to follow them into the army found, as George Borrow's father did, that commissions were exceedingly hard to come by except through influential connections. Hence there were plenty of men, with no other means of earning a living, ready to serve overseas if they could get the chance. There they might find careers more open to talent than at home. Meritocracy came in earlier, though never completely, in the hard school of warfare on imperial frontiers than on Horse Guards Parade. At the empire's very birth, before the end of Elizabeth's reign, one of the recommendations offered to the public on its behalf was that it could give scope to energies smothered at home. Even purchase of commissions, which stood in the way of many, long reviled but not abolished until 1871, was defended in 1840 by an enquiry commission headed by the Duke of Wellington with the argument that it allowed men to reach responsible positions while still young enough to be active, and that this was vital because of the amount of colonial service to be performed, in every sort of climate.

At that moment 77 out of 103 infantry battalions were overseas, 20 of them in India, a circumstance 'unexampled in any army that is or that ever was in the world.'⁷ They forgot Rome.

In nineteenth-century England estates still went to eldest sons, while fortunes or competences made in business or the professions continued to be portioned out; so impecunious younger sons came largely from gentry, and later in the century when rents dwindled under competition of cheap grain imports they could count still less on family support. Other aspirants came from modest middle-class backgrounds. They might find their best openings in the technical departments, scorned by those of bluer blood. For a country incubating the first industrial revolution, England was for long strangely backward in gunnery and military engineering, but now advances in technology were giving these branches an impetus. Scarcity of alternative occupations made the army, like its sibling the Church, very often a hereditary profession. Among families to which the overseas army was their bread and butter and their world were the Pennycuicks, whose head, a lieutenant-colonel, fell in 1849 at Chilianwala, fatal to so many, along with one of his eleven offspring. A youngster stationed thousands of miles away at Bloemfontein heard the tidings, and shed a tear for 'poor little Pennyquick who was at school with Jem and myself', and for a brother of his, another school-chum, lately dead of yellow fever in the West Indies.⁸ Sir Francis Younghusband, of the Tibet expedition of 1904, came of an old Northumbrian family, and was son, nephew, or brother to five generals.

While troopships moved slowly and cumbrously by sail, overseas duty was oftener than not prolonged, and one colonial posting might be followed at once by another. It was common for a regiment to stay twenty years in India, as the 69th, an ancestor of the Welch Regiment, did. The 17th Lancers were there from 1822 to 1847, the Green Howards in Ceylon from 1796 to 1820, the 65th in New Zealand from 1845 to 1865. In the minds of officers who spent most of their lives in the outposts, the Britain they knew steadily receded into the past, their Englishness became semi-petrified. Lord Wolseley was the son of a major who died when he was a boy, and had to get on by way of Burma, the Crimea, the Mutiny, the second China War, west Africa, Egypt, south Africa. Sir Redvers Buller had a higher starting-point, at Eton, and served in seven campaigns in three continents, another of the many generals who returned to London from time to time, as Shakespeare expected Essex to do, bringing rebellion broached upon their swords. Baden-Powell joined the 13th

Hussars in India, and served there and in west Africa and Matabeleland before winning fame as defender of Mafeking. A bizarre existence might mould a bizarre mentality. Britain's conquest of India was one of the most abnormal, unnatural events in history; only individuals somewhat unbalanced, as well as full of energy and drive, could have accomplished it. In the later years Kitchener shared with many others in the British and French military castes a kind of Orientalizing obsession, a 'sado-masochistic romantic involvement with the Middle-East'.[9]

For joining the ranks poverty was the chief inducement, but recruiters did their best to paint the charms of army life in the brightest colours. A recruiting-poster of the late Napoleonic period invited 'Dashing High-Spirited Young men' to join a corps under the command of General Guyler, 'an officer to whose distinguished Merit no Language can do Justice', and pointed out that its first battalion was at present in Java, 'where their Prize Money will be almost INCALCULABLE.'[10] Borrow fell in with a sergeant collecting men for the EIC by promising a carefree life of knocking darkies on the head and amassing wealth. To such rhetoric the man in the street's image of India must have owed much. Disenchantment might be rapid. 'Oh, how often did I wish myself in my native country again', a man sent to India in 1845 recalled: he had joined the year before at twenty, heedless of warnings from his father, an old soldier.[11]

In the first half of the century Scotland and Ireland supplied a disproportionate part of the army, both officers and men. Cadets of Scots landed families were poorer than in England; tacksmen of Highland clans often went out into the world with the Highland regiments, like the Grants whose most distinguished representative in India rose to be General Sir James Hope Grant. Among the Dalrymple Hays commemorated on family tombs in Glenluce Abbey are three brothers born at Dunragit between 1829 and 1837, 'whose bodies rest in distant lands awaiting the resurrection of the dead': one died in 1864 an army captain in Sierra Leone, one in 1872 a magistrate in Australia, the third in 1881 a colonel at Poona. Between 1797 and 1837 ten thousand men from the Isle of Skye served, among them 66 generals and colonels and 600 other officers.[12] More Scots than others may have risen from the ranks: they were less illiterate, and hungrier for success. At the capture of Lucknow in 1858 the adjutant of the 93th Highlanders was a former private, an Inverness ploughman. He was said, with Gaelic exuberance, to have despatched eleven mutineers with his sword. Colin Campbell, whose real name was Macliver, was the son of a Glasgow carpenter. He was one of a bevy of Scottish commanders who took part in the crushing of the Mutiny, in not a few cases with a brutality verging on sadism.

Anglo-Irish officers, far more still, had imperialism in their blood and bones. The gentry many derived from were scions of the conquerors of Ireland in Elizabethan and Cromwellian times. Henry and John Lawrence were two of the twelve children of an Irish Protestant officer who fought at Seringapatam in 1799. Nicholson, another of the butchers of 1857, was born in Ulster and brought up there by his mother, the poor widow of a doctor. He hated India and Indians, and seems to have suffered from morbidities, characteristic perhaps of classes imperialist by nurture. Roberts was born in India, but came of a Protestant family of Waterford, whose graves can be seen in a mouldering church there once occupied by a Huguenot congregation; among the names is that of a Lt-Col. Roberts of the Madras army who died in 1875. Modes of repression practised in the conquest of Ireland, and resorted to in face of Irish revolt down to the end, were carried at times of stress into imperial government as well. The hanging of Afghan patriots at Kabul in 1879, or the bloodthirsty repression in the Punjab in 1919 under Governor O'Dwyer and General Dyer, echoed some of the violence of centuries of British rule in Ireland. Roberts must have had in mind the number of Anglo-Irish officers in India when he defended the 'Ulster rebellion' in 1914, and warned of grave consequences in India if the Liberal government persisted in granting Home Rule to Ireland.[13]

Between 1854 and 1914 the number of Scottish and Anglo-Irish generals fell a little, that of Scots and Irish other ranks vastly more. Of these two the Irish, mostly Catholics, had been far the more numerous. In 1832 they constituted 42 per cent of the army, an alarming figure when nationalist agitation was gaining ground. Famine and emigration reduced it by 1912 to 9.1 per cent. 'The late-Victorian army was always predominantly English';[14] this must have made it easier for Englishmen to love it as they were coming to do, the London populace most noisily. Throughout, it was very seldom that Irish soldiers gave any sign of being affected by anti-British feeling. As against Afghans or Zulus, their English and Scots fellow-soldiers were their comrades. Conan Doyle, a romantic empire enthusiast, wrote a tale, *The Green Flag*, about an Irish seditionist who sees the light and stands loyally by his regiment when it is surrounded by a Sudanese horde. John Redmond, the Home Rule leader, was fond of talking about how much of the work of empire-building his countrymen had done; as soon as the Great War broke out he pledged his support. To the Irish temperament the lure

21

of excitement may have had a more than usually potent appeal. 'Most of us went for the adventure – to see what was on the other side of the hill', said one veteran of the Connaught Rangers, disbanded after mutinying in India in 1920.[15]

By and large the rank and file of the British army was composed of riff-raff, and was accorded the kind of treatment it might be supposed to deserve. In the 1830s, an officer who made his début then wrote, not one man in twenty could read or write. In the West Indies in his early years, by midday 'the guardroom was crammed with drunken men, cursing, fighting, etc.'[16] They were kept in some sort of order by court-martials, very haphazardly conducted, and savage floggings. 'Flogging in the army ought to be abolished', a private in India thought in 1849 after watching a man being punished for drunkenness; he recalled a man flogged for the same offence in Ireland, who from being one of the smartest men in his regiment 'became morose and sullen, and died of a broken heart' in north India.[17] Just before the final abolition a private wrote home from Zululand: 'They are very strict out here, and flog men for very little', purloining gin for instance.[18] Mechanical drilling – much less in use by the French army after the Revolution – was the milder side of a rough and ready process of turning the flotsam and jetsam of society into soldiers. Kipling spent sunny days in the Indian hills lying on a bastion to look on approvingly at the licking into shape of an awkward squad fresh from England by rough-tongued NCOs.

Considering all this, the army fought astonishingly well when called on, thanks to its blend of discipline with an inarticulate patriotism and, increasingly, racial pride or arrogance. In battle soldiers could feel for a brief hour that they were after all bold Britons, champions of a great nation, earning the applause of their country-men. He and his friends in Java in 1811 'would have faced the Devil and his dark Legions had they ventured upon us', one wrote dramatically.[19] 'I would never roam again if I was at home', another wrote from India to his sweetheart; but when it was time to be up and doing he was proud to declare that the besieged enemy would not risk themselves out in the open, 'for they have found out already to their own cost that British Bayonets are made of pure steel and when in the hand of an English soldier nothing can withstand it'.[20] He saw no incongruity between this sentiment and the pious reflections he often indulged in.

There might even be a chance of a reward, a small share of Prize-money or something else. After a brush with some Boers in 1848 Sir Harry Smith, taking leave of his little brigade, 'made a long speech to us giving each man a pair of boots, socks and shirts, a present from the Queen as he called it and bid us all goodbye amidst the most tremendous cheering you can fancy.'[21] In 1841 when the order to march on Multan was given 'The men welcomed the news with a loud hurra! All hands seemed in good spirits', one of them tells us.[22] This cheerful alacrity could glow still brighter as treatment of privates, and relations between them and junior officers, improved. By the end of the century it could be affirmed that these relations were more cordial than under any other flag, especially overseas. Officers and men 'always regarded each other as comrades', General Dunsterville – Kipling's 'Stalky' – wrote;[23] and it was probably least untrue during active service in the wilds, when survival depended on mutual trust. For sailors too a fight was at least a break in their dreary monotony, and a chance to work off on the enemy resentments accumulated by daily hardship and neglect. When a squadron was fitting out in 1816 to teach the piratical Dey of Algiers a lesson, thousands volunteered.

iii. Royal and Company forces in India

Empires brought with them a need for specialized troops permanently ready for colonial duty. Of all these the most remarkable was the East India Company's army, and its post-Mutiny successor, or rather its three armies based on the 'Presidency' towns of Calcutta – the capital – , Bombay, and Madras, the first far the biggest, the second the smallest. Each before long had royal troops attached to it; from 1779 there were always some royal regiments in India. From the outset relations between their officers and the Company authorities were apt to be strained; likewise between them and the Company's officers. In the midst of the cataclysm of 1857 British fortunes came near to being wrecked at Peshawar by a childish dispute over seniority between a royal and a Company commander.

For the rank and file a cantonment (this French term came into British use in India, though not at home) must have been a wretched place to live in by comparison with a Roman fort and its baths and sanitation. Outram was one of very few, before the Mutiny at any rate, who wanted to see conditions improved, and soldiers' good qualities allowed to blossom: India needed civilized men for its guardians, he urged. He was a pioneer in organizing sporting contests, and awarding prizes, as he did during his Persian campaign in 1857; and he wanted the men's wives to be treated with more respect.[24] Few soldiers had wives, however. Heavy drinking of crude spirits was the commonest refuge from their hard lot. Under stress of crisis it worsened; during the Mutiny there were scenes of helpless intoxication, women as well as men succumbing.

Officers in India by contrast led pampered lives, waited on hand and foot by servants whom they too often kicked or thrashed; but they had perennial grievances over pay and prospects. In 1809 officers of the Madras army mutinied over the withdrawal of some financial privileges. Fresh regulations in the 1820s called out fresh and loud objections. An investigating committee reported in 1831 that the majority were weighed down by debts incurred in their early, low-paid years, which they could never shake off. Concessions were granted in 1837, but grumbling went on. There were some compensations, and some plums to be had. One of the first Indian words picked up, along with solider stuff, by the British was 'loot'. Indiscriminate plundering made for disorder, and efforts were early made to regularize it into collection of 'prize-money' by 'prize agents', for distribution according to rank.

By the early 19th century there was, a Lt-Gen. Wetherall with a grievance about the Java expedition of 1811 impressed on the Treasury, a 'long-established usage', such as by long continuance 'assumes all the force and power of a law.'[25] One eighth was reserved for general or flag officers, with a double share for the commander-in-chief. There was an unedifying wrangle after the Deccan war of 1817-18 as to whether the prize-money should go to the troops which fought in it, or be shared by the entire army, in which case the Marquess of Hastings, who was commander-in-chief as well as governor-general, would be a sharer; as in the end he indeed was.[26] Sir Charles Napier as conqueror of Sind came in for £70,000. Sanguine hopes were not seldom dashed. After the fall of Bharatpur in 1825 the Rajah's celebrated jewels turned out to be less magnificent than fancy had painted them, and it was learned or suspected that 'a fourth of them have not reached the Prize Agents.' Those officers who had sold their shares in advance may have congratulated themselves.[27] Still, the general got £60,000, privates £4 apiece. At Mandalay in 1886 the prize committee was chagrined at finding that its haul from the famed palace treasures came to no more than about eight lakhs of rupees. Much or little, an objector maintained that it might take ten years for a claimant to get anything at all: the mode of administering the funds was 'infamous'.[28]

Another avenue to fortune was through political appointments,

24

such as missions to Indian courts. Here Company officers had the upper hand both of royal officers, less well versed in Indian politics, and of civilians, absorbed in their own sphere. One consequence was to strengthen the army's close links with, and at times give it control of, the government's external policies. Its discontents swelled the pressures making for expansionism, and deepened when there were years of inactivity and 'the army looked round in vain for employment'.[29] It was with 'shouts of joy' that a reckless group of aspirants hailed the coming of the first Burma war, and with 'uproarious applause' that they drank 'the well-known professional toast of "Prize-money and promotion", and the more barbarous one of "A bloody war and a sickly season"'.[30] A dash of youthful bravado may have entered into their jollity. In 1863 the viceroy was critical of his governer of Bombay, Sir Bartle Frere, as hasty and restless and too much under the sway of frontier officers avid for medals.[31]

Sepoy regiments, from 1824 of about one thousand men, formed the bulk of the Company's armed strength. They were run on very much the same lines as in a European army, far too much so in the view of some. Uniforms were complicated, cumbrous, and obviously unsuitable to the climate. Flogging was abolished in 1837, but restored in 1845 after an outcry by the martinets. Outram was again progressive in wanting the sepoy to be treated more as a human being instead of, his biographer wrote, 'merely as so much clay in the hands of that masterful potter the drill-sergeant'.[32] Such treatment might have been expected to deter entrants, most of whom were Hindus of high caste, Brahmin or Rajput, instead of outcasts like so many British privates. They lived in separate huts, often with their families; an advantage in some ways, but the huts were dismal makeshifts, and their sanitary conditions seemed to Florence Nightingale vile even by comparison with the British barracks; medical care too was even worse.

In 1842 the Bengal army had on its rolls 67,000 Hindu sepoys, of whom 53,000 were of high caste, and only 12,000 Muslims: the formerly dominant community was more reluctant to serve an upstart government. It was recruited outside Bengal, whose people were not reckoned a martial race; the men came from higher up the Ganges valley, from Bihar, the autonomous kingdom of Oudh, and from much further still. They were of impressive physique, an observer felt, by contrast with 'the pigmy and puny Madras and Bombay sepoys.'[33] Another, who saw Madras soldiers in action, judged them 'very respectable troops', even if with nerves 'not of the same iron structure as those of their European brethren'.[34] Mercenary service was a time-honoured tradition in an India always bristling with superfluous armies, or armed mobs. For a change, the Company paid regularly, even if pay was slender. But it was a drawback, rankling more as time went on, that no sepoy could rise above the very modest status of a 'native officer', and the senior grade of subadar could scarcely be reached before the age of sixty. Men who had got as high as they could were increasingly conscious of the disparity between their pay and position and those of the junior-most British subaltern, and also between their pay and what Indians in the Company's civil employment could earn.[35]

There was not much in the behaviour of most of their British officers to soothe such bitternesses. Cadets came out to take command of Indian soldiers with some rudimentary training in arms at the Company's seminary at Addiscombe, but knowing nothing of the country or its people. From 1824 the number of officers allotted to each regiment was 23, a liberal enough allowance, but it was notorious that some were always missing, having bettered themselves by going off to other duties. As for relations between sepoys and British troops, occasionally in the heat of action a degree of comradeship might assert itself. In the second Sikh war when Private Waterfield's regiment passed on the march the camp of the 72nd Native Infantry the men halted, and saluted it with hearty cheers. 'This Regiment had fought gallantly by our side, and would face a forlorn hope cheerfully with us.'[36] Any such ebullition was a rare gleam, and there was nothing in peacetime to sustain it.

iv. Foreign armies

Russian serfs carried off from their villages for long-term service could be trained to blind obedience and endurance. Whether ranged against foreign enemies or rebels at home, this army was 'a terrible weapon ... whose units were just human enough to take and execute orders, but were machines in every other respect.'[37] Like all other tsarist personnel the officer corps had a heavy proportion of Germans, mostly from the Baltic provinces. Many reached high rank, to the displeasure of the Slavophiles. Among the Russians the traditional backbone of the corps was supplied by the serf-owning landed class. Professional education and qualifications in the first half of the century were very low, and general culture not much better. When Tolstoy served in the Caucasus the officers he fell in with were uncongenial company, their leisure devoted to gambling and women.

Middle-class men were coming in, and were likely as elsewhere to be attracted to the technical branches. It was understood that a literate sergeant-major of twelve years' standing might be commissioned; in practice this rarely happened.

Frontier requirements were giving birth to something like a separate colonial establishment, battle-hardened and less hidebound by routine. Here men with Russian instead of German names were oftener to be found at the top, like Yermolov who was given the Caucasian appointment in 1816. Soldiers may be supposed to have preferred this, and Yermolov represented the kind of rough paternalism that formed part of Russian military habit. Like the great Suvorov whose apprentice he had been, he did his best to foster loyal feeling among his troops. He got the government to stop sending criminals and army offenders to fill up his ranks, though putting vagrants and undesirables into uniform as a means of getting rid of them persisted. It was applied also to political suspects, like Herzen's fellow-students who were sent to the Caucasus to do service in the ranks. Their radicalism could not be expected to inspire any brotherly feeling towards alien peoples, and these two young men performed their duties faithfully and won commissions.

In the 1830s the chain of Cossack military settlements was being given an orderly regimental structure, without losing its old fraternal bonds. Each unit had a fortified headquarters, where married men were stationed and did productive work in their spare time. Each had its own tailors, cobblers, and the like; Russian like French peasants were versatile odd-job men. All the officer corps of the Caucasus formed a corporation; later on another took shape in Central Asia, and between them jealousy was rife. Skobelev is said to have suffered from shortage of supplies in Turkestan because he had to draw them from an uncooperative Caucasus.

To a standing army of something like a million serfs, native levies could make no such addition as the sepoy army to Britain's strength. But there was from the first an interplay of European and Asiatic in the tsarist state, including its ruling class and army. Some tribesmen, like the Bashkirs, were early subjected to conscription. To Napoleon's aide-de-camp Ségur, captured in East Prussia in 1807, the whole Russian army seemed a horde of 'Tartars' or 'savages', and there really were thousands of Kalmucks and others for him to see.[38] In the 1813 campaign Bashkirs were nicknamed by French soldiers 'Les Amours', or Cupids, on account of their bows, the last ever bent in European warfare. Pushing through the Caucasus, the Russians were not slow to make use of Ingush and Ossietin and suchlike

27

fighting-men. Paskievitch employed regiments of local cavalry to good effect in his Persian and Turkish battles in the 1820s; Yermolov sometimes enrolled auxiliaries with a view to sowing hostility between one tribe and another, in the spirit of numberless colonial conquerors.

Lines of race were far less closely drawn than in British territories. Cossacks often came by local wives, and a mixed progeny resulted. An Ali Khan was easily metamorphosed into an Alikhanov. Individuals of any breed who proved trustworthy and able could rise high. Yermolov entrusted an important post to a Major-General Madatov, from Karabagh, who won distinction in the Napoleonic wars.[39] When the son of Shamyl Beg, arch-rebel of the Caucasus, was restored in an exchange of prisoners after sixteen years in Russian custody, the young man, who had become a cavalry lieutenant, is said to have pined away and died in the exile of his birthplace. Georgians and Armenians in Transcaucasia were even more readily inducted into Russian life. They were Christians, looked more or less European, and had not been deprived of independence by Russia but taken over from Turkey or Persia. Not all, it is true, were willing to accept their new position, and the Georgian Military Road was built in 1804 to make Russia's hold on them firmer.

In 1855 Marx wrote of the French peasantry as, since 1789, 'the great supporters of war and war-like glory', and linked this with rural over-population. Soldiering was a respectable occupation. There was far less than in Britain of regimental continuity, but more pride in the army, one and indivisible. Still, there was increasing reliance on poorer regions, which as in the British Isles might belong, like Brittany and Corsica, to ethnic minorities. Socially France after 1789 was more egalitarian than Britain, but the distance between officers and men was kept wide enough to prevent any lack of respect for authority. In France as everywhere, but more sharply than in most armies, there were cleavages also within the officer corps. Some came from the old noblesse, and under republican rule might be viewed with mistrust as Catholic and royalist; others were from the professional middle class, or from lower down. Any NCO was eligible for a commission, but if he got one he seldom rose much further, and was unlikely to be welcomed by his new colleagues as one of themselves.

A French soldier's light-heartedness – in British eyes, frivolity – was not proof against the ordeal of being kept far from home for a long spell; phlegmatic Englishmen may have been better equal to it, just as they made better emigrants and settlers. This was a persuasive argument in favour of a long-term professional army, as France's tended to become through conscripts being allowed to provide substitutes, and for special formations of the kind that evolved at the end of the century into an *armée coloniale*. Here as in Russia, meeting colonial needs could be at the same time a means of purging the country and the army of unwanted members. Criminals might be given the option of joining the *bataillon d'Afrique*, a military labour unit. Algeria provided, it was noticed, 'a kind of drain to run off the evil effervescence and unquiet spirit of the French army', with the unruliest packed off to the wildest frontiers.[40] It was such representatives of Christendom that Afro-Asian peoples too often came in contact with.

A broad stepping-stone towards a colonial army was employment of aliens. Before long in Algeria bodies of 'Zouaves' were enrolled; the name was that of a Kabyle tribe of swordsmen, but from 1840 their membership though not their costume became European, an assortment of adventurers from France and many other countries. Their chief field would be colonial warfare, and this was still more the case with the Legion, founded in 1831. Napoleon III added a Swiss company to it; three centuries of Swiss in the French army inside Europe had only just come to an end. Algeria was the Legion's starting-point, and always its principal home: its main base from 1845 was Sidi-bel-Abbès, south of Oran. From there its battalions went wherever the French flag went. Their contribution to the work of blood and iron was so great that it must seem doubtful whether the empire would have been possible without it, any more than the British without its sepoys.

As everywhere, colonial service attracted officers of specific types. Those who had to work their way up by solid performance looked to it as providing, in ordinary times, most opportunity. Bugeaud, the man who clinched the conquest of Algeria, began as a private of the First Empire and ended as a duke of the July Monarchy. He was noted for his attention to his men's welfare, shared their privations, made officers march on foot with them. There were such commanders in all armies, whose care for their own men was no assurance of any humanity towards the enemy. A galaxy of individuals who achieved fame and fortune made the Legion their ladder. Because it was nearly always smelling powder somewhere, and nearly all its leaders except the junior-most had to be Frenchmen, it could be a quicker route than any other. A typical figure was Saint-Arnaud, ruined by cards and women in Paris, a daredevil hero of the Legion in Algeria, commander of the French army in the Crimea. Four other marshals

29

cradled by the Legion were Canrobert, Pélissier, Bazaine, and MacMahon.

One of Napoleon's daydreams at the time of his foray into the East was of going on to subdue Asia with an army of Greeks, Armenians, Arabs, keeping his Frenchmen as a praetorian guard.[41] He formed a 'Mameluke corps', including Copts and miscellaneous, of men who accompanied the withdrawal from Egypt; a visitor to Paris in 1802 thought it the most dazzling unit on view in a parade. Africa, northern and then also western, was to be France's chief colonial recruiting-ground, as India was for Britain whose sepoy army must have stirred French envy. In Algeria a familiar motive was provision of employment for fighting-men who might otherwise be troublesome. When a reorganisation of the army was carried out in 1841 three battalions of *Infanterie légère d'Afrique*, first embodied in 1832, and three of *Tirailleurs indigènes*, were found a place. In the previous ten years the *Chasseurs d'Afrique* had grown to four regiments; there were three of Spahis, or native horse.

In the matter of promotion French policy was more liberal than British, less than Russian. Most Spahi officers were French, but Arabs could be lieutenants. A few might rise higher. General Yussuf was an Italian-born who had turned Muslim as a slave, joined the French when they came, and made his way up by intrepid conduct to the head of the division. A force of 4000 invading Dahomey later on, composed of Legionaries, African *tirailleurs*, and a few Frenchmen, was led by General Alfred Dodds, a mulatto born in Senegal. But a British army visitor to Algeria just before the Indian Mutiny felt that the French, a more military nation, showed more foresight than his countrymen in India by making it a rule that half the NCOs in every unit should be Frenchmen, and that all artillery should be in French care.[42] Tactics of dividing and ruling were not overlooked. Berbers were enlisted as a counterbalance to Arabs; in western Africa the French, like colonialists in many lands, gave preference to certain districts and ethnic groups, which could be played off against the rest.

1815 found Spain engaged in a vain struggle to keep its American dominions. Cuba and Puerto Rico were left to it, as well as the Philippines. A Spanish radical writing in 1862 held that his country would be better off without these remnants, just as it was better off without South America, and regretted the public delusion that their loss would mean ruin.[43] One vested interest bent on keeping them was the army. With an aristocracy too effete for any real exertion, the officer corps was mostly middle-class, and because of economic torpor and lack of other openings it was always overcrowded. As competition intensified, service in the colonies grew more attractive; nests could be more expeditiously feathered there, by licit or illicit means. High posts were lucrative, most of all the captain-generalship of Cuba, a plum whose possessor regularly came home with a fortune. One such was O'Donnell, who went on to become prime minister, field marshal, and leader of an invasion of Morocco. He came down heavily on black rebels, but winked at the slave trade carried on in breach of treaties with England, in return for bribes from the Cuban planters.

Conscription by drawing of lots, the hated 'blood-tax', brought cheap soldiers to the colours for eight years, if they survived so many in their insanitary barracks. Few had any wish to be sent overseas, but the Caribbean possessions had to be vigilantly guarded for fear of American attempts to snap them up, as well as of slave revolts. In 1858, when there were 118,000 soldiers in Spain, there were more than 25,000 regulars in Cuba, besides local militiamen, and nearly 4000 in Puerto Rico. In the remote and less exposed Philippines all the armed forces at that date, a total of 11,500 men, were raised locally, except for an artillery brigade and the senior officers.[44] When Filipino nationalism dawned, a patriot alleged that too many of his fellow-countrymen had been carried off, in the earliest days as archers or seamen, to be used in wide-ranging Spanish expeditions from which they seldom returned.[45] They were allowed little chance of bettering themselves by service; the risk of their getting out of hand was too great, when reinforcements from Spain would take so very long to arrive. A Spaniard sent out on a mission of enquiry in 1842 – Sinibaldo de Mas, not personally reactionary – was emphatic in his report that no native in the army ought to be allowed to rise above the rank of corporal, and that it was safer to trust the most worthless or ignorant white man as an officer than the most capable Filipino.[46]

Portugal, with Brazil gone, was left with only scattered scraps, mainly coastal strips of east and west Africa, requiring few forces to police. Intrusion into the African interior only came later on, in the wake of the 'scramble for Africa' initiated by stronger countries. Then as in all earlier times Portuguese manpower was scanty, and had to be supplemented by native levies and auxiliaries. Holland too had only a small population to draw on, and a naval but no military tradition; and white men in the East Indies were easily bowled over by climate, disease, and their own excesses. Recruitment of native forces, not all of them voluntary, began betimes; it was concentrated not on Java but on outlying islands like Amboina and the Celebes. A Frenchman in Dutch service reckoned the Macassars and Boughis the best fighting-men in the Celebes, their first onset 'furious and often irresistible'. The former anointed their swords with poison; the latter, tall and well-built, had for centuries been soldiers of fortune as well as traders over a very wide tract of eastern Asia, and were reputed as faithful as they were courageous.[47]

v. Arms and the men

Colonial theatres had their share in improvements in weaponry during the wars of the Revolution and Napoleon, and still more in the next forty years when there was scarcely any fighting in Europe. At the Dum-Dum arsenal near Calcutta Cornwallis watched successful trials of shells which exploded on contact, and there was jubilation over the Bengal Artillery hitting on a solution for a problem gunners had long been wrestling with. It was not to be Dum-Dum's only contribution to the repertoire. In Britain Colonel Shrapnel was making a parallel invention, an anti-personnel projectile exploded in the air by a fuse, the secret of which long remained a British monopoly. Another fertile mind, that of Sir William Congreve, devised in 1808 the rocket-shell, tried out in the Peninsula and in the war of 1812–14 with America. Rockets proved hard to keep on course, and Wellington rejected them, but their very unpredictability, their veering and swerving flight, and their noise, might be unnerving to opponents, those particularly to whom they were their first introduction to western science. They came in fact to be earmarked chiefly for colonial fighting.

They could be an asset for instance at close range in jungle fighting when cannon could not be brought up: firing-tubes were quite portable. They were regularly handled by parties of bluejackets ashore, and became very much a naval speciality; in some respects the navy was readier for innovation than the army. Organizing Chile's naval squadron in the war of independence from Spain, Cochrane was a keen experimenter with fireships and mechanical contraptions, and had rockets made by an English engineer who had worked under Congreve.[48] Other British seamen frequently seen ashore were marines – from 1802, in recognition of their value as a naval police, Royal Marines. Their new colours of 1827 displayed a globe, denoting the world-wide range of their vocation. They might be called forerunners of today's paratroopers, being under only lax discipline, which went with their 'free use in "backward countries" on the more defenceless peoples'.[49]

In naval power Europe had eclipsed the rest far more completely than on land. Industrialism and steam soon made this superiority more crushing still. In December 1825, aboard a troopship crossing the Bay of Bengal at the time of the first Burma war, the pilot looked in at the cabin to say a steamboat was in sight. 'In an instant the dinner table was deserted, some servants and plates overturned', in the rush to get on deck and view the prodigy.[50] Quite soon it became a commonplace. All countries with colonies or desirous of them had need of warships, the more up to date the better. Holland's navy had scarcely any function except in the Archipelago. Spain had intermittent fits of trying to regain its strength on the waves. In 1862 it could claim fourth place among the European powers.

Amid many new departures, the old hard core of battle equipment was altering very sluggishly in the first half of the century. The British firearm in standard use during the Napoleonic wars was sometimes known as the 'East India' model. A man who entered the army in India in 1840 found target practice with this venerable flint musket a farce – 'the direction the ball took depended entirely upon which part of the barrel it touched last.'[51] Naval gunnery improved very little in either range or accuracy between 1550 and 1850,[52] and both here and in naval construction industrial Britain was slower than France to deploy its new resources; being in the lead, it felt no need to hurry. Conservative inertia showed still more obtrusively in the uniforms carried out from Europe to uncongenial climates, expressions of a deep-seated conviction that the outer man mattered more than the inner. Royal troops in India could not be drilled at all in hot weather, the governor-general Dalhousie complained in 1852, because of their 'cruel and preposterous dress', so that officers had nothing to do except play billiards and drink brandy.[53] Company troops were rather more free and easy, and on active service 'great license' was allowed. French costume, already liberalized by the Revolution, was further simplified by the Algerian wars.

Bad old ways might be compounded by intercourse with Asia. Adoption of its even more cumbersome baggage-trains, most wholeheartedly by the British in India, is an example. As a Frenchman pointed out in 1845, a British army there of twenty-five to thirty thousand men required sixty to eighty thousand baggage-animals. 'Even a young ensign is obliged to adopt the style of a nawab, or submit to unpleasant criticisms': even at war, Britons – unlike Russians – must enjoy 'le comfort Britannique'.[54] This often entailed severe demands on a territory's food and fodder, and friction with its people. Drivers or porters in large numbers had to be found and kept by hook or by crook. When the Bombay army was entering Afghanistan in 1839 Outram had to deal with a strike of more than two thousand camel-drivers collected from Kutch; he did so by flogging one batch after another till they all gave in.[55] Such methods persisted much later. In 1894 hundreds of camel-owners and their animals were 'impressed' for an expedition on the north-west frontier. They refused to move until, as the commissariat officer complacently recalled, 'the ringleader was given two dozen and thereafter there was no trouble whatever with them'.[56]

Until, and even well into, the 19th century, Europe's successes against its less sophisticated opponents seldom owed very much to equipment beyond the other side's ability to duplicate or to adopt. They owed far more to organization, discipline and morale. Muskets might be poor things, but volleys of controlled firing could be daunting to enemies accustomed to loose off their own pieces at random. But to a very remarkable extent the decisive weapon was the bayonet, descendant of the pike which it supplanted early in the 18th century. French soldiers gave it the endearing pet-name of 'Rosalie', or Rosy, from its blushing hue on the battlefield. A British ranker long in India referred to it affectionately as 'the queen of weapons', 'that ugly bit of cold steel'.[57] British troops always plumed themselves on their handling of it; so did Russians, whose attachment to it went back to Suvorov. In both cases so crude a weapon may have been best suited to soldiers drawn from the lowest classes.

Its gory career in India is recalled by the slang phrase 'bundook [*banduq*, musket] and spike', which turns up in one of Edmund Blunden's poems of the Great War. For generals the temptation to rely on its sweet simplicity, oblivious of all more head-straining considerations, was one that many, down into the Great War, gave way to. Sir Hugh Gough marching into the Punjab talked disparagingly of cannon, and declared his intention of trusting to the bayonet. Some justification for his philosophy might be found in a soldier's verdict after the battle of Gujarat that the Sikhs with all their skill and manhood 'could not stand the shock of cold steel'.[58] Britain's sepoys were trained to use it, but during the Mutiny it was common in hand-to-hand fighting for the less effective Indian *talwar* or sabre to be pitted against it. It ought not to have been too difficult to counter it as Highlanders were learning to before 1745, by 'taking the opposing bayonets on their targes and flicking them aside.'[59] In the fray near Kandahar in September 1880 Afghan 'fanatics' hit on the same expedient. But westernizing Asian armies were discarding shields, while irregulars often failed to make use of them. Some Sikhs tried to catch hold of the blade with their left hands.

It puzzled Callwell, the British army's expert on colonial warfare, that so many Africans and Asians had wielded swords and spears all their lives, yet 'The bravest of them turn and flee before a bayonet charge.'[60] Something must be allowed for the moral ascendancy gradually built up by the white man, which might make him seem irresistible face to face. But stabbing weapons have been congenial only to troops as well drilled in combat in close order as Romans, or Zulus. To face them requires, it would seem, bravery of a special kind, different from that of the soldier exposed to missiles, however deadly, or to cutting weapons; the psychology – or physiology – of such reactions deserves more study. Boers were valiant enough, but they were amateur warriors, not trained with the inhuman European rigour, and could be thrown into disarray by a bayonet attack. They did not resort to the weapon themselves; they probably thought anything like it only fit for the natives they were accustomed to pick off from a distance with their rifles, and would have considered it undignified to get into a scrimmage with them.

Curiosity about strange weapons of other continents was filling shelves in regimental or public museums. Sheffield has a 'Naga crossbow', and a Sikh 'war quoit' or sharp-edged ring for throwing. It is seldom that we hear of these contrivances doing much damage to western invaders. It is perplexing that more damage was not done by a weapon once the queen of Europe's own battlefields, the bow. Its supersession by firearms (in sixteenth-century Europe too) may have owed more to their novelty and self-advertising noise than to strict utility. With his firearms the white man's shadow fell across Afro-Asia well in advance of him. In many regions, thousands of miles apart, they met with the warmest of welcomes from those who could hope to possess them. Incas and Aztecs may have been stunned by the sudden apparition of gunpowder, but Asia and much of Africa had plenty of time to get used to it, and only rarely seem to have been stampeded.

Because European weaponry was evolving in many ways so languidly, there was opportunity for Asia to catch up, and some advantage was taken of it; most efficiently by the still independent States of India, and in the department, artillery, where only small numbers of men were called for. At the battle of Maharajpur in 1843 Maratha gunnery came up to the highest European standard; Gough remarked that the artillerymen seemed to worship their guns, and an officer present called their firing 'quite beautiful'.[61] They were an élite; it was far harder for the bulk of an Asian array to master new weapons, still more to learn tactics appropriate to them, hardest of all to acquire the kind of discipline these called for; the old tumultuous rushes were of no use now.

Eastern nations, Pasley thought, might deserve to be called more, not less, warlike than Europeans.[62] They were perpetually at war among themselves; many had long been in contact with Europe. Yet their military organization remained rudimentary, and so fragile that the third-rate human material sent out by Britain was able to effect and then maintain the conquest of India with comparative ease. At Maharajpur the bull-headed British commander sent his men forward to break through three successive defence lines under heavy fire. It is only one of many victories hard to comprehend; it seems to imply the thews and fury of the heroes of Valhalla in an army of ill-fed, disease-ridden alcoholics. There is proof here of an immense disparity, far less in equipment than in everything that enables large numbers of men to combine and act in concert, whether in military or in civil life. In Asia's non-national States war had been for very long the business of professional soldiers; in Africa, as in the skirts of Asia, all men were fighting-men. In neither case could they often hold together for long. Governments and treasuries were unequal to the strain of a prolonged conflict, and tribesmen soon wanted to disperse, the more quickly when they had booty to carry off with them. Only a new social order, or a vision of one, could provide the remedy.

3

INDIAN WARS

i. Conquest completed

Achievement of paramountcy in India cost the British many more
small operations after 1815, but also some on a grander scale than
in any colonial fighting anywhere else, and rivalling Europe's own
battlefields of before 1789. In a final contest with the loose Maratha
confederacy, there was sturdy fighting in central India at the end of
1817, though in the open field the Marathas of Nagpur could now
make little showing. Like so many others in Asia, their rulers had
come to depend overmuch on foreign mercenaries; now their Arabs
were mutinous for want of pay, and seized the palace. Behind the city
walls the defenders showed far more spirit, and after the siege guns
opened a breach an attempted entry failed: the storming party was
'too small and badly officered', in one spectator's view, information
about enemy dispositions was poor, and altogether he was disgusted
that a more telling result was not obtained, against a despised enemy.[1]
A rump Nagpur survived for another generation. But the Peshwa,
titular head of the confederacy, was eliminated, and western India
brought under British rule. Maratha soldiers were immediately
added to the British pay-roll.

An epilogue, which again demonstrated how resistant India's huge
fortifications could still be, was the siege of Bharatpur at the end of
1825. This stronghold of Rajputana, west of Agra, had repulsed three
British assaults in 1805. Their memory had to be wiped out, and
preparations now were prodigious. A future general, T.J.H.Pearson,
making his first trial of war with the 11th Light Dragoons, was
impressed by the 'magnificent park of artillery ... one hundred and
fifteen pieces of battering ordnance and mortars', and some
howitzers, more guns than had ever been gathered together before,
as well as 21,000 men; and it was the commander-in-chief, the
Peninsular veteran Lord Combermere, who was taking charge.[2]

Fifteen miles in circuit, it was said, the walls were a formidable barrier, sheltering a large garrison with plenty of guns – firing cannon-balls many of which had been fired at Bharatpur by Lord Lake's army in 1805, and carefully collected. Some damage was done to the ramparts by the British batteries, but it was observable that their material, mud baked by centuries of hot sunshine, was 'very adhesive', crumbling when hit 'instead of, like masonry, coming down "en masse"'. Meanwhile rumours spread of mutiny threatening in several sepoy regiments, because of a story of wounded men being murdered in the hospital; 'should we therefore meet with a single repulse', Pearson said to himself, 'we may expect their desertion to the enemy.'[3]

Mining was resorted to, at first ineffectually, but a second explosion opened a practicable breach. 'We mounted the walls like Tigers', Private Edward Foster wrote, 'and advanced rapidly amid the noise of the thundering cannon.'[4] Pearson heard the band playing 'The British Grenadier' as the assailants forced their way into the town, against stiff though brief hand-to-hand resistance. Enemy gunners 'were according to custom dying at their guns and refusing quarter'.[5] The cost to the winners was nearly 800 killed or wounded; it must be supposed that in nearly every colonial contest the wounded on the European side had a somewhat less bad chance of recovery than their opponents, even when victorious. Thus fell, Foster concluded proudly, though three fingers of his right hand had been smashed, a fortress which was 'a terror to all India, and never was believed it could be taken, but however we let them see to the contrary.'[6] Inevitable looting followed. A sepoy named Sita Ram thought that 'many *sahibs* acquired very valuable property.' He himself took a dead woman's necklace; two English soldiers snatched it from him and divided it, but he got half of it back when he came on its ravisher dead drunk.[7]

When the Mughal empire faded, backward and isolated Sind was overrun by Baluchis from the deserts west of the Indus, as fertile land has so often in history fallen to men of the wilderness. Three branches of the Talpur clan ruled over the valley, with a following mostly of Baluchi mercenaries or men raised by Baluchi fief-holders, accustomed to fight more with sabre and lance than with firearms. In 1839 Britain felt entitled to treat the province as a base for war against Afghanistan, and when this ended in failure Sind offered a consolation prize. Sir Charles Napier, a soldier new to India, was chosen as 'a congenial representative', in Lyall's words, 'of demands that were likely to produce war'.[8]

At Miani on 17 February 1843, near the capital Hyderabad and the river, Napier's force of 3000, with only one European regiment, encountered a far more numerous enemy, in a strong position with flanks sheltered by long walls and groves. An artillery duel was quickly settled: Sindi fire was silenced, while men exposed to the British cannonade fell in heaps. Some of the Baluchis rushed out from cover, and with only sword and shield, 'in more than one impetuous onset, shook and forced back the British line': repeatedly the sepoys had to be rallied, and even the European troops, more proficient with the bayonet, gave ground. So wrote Major Waddington, the senior engineer, who saw Napier exposing himself as he went forward to hearten his men. A cavalry charge was hampered by the confined space, but proved decisive, though only after an hour's obstinate exchange of blows over a dry ditch. In the end this was crammed with dead and dying foemen, most of whose cotton clothes caught fire from their matchlocks: 'their scorched and writhing bodies presented a shocking spectacle.'[9]

On the British side 6 officers were killed and 13 wounded, a high but not unusual figure in proportion to the 56 other men killed and 181 wounded. Enemy losses were vastly heavier, 'a plain proof', Waddington felt, 'of the superiority gained by discipline, and especially by one of its results, a rapid and well sustained fire.' But whatever the defeated lacked in science, they had no lack of courage. 'Seldom perhaps has the determined valour of the Beloochis on that occasion been surpassed.' Next year when Napier held a durbar in the Hyderabad fort, a newcomer was taken aback by the unimpressive aspect of the Sindi and Baluchi chieftains, a 'dirty, seedy assemblage' looking as though 'an Irish regiment with sticks would have licked them all.'[10]

From a new capital, Karachi, an Indus flotilla of steamers was soon ready to carry troops and stores to any point up the valley where they might be required. In the wilds of Baluchistan much desultory scrapping followed. Jacob, organizer of the Scinde Horse or local levy which patrolled the borderlands, found the task frustrating: 'a most harassing and disagreeable service', chasing a pack of 'cruel bloodthirsty cowards' who hid and ran instead of giving their pursuers 'a little honest fighting'.[11] It was the perpetual complaint of European soldiers hunting guerrillas. In a clash in 1847 however Bugti tribesmen stood and fought until 560 were killed and only a remnant of 120, most of them wounded, surrendered. The British loss was two killed, nine wounded; as in many cases, an outcome hard to comprehend.

39

Last refuge of Indian independence, the Punjab was struck down almost at once after Sind, by dint of a far more strenuous effort. Its Sikh ruler Ranjit Singh died in 1839, and without him his raw new kingdom could have no stability. It was the army created by him on European lines that came to the front. It wanted more pay, and feared disbandment if peace went on, but was also the champion of the Sikh community, the Khalsa, against enemies without and a ruling group riddled with faction and treachery within. As a blend of praetorian guard and New Model Army, it was like no other Indian force except the rebel sepoys of 1857, and there are interesting points of comparison between the two. To elect *panches* or committees came naturally to the Sikh soldiery; a political programme, on the other hand, may have been even further beyond its horizon than that of the men of 1857.

Fear of a revolutionary and better-paid Sikh army infecting the Company's sepoys may have decided Hardinge, the governor-general, to force the issue; and it may have been British preparations on the border that impelled the Sikhs to strike first, as they did at the end of 1845 by crossing the Sutlej.[12] Their antagonists were not expecting a stern test; an army run by committees must have seemed to them a rabble. Sir Harry Smith, at the head of one marching division, 'a somewhat obstinate old gentleman' in the words of an officer, 'thought it would be undignified for him to go out of his way in order to avoid what he called "some black fellows"'.[13] Experience taught him better. There was little manoeuvring or finesse in this war, but four pitched battles in rapid succession from December to February. It has been called not inaptly a collision between 'lions led by asses'.

For the most part the Sikhs adopted defensive tactics, with field works to cover their array. Their powerful artillery was well served. In each encounter they were forced back, but at considerable cost; the second, Ferozeshah, was 'the most bloody and obstinate contest ever fought by Anglo-Indian troops'.[14] It lasted for thirty-six hours; in the end the Sikh commander incomprehensibly retired from his strongly entrenched position, but leaving a shaken British army. There were hard words for the sepoys, among whom there were a good many desertions. But from what Pearson – now a seasoned campaigner – heard, more than one of the seven European regiments also 'staggered and reel'd under the enemy's artillery fire', and some Company officers (he was a Queen's soldier) 'ran clean to Ferozepore, amongst them men of family'.[15]

At Aliwal on 28 January, 'a lovely morning', on 'a beautiful plain',

Sir Harry's critic, one Pughe, saw most of the enemy infantry and gunners bolt as the British advanced.[16] His account and Pearson's illustrate the difficulty of making out what really happened when different witnesses sound as if they had taken part in quite different battles. In Pearson's version, 'even the Peninsular heroes say they never saw more severe fighting.' The British had 10,000 men, far fewer than at Ferozeshah, and only three European regiments, facing he believed 40,000, with more than seventy guns, 'and a brave enemy they have proved themselves to be.'[17] At Sobraon on 10 February the British, reinforced, dislodged them from their last foothold south of the Sutlej. They fought hand to hand, 'like what they are, gallant soldiers', but thousands perished as they tried to escape over a deep ford, with twenty-four cannon firing on them.[18] Pearson like many others was bitter at the blunderings of Sir Hugh Gough, the elderly Anglo-Irish commander, and at a dinner given by him after Aliwal was nauseated by the 'whole basketsfull of praise and flattery' exchanged, a large part of it undeserved.[19] Gough's reward was a peerage.

Before the end of February it was all over, and Lahore occupied, the victors seemingly welcomed by a fair number of the people, among whom Sikhs were only a warlike minority. They had saved the Punjab from immediate annexation; instead a veiled protectorate was set up. Political confusion went on, until in April 1848 a fresh conflict was started by the revolt of Mulraj at Multan, between the Punjab and Sind, where his father had been governor, and where he was speedily joined by unreconciled Sikhs. Troops were concentrated for a siege of the town and citadel. With the hot weather coming on, some of them had a dreadful march, like the detachment young Corporal Ryder of the 32nd Foot was with. 'One man fell dead. He was relieved from this world of trouble, and many more wished for the same fate.' Water-carriers who were impressed bolted. When a well was reached there was an ugly scene of desperate men struggling round it for a drink.[20] Such hardships were among the very worst that campaigning in hot climates entailed.

Villages round Multan had to be cleared. 'I would have given the world, at that moment, to have been in England', Ryder confesses about his sensations before one assault; all his sins thronged into his memory.[21] (He got back safe to England, and made haste to quit the army.) Outside the city some comic relief was afforded by the crew of a 'sailors' battery' and their drolleries: 'a lighter hearted lot of fellows never fired a gun', commented another soldier.[22] At the opposite extreme was the explosion of the magazine in the fort, caused some said by a ten-inch shell falling into it. A young officer, Charles Pollard, was returning from a night in the trenches when he suddenly felt as if 'seized by the two shoulders and hurled back by some gigantic, irresistible force'. Staring up he saw 'a strange dense mass like a rude column, black as ink', rising slowly and then 'assuming the form of a gigantic tree'. On both sides the batteries which had opened at sunrise ceased, 'and a dead silence ensued'. When the besiegers resumed their fire it was promptly answered from the fort by 'the gallant Sikh artillery men, who seemed not one whit disheartened by the catastrophe.'[23] They were 'beautiful shots', by another testimony, countering salvos 'with wondrous precision'.[24] More than most of the business of war, gunnery had for connoisseurs a true aesthetic quality.

'Seldom or never in any part of the world has a city been exposed to such a terrific shelling as the doomed city of Multan,' a military historian wrote in 1852.[25] Mining too was being carried on, under a galling fire, and when finally in January the town was stormed it was hideously sacked by an infuriated soldiery. Ryder saw women as well as men shot down, or raped, as the fierce scramble for loot went on. 'Our men now appeared to be brutish beyond everything, having but little mercy on one another – still less for an enemy. ... Our native soldiers were much worse, and more brutish; but they were more to be excused, as they were natives.' Officers were too few to stop the frenzy, 'and some of them were equally as brutal as the men.'[26] For another three weeks the citadel held out; it endured 36,000 missiles, including 21,000 shells, before surrender came.

Meanwhile the men of the Khalsa had flocked to arms again. They entrenched themselves on the Jhelum in a strong jungle position, well supplied once more with guns, at Chilianwala. Gough's head-on attack on 13 January was unusually inept, and incurred losses – about 650 killed and 1700 wounded – which raised an outcry in England, though far smaller than what Asian and African armies had to suffer on countless stricken fields. To make it worse there was a panic flight of some cavalry regiments. The Sikhs lacked the generalship needed for victory, and not many weeks later, at Gujarat, met with total defeat, in spite of desperate efforts and a charge against the British guns. A youngster whose letters home were published under the name of 'A Subaltern' watched the massed British batteries pounding the enemy at 300 yards, and the Sikh gunners replying 'with great spirit and precision.'[27] Ryder was less impressed by their accuracy than by the way they 'stood and defended their guns to the last. They threw their arms round them, kissed them, and died.'[28]

Heavier weight of metal gave the day to the British with a loss of under a hundred killed; on the other side thousands fell, many of them in a ten-mile retreat harried by cavalry and horse artillery doing 'awful execution'.[29] After it was over 'Lord Gough came amongst us, and was very full of jokes', says Ryder.[30] Dalhousie, now governor-general, was not given to joking, but he hailed a triumph calculated 'to impress the native enemy with a sense of our invincibility, as arising from military science, and vast military resources, apart from courage and dash.'[31] Before long the Sikhs gave in, and he was able to report gleefully to the Queen their 'absolute subjection and humiliation'.[32] The Punjab was annexed; Mulraj, sentenced to transportation, died on the road to exile.

ii. India expanding

In some other directions the British bayonet was finding its way beyond the confines of the old India. An early episode was the war of 1814–16 against the Gurkha military oligarchy in Nepal. The Gurkhas were learning something of European drill, and band music, from sepoy deserters, a possibility the Company was always nervous of. For its men this was their first sharp bout of mountain warfare, and was not much relished, both because of the steep slopes and forests and because the Nepalis defended their stockades and other strong-points with great spirit. Sepoys could not easily be got to stand against their whirlwind charges. Still, by degrees the ponderous machine wore down its opponents, and annexations carried the frontier up to and beyond the Himalayan watershed. Nepal's leaders were willing to accept a relationship which made their country a new Hesse, a supplier however not of conscripts but of volunteers goaded by poverty. Most of them were aboriginal tribesmen from the mountains. Like Highlanders they were accustomed to the authority of clan chiefs, easily exchanged for that of British captains; this was always a factor in the moulding of useful native troops.

Like Nepal before 1816, Burma could be viewed as a trespasser on Indian soil, a menace to the country whose protector as well as master Britain now had to appear. A new Burmese kingdom founded in the 18th century by a military chief was expanding round the Bay of Bengal, and across the hills into the decrepit principality of Assam. War broke out in 1825. For the British it was a move into the almost unknown; for sepoys, still more so, and there was a mutiny of some who objected to being sent overseas, as Roman soldiers are said to have jibbed at being sent to invade Britain, outside their familiar world. Most of the sepoys employed were from the Madras army, more amenable than those of Bengal. Sir Archibald Campbell, in command, one of many Scots and empire-builders who made their name in the Peninsular War, knew very little of anything eastern. His army looked forward to a welcome from the people of Pegu province, round Rangoon, as liberator from the sway of Upper Burma. There was no sign of a welcome, however. Rangoon was occupied, but its population as well as garrison vanished into the interior. On other occasions later on Burmese forces evaded capture by mysteriously disappearing in the jungles; 'in such matters', Ensign Doveton of 'the Lambs', or 1st Madras European Fusiliers, could not help thinking, 'a barbarous foe will beat a civilized opponent hollow.'[33]

With no people or market left in Rangoon, there was no food to be bought, and outside the town the enemy was practising an early version of scorched earth tactics, without regard to any hardship inflicted on the inhabitants. Usually well-nourished officers were reduced to living on the same meagre rations as the commissariat could supply to their men, and had to pay much more for them. The rains limited fighting to scuffles in the neighbouring jungles, and then at the close of the year the famous Burmese general Maha Bandula, recalled from Assam, gathered an army for an attempt to recapture Rangoon. His corps moved to their stations with commendable 'celerity, order and regularity'.[34] They were repulsed, none the less, and in the withdrawal Bandula was killed by a shell, greatly to the relief of his pursuers who had come to think of him as 'a sort of sable Bonaparte'.[35] His host then broke up, as frequently happened in Asia when a leader fell.

The invaders pressed their advantage, launching blows in several directions. Most formidable of the obstacles met with were stockades, more elaborately constructed here than in any other of the many forest lands where such wooden fortresses were built. They sprang up 'like mushrooms' wherever the British turned. Larger ones might have a ditch outside the rampart, and beyond it an abatis studded with stakes; and there might be flank bastions, and light guns mounted in trees, as well as heavier ones on the walls. In some cases fox-holes or trenches for four or five men were dug close by for support. One lesson learned was the need to carry scaling-ladders. The Burmese armoury struck Doveton as more like a museum than an arsenal, with guns from all epochs and countries, muskets chiefly condemned EIC stock.[36] (Fifty years later an expedition into the Lushai Hills captured among other pieces a musket with the

Tower-mark 1782.)[37] Burmese gunnery was poor, though there seemed to be some mercenaries from outside to assist with it. Swivel-guns and jingalls 'were generally fired with considerable precision.'[38] Most of the men had no better weapon than a heavy knife, or *dah*. 'They are individually brave', another officer tiro, Pennycuick, wrote, 'but they are entirely deficient of that collective courage which is the effect of discipline.'[39] Discipline did not deter a few European soldiers from going over to the enemy, beguiled by hollow promises and feminine charms.

Repeated defeats and heavy losses were demoralizing, but to compel the government at Ava to come to terms it was necessary to advance far inland. The Irawaddy offered access; Marryatt, a rising young sailor, seems entitled to the credit for a small paddle-steamer being included in the flotilla. This had to face bulky 'war-boats' crowded with men and carrying cannon, and fire-rafts loaded with barrels of petroleum and other combustibles, a new sort of Greek fire. Not until early in 1826, when the British reached Gandaboo, within forty-five miles of the capital, were they able to extort a treaty. It left Pegu still Burmese, but Britain gained the rest of the coastline, Arakan to the north and Tenasserim to the south, and a protectorate over Assam. Of 40,000 men who took part in the invasion 15,000 were dead, mostly from disease. Of the 'Lambs', 600 out of 900 were no more. It was their young sprigs who toasted so jubilantly, when war broke out, 'a bloody war and a sickly season'.

By 1852 it was time for another bite; early that year Dalhousie let himself be drawn, not too reluctantly, into war, by a blustering delegate, Commodore Lambert. For diplomatic business sailors or soldiers were rarely a safe choice. Dalhousie's father was a Peninsular general, he had wished to bear arms himself, always took a keen interest in military affairs, and usually felt that he understood them better than his commanders. His man for this occasion was General Godwin, aged seventy, who looked back on the rambling war of 1824–26 as the perfect model. Dalhousie was displeased by his neglect to gather information; this was the weakest point in all British campaigning, he believed.[40] Inadequate reconnaissance has been called the classic deficiency of warfare in nineenth-century Europe, and in the back of beyond it was harder to make good.

This time there were steamers to carry troops across the Bay, the Bengal and Madras armies each contributing two European and four sepoy regiments. Two Sikh units were the first to volunteer, and Sikh mounted irregulars acquitted themselves well in the fighting. Rangoon was again the initial target. A strong naval force was assembled, and a tremendous bombardment of the defences carried out. Enemy firing, kept up at first with 'considerable dexterity and precision', was quickly silenced. At night the spectacle was 'terribly sublime', and 'fearful execution' was done.[41] Among the projectiles were 'carcasses', the same huge incendiary devices that the navy employed in the bombardment of Falmouth in New England during the American rebellion in 1775. Army and navy did not always co-operate smoothly, but this time Dalhousie considered that they 'worked beautifully together', notwithstanding Godwin's 'petty jealousy'.[42]

Most dramatic, and a thrilling story for readers in Britain, was the storming in April of the Golden Pagoda at Rangoon. It was perched on a low hill, with three stockaded terraces and rows of guns, some of heavy calibre, round it. The assailants had to make a dash across half a mile of valley to reach the foot, but they were covered by naval guns on the river. Only twenty men were killed, though among these were three officers, and two more officers died of sunstroke, before the enemy 'fled in all directions before the British bayonet.'[43] Godwin's despatch however made a point of the way his men on the march were harassed by jungle skirmishers, which never happened in the previous war when the Burmans stayed behind their defences. Some of the troops had rehearsed attacks on stockades at Calcutta, and they were ready to tackle the grand one close to the pagoda, about which many tales had been told. It was taken by storm, despite massive timbers proof against any cannonade.

From May to October was the rainy season, which hindered but did not suspend operations. Godwin seemed to his detractors to be marching and counter-marching instead of striking a knock-down blow. This 'subalterns' war', as it came to be known, was a flurry of raids up one river channel or another. There was no new Bandula to take the field, but also no sign of the Burmese coming to heel, and Dalhousie grew impatient: 'the beasts don't give in. ... *I can't get a result.*'[44] Finally, at the end of 1852, Britain simply declared Rangoon and Pegu annexed, thus completing its occupation of the coastline, without any peace treaty. This was felt to be unsatisfactory, and must be part of the reason why it took ten years to reduce the new possession to order. More galling to the army were long delays in London about promotions promised by the commander-in-chief, and by the end of 1853 officers were ready 'to despair of getting anything at all.'[45]

iii. The Mutiny

In 1844 there took place a mutinous outbreak in Sind of sepoys of the Bengal army objecting to being stationed there, so far from home, or wanting extra pay. Some executions were the retort, but sundry European officers were shown in a bad light, as negligent of duty or given to ill-treating their men. In the next dozen years a series of disturbances broke out here and there; this had happened sporadically since the foundation of British power, but now it was worsening. In 1850 Major Hodson, of Hodson's Horse, wrote of Napier, now commander-in-chief, being 'frightened, as he well may be, at the fearful want of discipline in the native army.'[46] Dalhousie laid the blame on slack or senile officers. 'The sepoy is a child in simplicity and biddableness, if you make him understand his orders, if you treat him justly, and *don't* pet him overmuch' – as he suspected Napier of doing.[47] He was always of confident temper, and his diagnosis, his notion of the childlike sepoy, was far too simple.

In 1857 a war of races exploded. It was the only time in the century when a native army trained by Europe rose up against its masters. This one had close ties with the peasant or petty landowning classes, and could share and voice their grievances. It was a national movement before India had any words to talk of nationalism. It could not affect the whole country, or much more than the old 'Hindostan' of the upper Ganges valley, homeland of the Bengal army. For the insurgents to flock together at Delhi was a strategic error which revealed the exaggerated importance Hindostan's old capital had for them. Politically it was a backwater, a city of the past. They failed to strike at Calcutta and western Bengal, the centre of British power, and risings in the backlands of east Bengal were isolated. Very important also, they failed to seize the initiative in the lately conquered Punjab, where they were nearly as much strangers as the British, and where British forces were in strength. An illustration is the rising of the 14th N.I. at Jhelum on 7 July, of which an officer's account has survived. After some fighting the rebels carried off part of the magazine and barricaded themselves in a nearby village, where they not only beat off an attack but captured a gun and turned it on their opponents. But then their nerve seemed to fail them; in the night they scattered, many were soon rounded up, 'and those not yet executed will receive the punishment their misdeeds merit.'[48]

Even within the Bengal army some remained faithful, or submissive. Of the 1700 defenders of Lucknow about 700 were sepoys, unaffected by rebel blandishments. But on the whole there was a high degree of solidarity; it was noticed how strong among the sepoys was their sense of belonging to the *Fauj*, the army as an entity with a corporate will, a quality which made it a microcosm of an Indian nation still to be born. Leadership was another matter. Not much could be looked for from the native officers, with their lowly status, made worse by the fact that in the Bengal army they were promoted by seniority; to Outram, of the Bombay army where promotion went by merit, they appeared 'old imbeciles merely, possessing no control over the men'.[49] In 1857 talent might emerge out of the ranks, from which it had not been creamed off, but there was scarcely time for it to assert itself, except locally, and outsiders might come to the front. Among the few individuals whose names are remembered, several were Muslims, among them Mohamed Bakht Khan who is described as a Wahhabi, or Muslim revivalist. Islam had an ideology of holy war ready to invoke, but one more productive of energy than of ideas, and only a minority of sepoys were Muslims. Of Hindus who distinguished themselves, 'Tanti Topi was a marvellous guerrilla warrior', in Malleson's opinion,[50] but he was not a sepoy, and fought in central India.

So far as fighting was concerned, sepoy performance extorted many unwilling British tributes for skill as well as courage and resolution. In very few other contests anywhere did European troops have to face such well-served cannon or steady musketry. At Bithur the 42nd NI defended themselves so firmly from behind their breastworks that Havelock had to confess 'he had not seen firing kept up so well' since Ferozeshah in the first Punjab war.[51] For the sepoys, in view of their lack of an organized command, the most promising tactics were those of obstruction and harassment, and sometimes these were adopted. A British detachment on a short march from Meerut to Arrah lost more than half its effectives to invisible foes lurking behind trees and walls, in the style of the American Minute-men of 1775. Too often however the rebels chose to stand their ground and offer battle. This was what they were trained for, and they might trust too much to weight of numbers, or need to reassure themselves by standing together in masses. On these occasions they were always driven off the field, and often pursued with further and heavier loss. If altogether the Mutiny cost the British forces a mere 11,021 lives, 8987 of them from sickness,[52] the rebels really succeeded in killing remarkably few. With all their advantages of knowledge of the ground, and popular sympathy, they ought to have been able to do very much better.

Defeat in the open, and the absence of experienced leaders, helped

48

to confine the bulk of the sepoy forces to siege work, at Lucknow as attackers, at Delhi as the attacked. In either case they had cover to fight behind. Sir Colin Campbell advancing to the relief of Lucknow in March 1858 was impressed by finding a chain of palaces and courtyards linked together into a well-designed fortification, and his men soon realized that every house and mud wall facing the river was looped for firearms, often very well aimed. On the other hand the rebels had omitted, as young Roberts wrote home, to erect a flank defence at a crucial point, and thus allowed their assailants to enfilade a position 'perfect in every way but for this one grand mistake.'[53] Lack of any regular staff must have made such errors easy to fall into.

On the Ridge the cannon and ammunition collected by the British seemed enough, someone said, 'to grind Delhi to powder',[54] and inside the city quarrels and divisions spread as the siege went on. Yet General Wilson found it in the end a prickly morsel; 'this street fighting is frightful work', he lamented, 'and Pandy is as good a soldier at that as our men'.[55] Roberts was left by the experience with 'a lasting prejudice against street fighting in any form'.[56] Regular soldiers have very seldom relished it, whether in overseas campaigns or in coping with revolutionaries and barricades nearer home. There was similar distaste for the guerrilla fighting of the final phase, going on well into 1858, with bodies of rebels who showed both initiative and courage in laying jungle ambuscades or cutting communications. They were only worn down by firepower, and by intimidation of villagers suspected of aiding them. To the youthful Wolseley this sort of hole-and-corner scuffling seemed inglorious, though risky enough, 'quite derogatory to a soldier's profession'; and he could not help feeling some admiration for the enemy's stoical resolve.[57]

If the sepoys had few good leaders, the British had far too many bad ones. All governing classes tend to drift away in time from reality into fantasy, but in India this was magnified by their being strangers, and in the old provinces they had sunk into a sun-dazzled dreamland. There was confusion at Cawnpore at the outset, and panic at Simla where groundless rumours set off a *sauve qui peut*. It was mostly in the freshly won north that men of action were to be found, with a brutal realism appropriate to the emergency. There was not much in the way of brilliant strategy. In the first relief of Lucknow more than a quarter of the two thousand in Havelock's force became casualties, because he went at the well-defended town with a blind rush. Wrangling and jealousies were chronic. Neill's insubordinate attitude to Havelock was 'indefensible by any standard of military decency.'[58] Junior officers carped at their fumbling superiors – 'heaps and heaps of muffs and old women', as one dubbed them[59] – commanders harped on their juniors' incompetence. All showed up best in the open, where little subtlety was called for, only determination, with guns well up in front on the two wings and cavalry ready to charge. Thirst for revenge ensured that all successes were thoroughly followed up, and retreating 'niggers', as they were habitually called, given no respite. Energetic pursuit was a hallmark of European colonial practice, Callwell was to emphasize. 'Asiatics do not understand such vigour and are cowed by it.'[60]

In the Punjab and the north-west the British, after disarming unreliable sepoy units, were able rapidly to collect new levies, including trained men from the old Khalsa army with no other calling to turn to and glad of a chance to get even with the sepoys who had helped to overthrow them, and Pathans and Afridis and Baluchis from the borders, athirst for plunder. It was one drawback of Delhi as rebel centre that it was a magnet for these northern barbarians, who would have had less stomach for a march on distant and unknown Calcutta. Reinforcement came from outside India too. Britain's imperial holdings dispersed over the globe could succour one another. Sir George Grey sent men from the Cape, and a contingent on its way to the China war was diverted to India.

'It was a fearfully savage war', an officer recalled in his memoirs. He was obliged to shoot thirty prisoners with his own hand, when his native soldiers refused the butcher's work.[61] G.O.Trevelyan in India a few years later wrote of how 'from the lowest depths of our nature emerge those sombre, ill-omened instincts, of whose very existence we had ceased to be aware.'[62] An Indian historian writes of Neill at Allahabad letting his men loose to perpetrate all the 'cruelties and barbarities which human ingenuity could conceive.'[63] The shadow lay over India for years to come. One day in the 1870s two British soldiers making their way through a forest in the Deccan fell into talk about the Mutiny, and worked themselves up into such a state of mind that they vowed to kill the first 'nigger' they met; they did so – a harmless tradesman jogging along on his pony – failed to keep their secret, and ended on the gallows.[64] Fear of a mutinous spirit spreading from one empire to another may be detected in a minute by the viceroy in early 1880 on the undesirable possibility of a British victory over Russia in Central Asia being followed by an anti-Russian rising, akin to 1857.[65] Well into the next century British soldiers coming out to India were given solemn warnings about the Mutiny, and how it might break out again.

iv. The new Indian army

Britain had won. 'It was a question of race', Malleson explained simply in summing up.[66] After the conflict, and long and acrimonious debate, it was decided not to have a separate European army in India, like that of the now abolished Company. From now on there would only be the regular forces of the crown, but more of them would be oriented towards India. Three presidency armies survived, until in 1895, after lengthy chipping away at a now outdated system, a single commander-in-chief was agreed on, with four regional commands. In numbers the British strength was greatly increased, and so was the proportion it represented, one third, of the total under arms. All artillery and arsenals were kept in British hands, a tribute to the good use the sepoys of 1857 had made of them. So essential was this deemed that in 1891 the War Office wanted auxiliary gunners, if required, to be Africans instead of Indians.[67] Finding the necessary manpower was not easy; it required that garrisons in settlement colonies should be as far as possible withdrawn, and their progress towards self-government was thus hastened. In 1876 there were 60,000 European soldiers, with a very high complement of 3000 officers. Native troops numbered 123,000, with only 3400 officers, a much lower ratio.

A further precaution was the mixing up of diverse elements in the sepoy army, on principles very deliberately of divide-and-rule. In the Madras and Bombay armies individuals were thrown together higgledy-piggledy. In the north, most regiments had different components, but to avoid too much communal friction, and complications about food, they were made up of 'class' companies, each of men from a single community. Only at the end of the century was there a turn towards more 'class' regiments, which could be expected to have greater solidarity. Many did develop a keen regimental spirit, whereas before 1857 it was the army as a whole that attracted allegiance.

The new sepoy army drew heavily on the northern areas where so many recruits were found during the Mutiny itself, and where nationalism, when it began to stir in Bengal and other provinces, found it hard to penetrate. Among the communities drawn on the Sikhs were prominent. At the outset the fact that Britons and other Europeans had helped to train Ranjit Singh's army made it simpler for Sikhs to be incorporated in the British ranks; now martial memories of Ranjit's day and earlier fed courage in a new cause, or courage for its own sake. Proudly telling an English private a story of twenty-one Sikhs holding a frontier post till all were wiped out, a

Sikh soldier added: 'surrender is a word we do not know or use.'[68] A file of Sikhs is among the warriors and scenes of battle carved round the plinth of Lord Roberts's equestrian statue in Kelvingrove park in Glasgow. 1857 gave a filip also to enlistment of Gurkhas. Nepal sent troops of its own to assist the British during the Mutiny, and its rulers were handsomely rewarded. From 1858 the Gurkha Brigade of later days was taking shape. Between Gurkhas and British soldiers 'a bond of good fellowship' seemed to many to establish itself with curious ease.[69] Allies from outside India were somehow different from subjects of the Raj, not inferiors as Indians were.

Fear of disloyalty could serve to justify determination, due as much to prejudice of race and desire to reserve commissions for British families, not to allow Indians to rise above their lowly officer-grades. As a sepoy who remembered the old times and may have looked back on them through a rosy mist, Sita Ram felt that the new British officers were worse than the Company's, treating their men roughly and making no pretence of liking them.[70] Enlistment dropped off. One remedy, in 1895, was a slight increase of pay, unaltered for a century. Beyond this, officers were coming to be expected to take a much closer interest in their men. The more relations with political India grew strained, the more needful were good relations within the army. In the late years of the Raj 'The company commander was looked upon as a father of a family'.[71] Recruiting districts harboured a firm attachment to the army. Service often ran in families, as it did among British officers and officials, so that a newcomer from Britain might be welcomed by old soldiers who had served under his father; it seemed a guarantee of the empire's permanency.

India's military centre of gravity was shifting towards the north-west, where beyond Pathan and Afghan lay the real enemy, Russia. This made goodwill within the army yet more vital. A visiting journalist perceived the dilemma on whose horns British rule was caught.[72] To ensure that British soldiers could beat Indian soldiers, at a pinch, they had to be equipped with better rifles. But if these Indians had to be sent into action against a European opponent, for them to be less well armed than the enemy would invite defeat. In 1900 it was decided in London – the viceroy, Curzon, still dissenting – to issue the same standard Lee-Enfield to all. Lord Minto, viceroy in 1907, with many years in the army behind him, still felt twinges of doubt about fidelity, and he was in favour of giving commissions to Indians in the hope of confirming it. Kitchener, his commander-in-chief, and Roberts, were not.

'The Indian Mutiny of 1857', a German diplomat wrote a good

many years after it, 'hangs like the sword of Damocles over Great Britain as regards her position in the world.'[73] To rebuild the army and the fabric of authority in India took time; there was a slowing down, though not cessation, of the imperial expansion in which Indian soldiers had so indispensable a part to play. In 1878 came the second Afghan war, a failure like the first if less catastrophically; and then, partly no doubt in order to make up for this, as well as to gratify gluttonous commercial interests, the third Burma war. Plans for a final round with Burma had been carefully worked out for years, before in November 1885 an expeditionary force of ten or twelve thousand was given the signal. One of the three brigades was contributed by the Bengal army, the others by the Madras army, now given another chance to shine. Roberts, commander-in-chief in Madras before reaching supreme command in India, held that only rude frontiersmen like Pathans, Sikhs, or Gurkhas were fit for really strenuous work; and Colonel G.S.White, at the head of the third brigade, privately thought his brethren of the Madras army, especially the more elderly, 'an indolent unmilitary lot', and the native troops 'sleepy'.[74] White was an ambitious Ulsterman, later field marshal; the commander-in-chief, Sir Henry Prendergast, was another of the ubiquitous Anglo-Irish. To make good any weaknesses, there were twenty-four machine-guns, and the enemy was to show 'a wholesome fear of the Nordenfeldt and its stream of bullets'.[75]

Since the last war the Burmese polity had been running down, and it was now easily toppled over. The invaders were coming up the Irawaddy, a naval flotilla leading the way and the army marching along the banks. These were protected by thick jungle, and the Burmans had some guns, and a number of forts, one of them a large brick edifice not far from the frontier, designed by Italian engineers. Its garrison of 1700 decamped, though there was bold defiance at a masonry fort on the opposite bank, the only real fighting of the brief hostilities. Other strongholds collapsed in turn as they were shelled from the river and threatened by troops moving round on the landward side. British casualties were negligible, Burmese quite light. On 28 November Mandalay was entered. The smartest Burmese move was the blocking of the channel further up-river with sunken boats.

Five years of guerrilla resistance followed, of the incoherent kind that seems endemic in regions where a regular monarchy and army have disappeared, leaving a vacuum. Disbanded soldiers took to the jungles, which afforded ideal cover though they made it hard for any concerted movement to form. The editor of the *Bombay Gazette*, Geary, who went to Burma at the end of 1885 as an observer, thought the trouble started from disorders due to food scarcities, which were turned into patriotic struggle by army shootings.[76] To the military mind, always antipathetic to guerrillas, real patriotism was unthinkable in a country whose army could be knocked out in three weeks with scarcely a blow struck. Any who held out could therefore only be criminals. 'One grows sceptical as to the tranquillizing effect of military executions', Geary commented, and in his view they were having a brutalizing effect instead on those responsible for them.[77] Some horrific details leaked out, and the authorities were obliged to order restraint – with what result might be hard to say.

In February 1886 Lord Dufferin, the viceroy, affirmed that Burma was opening its arms to the British. 'But by July', wrote Crossthwaite, looking back on his years as chief commissioner from 1887 to 1890, 'it had become evident that a considerable minority of the population, to say the least, did not want us.' This only induced him to admit that the unrest might at first have had 'some faint tinge of patriotism', after which it swiftly degenerated into dacoity, or brigandage.[78] Here as in wide expanses of Asia bandits were so numerous as to form a familiar element of society, almost at times a fourth estate. Their philosophy would be hard to define in any modern terms. Like the Irishman questioned about his politics they were *agin' the government*, and this was enough to entitle them to some esteem among common people who were never short of reasons for disliking their rulers. They were ready-made guerrillas, like Spanish smugglers during the Napoleonic occupation, and better fighters than most soldiers Asia could set on foot.

Notebooks of an officer invested with magisterial powers during the first year strike some hopeful chords. 'Villages quiet and people contented, information easier to obtain than formerly.'[79] But a later comer, A.G. Burn, found individuals who had done their tour of duty 'very pleased to get out of the country'.[80] He was soon aware of discords between civil and military, the latter irritated by captured dacoits being set free, partly thanks to bribes to interpreters; as a consequence, 'the innocent are in the future likely to suffer with the guilty as the men are not disposed to take prisoners.' It was government policy, he knew, to try 'to win over the population of the newly acquired territory more by kindness than severity', but the soldiers did not understand this. He heard of captives being kicked with heavy boots before being handed over to the police.[81] They may have been the luckier ones.

With frontier tribes too making trouble, and an extensive rising in Lower Burma, pacification required very much bigger forces than the original conquest. They swelled to 32,000, drawn from all three presidencies, plus 8500 military police brought in from India; very few colonial operations ever called for so many. Chafing at the 'long period of exhausting fighting to which no glory attaches', Burn was querulous about two of the Madras regiments; 'demoralization' in one of them, he heard it said, could be explained by its being full of unmartial Telegus. 'The Bombay troops are also not well spoken of', and even the Bengal army contingent he thought was not adding to its laurels. He was convinced that there were never enough British officers with native regiments.[82]

Like so many Afro-Asian states, Burma was far from homogeneous; a kite's tail of ethnic minorities was loosely linked on to it. When the time came for enrolling a local force in the usual manner, Burmans were written off altogether. A semi-official verdict was that they were 'intelligent and attractive, but temperamentally unsuited to the strictness and regularity of army life'.[83] They had soldiered well enough under Maha Bandula, and it seems probable that they were really regarded as too precociously nationalistic. Shans were left out, as too simple and peaceable. Karens were recruited, being at least smart and quick, but these Christianized folk of the south-east, nearest to Rangoon, did not take too kindly to discipline. Kachins, the most warlike race it was felt of the country, and the western Chins, who reminded some of Gurkhas, provided the staple. It was a further safeguard against Burmese revolt that policemen were drawn from the same stocks.

'How long would it have taken', Crosthwaite asked his readers, 'to subjugate and pacify Burma if we had not been able to get the help of the fighting-men from India, and what would have been the cost in men and money?'[84] The fact that from 1858 India belonged to the Crown instead of the Company made it more a matter of course to utilize its army far away from home, at Indian expense. There was now no intermediate authority to object to such use or misuse of Indian revenue. Without this facility, imperial adventures would have been less light-heartedly ventured on. John Bull might love his army and empire, but not well enough to want to pay for them. Bengal had been made to pay for too much of the conquest of the rest of India, at the cost of a relatively huge Indian debt piling up, nearly £45 millions by 1815. Then the process was repeated further afield, with all India footing a good part of the bill. There were always some protests, British as well as Indian. 'Perseverance in the attempt to burden the resources of India', Jacob wrote in 1842, 'with wars extending from the Red Sea to China will lead to nothing but ruin.'[85]

As national consciousness grew, there was a certain ambivalence in Indian attitudes. Pride in the army's successes was not lacking, and some business interests profited by them. On the other hand it was becoming a patriotic thesis that wealthy Britain was aggrandizing itself at the expense of the anaemic Indian exchequer, while Indians were not even eligible as officers. The second Afghan war cost £23 millions, and Gladstone was felt by his compatriots to be acting generously, by many of them over-generously, when he decided that Britain should pay five millions out of the total. India was resentful of having to pay for the third Burma war, and Gladstone was loudly reminded of his words in opposition, 'Let those who make war pay for war'.[86] A complex procedure was being worked out for dividing the costs of Indian troops outside India into ordinary, payable by India, and extraordinary, sometimes paid by Britain. A Royal Commission submitted a report in 1900 which Indian opinion found deeply disappointing; it held that all such spheres as the Suez Canal or Persia were of vital concern to India, which should therefore bear all charges arising there. On this issue, as on some others, there was a widening divergence in the later years between the two British governments, one in London and one – the old Company *redivivus*, it might sometimes look – in India. While Treasury and War Office displayed 'a pettifogging and huckstering mentality', viceroys and their advisers 'took throughout a consistent and strong stand' on India's behalf.[87]

4

BRITAIN AND RUSSIA: WARS OF THE BORDERLANDS

1. The Caucasus and the first Afghan War

Of all regions open to the men of empire, the most continuously competitive was the middle Asia stretching from the borders of Turkey to those of China, where Russians and Britons came closer and closer, more and more indignant at each other's felonious designs. Most of it at first *terra incognita*, it was explored only by slow, painful steps. A French officer, Ferrier, rashly endeavouring to make his way from Persia through Afghanistan to India in 1845 left a graphic picture of chaotic violence, now compounded by the rivalries, territorial and commercial, of the two powers. For a hundred years after the first alarm in 1807, much – far too much – of the energy of India's rulers was devoted to the grand riddle of whether Russia hoped to cross the desert and mountain barrier, and whether if so the enterprise was feasible. Ferrier believed it was. But an attendant danger, likewise foreseen by him, was looming up, that any close Russian approach would be the signal for rebellion in India. Cautious men wanted to await the Russians, letting them wear themselves out; the 'forward school' maintained that to do so would be ruinous, and the challenge must be met as far beyond the frontier as possible.

Anglo-Russian rivalries were hydra-headed, and had a western flank in the Caucasus and Transcaucasia, bordering on what was from the viewpoint of Europe the site of the Eastern Question. Conquest of the Caucasus was being pushed on in intermittent bursts, meeting its fiercest foes among the Chechens of the Daghestan uplands to the east. Both dense forests, concealing the villages, and *aouls*, fortified settlements perched on the mountain spurs, weighed heavily on the tsar's deputies; and there was a social pattern shared with many other primitive lands of women doing most of the useful work, leaving men free to amuse themselves, chiefly by fighting, so that they were always in arms, and thirsting for warlike fame.

57

Absence of strong chiefs among the Chechens left the way open for new protagonists to win their way to the front; though to assert their authority might require both an aura of religion, and merciless rigour.

In 1818 the fortress of 'Grozny', the Terrible, was built on the Terek river eighty miles west from the Caspian, by Yermolov, governor-general of Georgia from 1816 to 1827. A long series of forays into the Daghestan heights began. When they could be brought into play, cannon were of great use, being a novelty to the mountaineers. By 1832 the 'Cossack line' with its forts and guard-points stretched south-west from the sea of Azov for 466 miles. Troops serving in the Caucasus needed more initiative and self-reliance than could be imparted by the drill-ground training of most Russian soldiers. Yermolov knew how to make the best of them; and his preference was for the most ferocious methods as the most efficacious.

In reality he was overreaching himself with his burning of villages and hanging of suspects, and his term of office ended amid fresh symptoms of revolt; four years later there came on the scene one of the most demonic of all Europe's challengers, Shamyl Beg. He was the warrior chief of an Islamic sect or movement founded by his boyhood friend Kazi Mullah, whose disciples or Murids were the cream of his following. They were few in numbers, but the name came to be bestowed on all the rebels. Shamyl was an Avar, of the dominant tribe of Daghestan, with about a quarter of its half-million population, and his own tribe was his staunchest support. Others might have to be coerced, and he shrank from no measures necessary for the purpose. His rabid anti-Christian bent was not unnatural, but it prevented any combination with Christianized tribes in the hills.

Better planned and co-ordinated now, tactics were as before based on harassment of Russian columns and defence of lofty eyries. These tribesmen were much better shots than most of Europe's ill-wishers and it was when an expedition was homeward bound that it found sharpshooters swarming round it most venomously. Russian commanders could only endeavour to break their spirit by marching about and destroying villages and crops. For this they had to employ considerable forces. One expedition set out in 1837 with nearly 5000 infantry, 300 Cossacks, and a score of cannon and mortars; it suffered a thousand casualties. During four years of General Grabbe's campaigns 436 officers were killed or wounded, 7960 men;[1] a very heavy toll, or so it would have appeared to the British or French armies. The most celebrated siege of the war, at Akhoulgo in 1838, lasted eighty days and cost nearly 3000 casualties. Such stubborn defiance always inflamed tempers, and the final stage was stained by more than 'the usual horrors of Caucasian fighting'.[2] Numbers of Russians deserted; on the other hand the Russians could always count on some native levies, many of them irregulars supplied by khans or chiefs who submitted.

When Lermontov wrote, about 1840, things were at least a little quieter: formerly, his hero was assured by a veteran, one could not walk a hundred paces from a fort without being stalked by some 'hairy devil'. The Caucasus was beginning to be fashionable, attracting young men of rank who like Tolstoy might join in for a few seasons as cadets, dandies viewed with contempt by hardened regulars. But Nicholas I was waxing impatient at the slow progress, and in 1845 Count Vorontsev was sent, in the usual dual role of commander-in-chief and governor-general, with orders to put an end to the insurrection. He set forth, with some hesitation, at the head of an army of about 18,000. Shamyl's resources were worn down by the weight of the offensive, and his stronghold had to be abandoned in 1848 after three weeks of siege and a battering by 46 guns. An engineer captain who took part, and may have carried away some useful lessons, was Todleben, half a dozen years later the defender of Sevastopol. Shamyl was being seduced into the error of trying to emulate Europe, by a shift away from guerrilla mobility towards a regular force weighed down with cannon and paraphernalia. It was the usual drift of such movements, along with the self-elevation of their leaders, into top-heaviness. The Taiping rebels in China were exhibiting it on the largest scale.

When in 1858, after a lengthy lull partly due to the Crimean War, the new commander Prince Bariatinski set out to deal the final blow, many districts were ready to yield. Guerrilla warfare is an exhausting strain for both parties. Cornered in his last fastness, Shamyl fought until nearly all his remaining band of murids were killed, and then surrendered. He died in 1871, in the odour of sanctity, at Medina. So far as the degree of tribal unity forged by him survived, it benefited the Russians, who now had men broken to the yoke for subjects;[3] a paradoxical outcome to be seen in sundry other places, as in the Sudan where the British fell heirs to the Mahdi.

Meanwhile Russian power had been creeping eastward, round or across the Caspian, into the wastes beyond, and meddling further south with Persia. More than one line of its advance seemed to the British to point towards Afghanistan, where Dost Mohamed had made himself Amir in 1818. Of the eternal triangle of Afghan politics, Kabul-Kandahar-Herat, he controlled only the first. He was trying to construct something like a regular army nucleus, including three thousand cavalry raised on a new plan, with fixed pay and horses provided by the government; also a thousand Qizilbashes, 'red-heads' or Turcoman mercenaries much esteemed in the whole region. But the country's real protection was the readiness of its warlike people to band together against intruders. Britain was unprepared for a reception scarcely ever met with in India when in 1838 fear of Persian and Russian schemes pushed it into an ill-conceived war. Its intention was to replace Dost Mohamed with a rival claimant, Shah Shuja. It turned into the worst disaster, except for the American revolution, in all Britain's imperial annals.

After hopes of Ranjit Singh joining and undertaking most of the work faded, Kandahar in the south-west corner was chosen as the point of entry. In a complicated combined operation, evidence of the government's ability to plan on a grand scale, a Bombay army contingent coming up the Indus, and making free with the territory of Sind, met at Shikarpur a Bengal army corps which had marched 450 miles south-west from Ferozepore, on the edge of the Punjab, likewise making free with the ruler of Bahawalpur's territory. Distant objectives always made transport the most gruelling problem, and the necessity of sending up huge supply caravans in April and May 1839, when the heat was already intense, led to crippling losses of men and animals in the waterless wastes, where forage was scarce and foragers liable to be molested. Memories of Burma rains may have come into Pennycuick's mind as he toiled up the Bolan pass, stinking with dead camels.[4] In the Kojak pass, Captain Backhouse of the Bombay artillery noted, 'many officers lost every rag, owing to their camels falling', and at one steep point it took three hundred men to haul an 18-pound gun.[5]

Before the end of April Kandahar was occupied without opposition, but also without any of the looked-for show of enthusiasm for Shah Shuja. There was a too prolonged halt here before the march north-east to Kabul was undertaken, at the end of June. After a fortnight of it Pennycuick saw numbers of camp-followers lying by the roadside 'quite worn out with fatigue, starvation or disease – some of them reduced to perfect skeletons and unable to stand.'[6] In all arduous marching they must have suffered painfully, more even than the soldiers. A pause had to be made to reduce the great fortress of Ghazni, with a garrison of two thousand. It proved to be poorly defended. When guns were brought up to pound the walls from two hundred yards there was no reply beyond 'a few straggling and ill-directed shots from cannon and matchlocks'. A mine blew up the gate, and within an hour both town and fort were taken with trifling loss; though Pennycuick witnessed 'a great slaughter' of those who refused to yield.' As another officer observed, it was necessary to capture Ghazni without loss of time, or 'the whole country would be up in arms against us.' He thought the enemy even more astonished than the British at the rapid downfall of defences deemed impregnable.[8]

Kabul was reached, and Dost Mohamed put to flight. The self-invited guests made themselves at home in a spacious cantonment outside Kabul, as though proposing to stay permanently and run the country through their puppet ruler. The longer they stayed the less they were liked. Shah Shuja had come back too much like the Bourbons in 1814, in the baggage-train of the Allies; and there was too much readiness to impose him on the kingdom by the mailed fist. When Outram was sent out on a punitive expedition against the recalcitrant Ghilzai tribesmen, and caught 112 of them, 46 of the most 'ferocious' of these 'banditti' were taken to Kabul and executed in front of the troops.[9] More than one reverse befell detachments sent out to scour the countryside, and it was not sepoys alone who showed signs of nervous strain. Backhouse had to admit that 'those who fight up here, will see quite as much funk and unsteadiness in the European troops of Her Majesty as in any others whatever.'[10] A 'sad disaster' recorded by another artilleryman, young Michael Dawes, jolted him out of the religious trance in which he went through the war, preoccupied more with chances of salvation than of survival. A force he was attached to collided with one of 7000 men on foot, led by Dost Mohamed himself, 'who advanced in the most determined style. Our officers did the same, but the troopers of their Reg.t instead of charging, as ordered, turned to the rightabout and fled in the greatest disorder.'[11]

Towards the end of 1841 disturbances were spreading, but no decision was taken before they reached Kabul itself. In January 1842 Burns and Macnaughten, the wrangling political representatives, were among those killed in a sudden rising. When the news reached Calcutta the governor-general, Lord Auckland, was seen 'walking up and down the verandahs of Government House in a most perturbed state'.[12] At Kabul it was realized that there was no alternative but withdrawal. There were 4500 soldiers, the great majority Indian, with a mass of sick and wounded, women and camp-followers. In harsh winter conditions, and under incessant attack, morale gave way, retreat became rout, and in the end the fighting force, reduced to a handful, was wiped out. A garrison defended itself in the fort of

Jalalabad at the entrance to the Khyber pass. It was under General Sir Robert Sale, who had won the soubriquet of 'Fighting Bob', but was now a used-up man of sixty, engrossed in endless consultations. Some of his troops were in poor heart, according to Backhouse, because 'both officers and men had not, have not, and never can have, one jot of confidence in the old superannuated fool that commands them.'[13]

General Pollock brought up reinforcements: he had to 'instil some pluck into his Native troops', who knew too well what had befallen their predecessors, by visiting and haranguing them.[14] In September 1842 they marched to Kabul; there were sights 'fearfully heart-rending' as they passed heaps of the last winter's corpses, and their gun-wheels crushed the skulls of dead comrades.[15] Joined by General Nott from Kandahar, where he had held his ground all this time – a Company soldier, 'a rather peppery old gentleman',[16] but solidly competent – they restored British honour by burning part of the capital down. Shah Shuja's murder made it pointless to continue; and the army was overstretched, part of it was away in China, security inside India might be jeopardized. Imperial ambitions were becoming too complex and inflated.

Tremors and echoes of the Crimean War ran through western Asia and India, and Muslim Africa; Burton heard gossip about it in Somaliland. During the conflict the Sultan vainly tried to arouse the Central Asian principalities of Khiva and Bokhara to their opportunity of assailing Russia from the rear and forestalling its threatened descent on them. But belligerent Russophobia stirred up in the Crimea incited Britain to pick a quarrel with Persia in the winter of 1856–7, and an expedition to the Gulf was resolved on; a piece of 'enormous folly' as it appeared to Jacob, in Sind, who was consulted.[17]

Most of the manpower was drawn from the Bombay army. What success was achieved owed most to co-operation between land forces and a navy beginning to be rendered more mobile by steam. Bushire, half-way up the Gulf, capitulated to their dual persuasion. Outram was now given command, and marched somewhat aimlessly inland; he was withdrawing, baffled, when he was intercepted by the Persian main army, at Khushab. One of its generals, with 3000 cavalry, 'kept well out of the way having a presentiment', an English traveller learned, 'that the Persians would be defeated.'[18] The day ended satisfactorily, 'the ground thickly strewed with dead and dying Persians', Surgeon Mills wrote.[19] Their guns performed not too badly, but their soldiers fired so high that when their shots hit anyone it was in the rear line. A feature of the encounter widely commented on was the destruction of an infantry square by a charge of the 3rd Bombay Cavalry. Jacob hailed it as refuting the notion that mounted charges no longer stood a chance against regular infantry.[20] British losses were, as so often, minimal, while mountains of equipment were captured. But Outram could do no more than return to the coast, and steam up to the head of the Gulf and through the Shatt al Arab. His opponents continued to make a poor showing. It was a handicap to them that Khuzestan was an Arab-speaking province. At Ahwaz, the capital, they mustered 6000 infantry, strongly positioned, and cavalry. Yet 'a few rounds from the gunboats sent the brave army once more flying, with swarms of plundering Arabs at their heels.'[21] It was the Persian army's last effort, except in Central Asia, before 1981.

ii. Central Asia and the second Afghan War

Russian intrusion into Central Asia began with protection for caravans against Kirghiz marauders. During the 1830s and 1840s control was being extended over the Kazakh steppes, lines of fortified outposts were creeping eastward. A fear, not to be wondered at, was growing that British enterprise intended to push ahead of Russian into the markets of Central Asia, whose value, like that of nearly all markets outside the West, was greatly overrated. It was as a rejoinder to the British march on Kabul that a first Russian expedition set out in the winter of 1839 towards Khiva, only to be beaten back by the climate; a catastrophe like the one Britain was to suffer a couple of years later. But the desiccated khanates of Central Asia were as little capable of combining against the tsar as Indian princes had been against the Company. Nasrullah Khan of Bokhara, most southerly and furthest out of Russian reach, was at odds with Khiva, and was starting on a long train of aggression against Khokand, with the sole effect of enfeebling his rival and making it easier prey eventually for the Russians.

Irregular horse were the best combatants of the steppes and deserts, when they could be got to fight under some plan, and the best plan for confronting the Europeans would have been to depend on skirmishing, delaying, wearing down. Instead these rulers committed their forces to pitched battles which they were sure to lose, because this was the only way their cumbrous and rusty machinery could function. In 1865 Tashkent was snatched from Khokand by the

Russians. It was a fortified town with a perimeter of sixteen miles, and contained 30,000 armed men and some guns; General Tchernaiev had no more than 2000 men and twelve guns. Audacity combined with discipline brought him success; startled by the boldness of his onslaught, the defence collapsed. Next year Bokhara entered the lists, impelled by the hegemonic claims it had set up; fanaticism playing on the ignorance and vanity of the mob helped to push the Emir on. The armies met at Yedshar, where some 40,000 Bokharans were on the march towards Tashkent. It was one more display of the superiority of quality over quantity. With only 3000 men, General Romanovski attacked unhesitatingly, and though hemmed in by the unwieldy masses threw them into panic by his firm advance, backed by steady cannon-fire. His twenty guns were seconded by eight rocket-firers, not often used except by their British inventors. In 1868 the decisive battle with the Bokharans was fought outside their second city, Samarkand, which was now annexed to a newly-created province of Turkestan, under General Kaufmann. Next year the Emir submitted to the tsar's overlordship; Khiva was reduced to a protectorate in 1873, after much briefer flutterings. Khokand was annexed altogether.

There were misgivings among British observers at the prospect of a native army in Russian employment. With swarms of Turcoman cavalry, it was said nervously, the Russians would hold Afghanistan at their mercy. It turned out that they were not in haste to enrol local forces which, in the conditions of Central Asia, might prove far less easy to lick into shape than in India. But anxiety about Russian proceedings continued to ferment. In 1876, with another Balkan war breaking out, the fertile fancy of the Tory premier, the ex-novelist Disraeli, conjured up the idea of an invasion of Central Asia from India, and the viceroy Lord Lytton, son of a novelist and himself a literary dabbler, and a diplomat unburdened by any knowledge of India or Asia, set about mobilizing an army for the purpose.[22] Far the greater part of human history has had the flavour of second- or third-rate fiction.

The grandiose scheme – 'reckless or even insane as it may appear' – was endorsed by experts as eminent as Roberts.[23] It had to be dropped, none the less, as impracticable, and great care was officially taken to bury it in oblivion. But it set in motion other trains of events, centring on Afghanistan where the Amir Sher Ali, uncomfortably placed between two fires, was suspected, quite mistakenly, of being in the Russian pocket. Lytton now had in mind an alternative, not much less drastic, solution – annexation of Afghanistan, or a good part of it, and the Indian frontier advanced to the Oxus. But the Balkan crisis ended, in 1878, before Britain went to war in November, and Disraeli and his colleagues seem to have had no clear notion of what they were about.

Two years of war fell into three phases or movements, all very *agitato*, while Lytton's grand design or fantasy crumbled away piece by piece. In the first, three columns entered Afghanistan, with a total of 706 officers and 39,000 men, scarcely adequate for what was in store for them. Two fought their way to Kabul, while the third entered the southern capital unopposed; but 1842 was not long in repeating itself. Rioting broke out at Kabul, and in September 1879 Sir Louis Cavagnari, another military diplomat, who had negotiated or rather dictated a treaty, was among the Britons murdered, or *killed* as we should say if they had been Afghans occupying London. Roberts had led one of the two columns to Kabul, and now marched back there, took control of the administration, and executed a large batch of Afghans accused of having had a hand in the rioting. But to find any reliable puppets, as a political base, proved impossible; and in July 1880 a force sent out from Kandahar was badly beaten at Maiwand by a younger son of Sher Ali, Ayub Khan. Once more in the role of avenging angel, Roberts hurried from Kabul to relieve beleaguered Kandahar and defeat Ayub, who retired a mile or two from the town at his approach. Activity then petered out in a general withdrawal. With a Liberal cabinet now in office, Kandahar too, despite loud army and Tory protest, was in the end abandoned, and Quetta remained India's forward base.

It was a war that placed transport and commissariat under heavy strains, to which they proved unequal. During the winter of 1879–80 Robert's garrison at Kabul had to be continuously supplied from Peshawar, at the cost of another hecatomb of baggage-animals, another frightful sum of physical suffering. In March it took 15,000 men to keep open the 160 miles between Peshawar and Kabul, leaving only 12,000 for occupation of the capital. Long-drawn lines of communication were always a heavy tax on an army's strength; Roberts on his way up through the Kurram valley in 1878, and again on his dash to Kandahar in 1880, was bold enough to cut loose from any base, and turn his force into a 'flying column'. On the second occasion marching had to be done mostly at night, to avoid the burning sun, and on short commons.

Since the previous war Afghanistan had been fashioning an army on modern lines, reasonably well equipped. It was accompanied into battle by varying numbers of tribal volunteers and of the jehadists

65

designated by the British 'fanatics'. It was committed by its leaders to a positional style of warfare to which the Afghan genius may not have been well suited. In a series of engagements it was always defeated except once, and, although the Afghans were as a rule posted in well-prepared positions, which the British had to attack, they suffered far heavier losses. British mountain guns played an important part, but the Afghans too had artillery, sometimes not badly managed. What must have told against them was the lack of experience. Roberts got the upper hand by a simple flanking manoeuvre which never failed to bring about a hasty withdrawal. It was a sort of instinct of tribal warfare reasserting itself; in the petty encounters of the mountains, to abandon a position once it was turned was a common convention.

At Maiwand Ayub Khan had a strong corps of regulars, with 36 guns, swelled to 12,000 men by tribesmen whose motives must have been the usual blend of hatred of the foreign intruder and hope of plunder; there were also some 'Ghazis', seekers of martyrdom and paradise. For once the Afghans, deploying in the open instead of pinning themselves down, seem to have displayed tactical skill. With the help of their far superior numbers they carried out an enveloping movement, and a frenzied charge by the Ghazis then overwhelmed the wavering enemy. General Burrows lost 1300 men and his guns. He came under censure for his too passive posture, and was demoted. Britain was saved from a further calamity by the devoted Scottish orderly who rescued a young surgeon, Dr Watson, with a shoulder shattered by a jezail bullet, from the 'murderous Ghazis'.[24]

In a massive night attack on the British fortified camp outside Kabul at Christmas 1879 the assailants were thought to have sacrificed some three thousand men, while the number of defenders killed was five. But the most breath-taking act of reckless courage was the charge of the Ghazis at Ahmed Khel, when General Stewart was intercepted on his way from Kandahar to join Roberts at Kabul, in April 1880. They came over a ridge, with nearly a mile to cross under artillery fire, and got right up to the guns, while shrapnel destroyed them in heaps. For a moment the British line was thrown into disorder, but in the end its losses were the usual bagatelle, 17 killed and 115 wounded against 1000 and more than 2000 of the Afghans. The general's son and aide observed that only a fraction of the enemy army of about 15,000 took part, and that it would have been better to lurk behind the ridge and then pounce on the baggage-train and cut the marching column in two. Cool logic could not keep him from paying tribute to the dead. 'It was a glorious sight to watch these swordsmen advancing under such a withering fire without a thought of halting. .... the actual piercing of our line was truly magnificent.'[25] It was with the same wondering admiration that other Europeans watched many other suicidal onsets; magnificent, but not war.

This struggle was the new Indian army's first acid test, and the experiment had its risks, especially the use of Muslim units in a country devotedly Muslim. One night early on there were eighteen deserters, and a court-martial had to be held on men suspected of treacherously giving warning to the enemy. On the whole, considering the length and vicissitudes of the campaign, the outcome was fairly reassuring; but by 1880 Roberts had to tell his government that discontent was spreading, and this must have helped to make it look for a way to extricate itself. At St Petersburg the general staff brought out a ponderous three-volume study of the war, laying heavy stress on British shortcomings as evidence that Britain would be unable to stand a major conflict.

In Central Asia defeat of the Khanates left Russia a more elusive foe to cope with in the Turcoman tribes of the deserts and their fertile fringes. A standard procedure of the Russians was to make sweeps and carry off flocks and herds of camels, 'as a means of bringing their antagonists to reason'.[26] But as Persia and the minor despotisms decayed, the tribesmen had grown stronger; it was part of a perennial ebb and flow of Muslim history. Among them the Tekke freebooters, scourge of all their neighbours, were in the ascendant, with the Akhal oasis as their base and that of Merv, to the south, also in their grip. At Merv the citadel was a 'gigantic structure' with walls about five miles round and earthworks nearly eighty feet high, but it was in poor repair, and its cannon were worthless. Such an edifice epitomized a whole condition of society, with rulers inside the wall and commoners outside perpetually at open or silent feud. Growing strength and their leaders' accumulated booty and ambition meant that the Tekkes were being drawn out of the security of their wilds, and exposing themselves to the antagonist now approaching.

A first lunge against the Akhal oasis in 1879 was a failure because nearly all the baggage-camels died, with the result that General Lomakin could only bring up 1400 of his 16,000 men for the assault on the Geok Tepe fortification. But battle tactics were also to blame, in the view of a Russian authority. They had been learned in the recent war with Turkey, where the troops had to advance against fierce fire, but once they reached the enemy's entrenchments the day was won, for the ill-led Turkish peasant conscripts were seldom ready to fight hand to hand. With the free Turcomans the opposite was the case: their fire was ineffectual, but when the Russians, coming on in loose order, reached their objective they were attacked by eager masses and hurled back.[27] Only their cannon saved them from annihilation. Abroad the Russians were blamed for over-confidence; cockahoop with easy triumphs they had coined a catchphrase: Asiatic strategy consists in running out of one gate as we run in at another. But a worse disaster for European arms quickly followed at Maiwand; again Russia and Britain were suffering reverses close together.

Commissioned next year to set things right, General Skobelev moved his men forward gradually, in small detachments, so as to be able in the end to bring to bear an adequate striking-force of 7000, with a sufficiency of guns. Had the Tekke Turcomans still possessed their old nomad mobility, it ought to have been within their power to cut off these detachments one by one. But they were turning sedentary, and for nomads an imposing fortress might have an attraction of opposites. Geok Tepe had enormous ramparts, nearly two miles round. It held out for a month, against bombardment and mining, before being stormed in January 1881. To rub in the lesson Skobelev ordered a massacre of the male population, the action of a Genjiz or a Timur, which struck terror into the whole region for a long time. He was one of few commanders, not British or French, to achieve international fame in the colonial field, and was frequently cited by Callwell (who does not allude to the massacre).

iii. The watch on the Indian frontiers

When Burnaby was at Orenburg in the course of his venturesome trip to Khiva in 1875, he was told that officers out there were always pining for action, being mostly poorer members of the nobility with no other chance of promotion, and hence tales of raids by natives, calling for reprisals, were always being concocted.[28] Ministers at St Petersburg often had scant knowledge of what was happening; presented with a *fait accompli*, they could scarcely reject it. On the other side of the mountains frontier soldiers and agents behaved much in the same way, or were accused of so doing – one of them, Algernon Durand, warmly protested – by 'a certain school' among their own countrymen. He appealed to his own experience in maintaining that even in the narrowest sphere a man was conscious of a 'terrible responsibility' weighing on him, and would never provoke strife out of 'paltry personal ambition'.[29] He himself was very open to the charge of doing this. At the same time, there is also truth in Lyall's dictum that men on the frontier were often blamed for acts of aggression really at bottom brought about by more impersonal pressures, economic or political greeds far away.[30]

On India's north-west frontier there was the happy situation of fighting always available for men who wanted to get on, in the tribal no-man's-land between India and Afghanistan. Here they had to learn new arts, akin to those picked up by the Russians in the Caucasus. Compared with their Baluchi neighbours, Pathans were hard to quell, not because of any strong organization but on the contrary because their tribal life was very democratic, with few chiefs capable of enforcing peace. In 1850 the Afridis were blockaded in their hill refuges and starved into submission; in 1852 when all else failed recourse was had to 'the policy of slaying and burning ... odious to us, as to any of our critics', Dalhousie insisted; and dissensions were sown among the clans by each being invited to make terms for itself.[31]

Promising as these moves seemed, from 1849 to 1879 a total of 37 expeditions were set on foot, in retaliation for raids but with an admixture from time to time of political motives. Careful planning went into them. For the Hazara expedition of 1860 general instructions laid down that each man should carry a hundred rounds, men of the Guides two hundred, and that 'No women or children or superfluous followers' were permissible.[32] That year there was a large-scale irruption of Mahsuds into the plains; they were driven back, and hunted into their fastnesses, their crops and their principal township burned. There were 450 casualties among the 5000 troops engaged. Far the heaviest losses were incurred in 1863, 238 killed and 908 wounded. A routine to deal with the turbulent was being worked out: blockade – light fines if prompt compliance was forthcoming – if not, punitive steps until terms were accepted. 'Such a policy', wrote a frontier official, 'is worthy of a nation the most enlightened and humane in Christendom'; it aimed not at extirpating savages but at gradually taming them.[33] Things may not always have worked so ideally. Another Briton spoke more bluntly of the duty 'to spread amongst these savages the power of that great civilizer the sword'.[34] Englishmen were getting more and more out of their depth with the economic and social problems of their India; standing guard on the marches was a manly, elemental task which they could comprehend and cope with. Indians might see things in a different light; mounting costs were disliked, and there was suspicion that border clashes were kept going by the government's desire to keep its soldiers in trim.

Army men were fond of talking of a 'scientific frontier', and the

'Durand Line' agreed in 1893 between Sir Mortimer Durand, India's foreign secretary, and the Amir Abdul Rahman was meant to constitute one. Its chief outcome was to alarm border tribes into fearing they were going to be annexed, and set off risings in 1897 along hundreds of miles of the border. Quite large tribal levies took up arms, though there could be no link among them except religious excitement, which the British were apt to mistake for the root cause. Several columns had to be sent out to restore what passed for order on the frontier. Young Winston Churchill was with one of them. It was a 'war without quarter', he wrote to his mother. 'They kill and mutilate everyone they catch, and we do not hesitate to finish their wounded off.'[35] The Tirah campaign, which lasted into the spring of 1898, involved an Indian army of over 40,000 men. It suffered some sharp buffets, though no grave defeat. Callwell wrote of hill fighting of this sort as 'almost the most trying which disciplined soldiers can be called on to undertake': in spite of the army's two generations of familiarity with it, new British troops did not take to it as readily as Sikhs, Gurkhas, or Dogras from Kashmir.[36] Tribal tactics were improving, and Pathans who had been in the Indian army and retired or deserted brought useful hints. It was known that modern arms were being secured by way of Muscat and the Gulf of Oman, and in 1911 an effort was made, with naval co-operation, to disrupt the traffic; not much came of it.[37]

A weary sequence of damaging raids and futile chases came to be nicknamed, after General Sir James, 'Wilcox's Week-end Wars'. Sir Michael O'Dwyer, who saw something of this frontier sparring when revenue commissioner at Peshawar in 1902, thought that what was wrong was perpetual chopping and changing, with each new political officer; but it was coming to be understood that what made Mahsuds and Wazirs raiders was the barrenness of their homelands, and the most sensible idea he had heard of was to copy the Russian achievement of pacifying the Caucasus by 'great military roads and well-placed garrisons', partly because construction work would provide jobs.[38]

On the north-east frontier, intervention in Tibet was set off by border disputes, commercial hopes, and the customary scare about Russian intrigues. Jotting down many years later his recollections as a junior officer, Brigadier Spencer wrote succinctly of the Tibetans: 'The high ups had no idea of the might of the British Empire (which no longer exists). Became impudent.'[39] One fear, shared by Roberts, was that Russian influence at Lhasa would unsettle Nepal and might divert Gurkhas away into Russian service.[40] Kitchener, then commander-in-chief in India, was not much perturbed, but Curzon insisted on something being done. In all the empires the constant habit of thinking in terms of prestige among native peoples must have made individuals responsible for decisions morbidly sensitive about their own prestige among the colleagues or subordinates always eyeing them. London had many reservations. It was just after the Boer War, and colonial coups were for the time being at least not the vogue. None the less, in 1903 Younghusband, an officer who had made his name by Himalayan exploration, was sent off with an armed escort as head of a nebulous mission.

There were months of stalemate on the border, and that winter about three thousand troops were brought up to strengthen the British argument. Not much more than a picnic stroll was expected, Tibetans being reckoned a cowardly lot. Their ruling class, adequately protected from its subjects by theocracy and superstition, had little need of an army. A Japanese religious student found that soldiers were so poorly paid, in grain, as to have to do other work to support their families; officers, like priests, could borrow from government at 5 per cent and lend out money at 15 per cent.[41] In India humbler folk felt less assurance about the enterprise. Younghusband found his camp-followers deserting, in expectation of disaster, and some of the ten thousand coolies taken into Tibet were 'practically an impressed gang'. Among the still more numerous baggage-animals there was, needless to say, terrible mortality.[42]

At Guru the way was blocked by a Tibetan array; the lamas, in one narrator's picturesque words, had 'turned loose on us soggy great hordes of the stout fighting material of the country.'[43] Younghusband tried at some personal hazard to get them to surrender their clumsy weapons, but when a shot was fired fighting broke out – 'to the delight of the troops', as a journalist frankly acknowledged.[44] It was a very one-sided affair, though Younghusband was upset at its being labelled in England a massacre. More than eight hundred Tibetans, nearly half their force, became casualties. 'The remnant simply turned and walked away with bowed heads.'[45] There was sporadic skirmishing round Gyantse, about half-way to Lhasa, and the fort was taken after a siege during which two of its guns, christened Big William and Little Willie, caused some annoyance.[46] One or two scuffles took place at unprecedented altitudes, higher than Mont Blanc, and the Gurkhas climbed a 2000-foot cliff in a snowstorm. Warm clothing and a rum ration kept the men going, and as Spencer was to say, soldiers of his time were not effeminate. 'In those days one bore many service hardships as a matter of course. Today [1965] soldiers write to their MPs.'[47]

They moved on to Lhasa, fortunately very much closer to India than to any Russian territory, finding no signs of the much talked-of Russian presence and meeting no further obstruction; though in negotiations with Tibetans on the way Younghusband complained – like a burglar reproving an uncivil householder – that 'the tone they adopted entirely ignored their serious breaches of international courtesy.'[48] He thought General Macdonald dreadfully cautious, and, he wrote from Lhasa, absurdly nervous about entering the capital, 'when with a loss of less than forty killed in action we have *killed* 2700 Tibetans.'[49] A treaty was signed in September, not amounting to very much. It proved, he declared, that in spite of jeremiads at home 'we not only can make friends by force, but we actually did.'[50] A Tibetan woman writer's testimony years later is that he really did make himself liked.[51]

5

WARS IN NORTHERN AFRICA

Conquest of Algeria was resolved on towards the end of the 1820s: the restored Bourbons needed glory, or the kind of blood-transfusion that war has so often given to monarchy. Early in 1830 a force of 30,000, with little cavalry but strong in artillery, was ready; volunteers came forward from other regiments. It landed unopposed near Algiers, whose army, about equal in numbers, rashly came out to face it and was routed with huge losses. Europe could applaud the overthrow of this place of ill fame, for centuries a pirate lair. Thomas Campbell the English poet was soon there to collect materials for a book. He was quite ready to admire the French, though their society would be even more agreeable, he sighed, 'if they would not so constantly and ignorantly boast of their resemblance to the Romans.'[1] But their procedures sometimes were reminiscent of Rome: harsh reprisals, taking of hostages, planting of settlements, and, most of all, road-building, an activity they plunged into wherever their flag led them.

What the French must have hoped was nearly the end of their work was only the beginning; their first ventures into the interior and the uplands brought swift retaliation. Few Muslim governments any-where offered much impediment to European conquest, and in nearly all India Muslims were only a minority. In north Africa, as in most areas where nearly all were Muslims, the people were ready for a dogged fight. The French reply was in true Roman style. One of the earliest of many successive commanders – Algeria was soon a graveyard of reputations – the Duc de Rovigo, ordered summary executions on the slightest suspicion, showed 'unnecessary cruelty' at places like Belida, sacked in 1831, and 'swept like a destroying angel over the Metidja',[2] the plateau fifty miles inland from Algiers. Campbell almost ceased to wish good fortune to the French when he read 'their own accounts of these absurd and brutal expeditions.'[3]

Cruising along the fascinatingly oriental coast on his way to Malta in 1831, Walter Scott gathered that they wished themselves 'well clear of their bargain', and speculated on their chance of being cornered and wiped out in the deserts like the emperor Julian by the Persians.[4] A year later he might have thought so with still better reason, for it was then that Abd el Kader inaugurated a struggle for independence which lasted with some intervals for fifteen years. In genius for war he was akin to Shamyl Beg; as son of a marabout or militant devotee, a descendant of the Prophet, and a *hadji*, a man who had made the pilgrimage, he had higher spiritual claims, though his own outlook was broadened by foreign travel. He was promptly acclaimed as leader, and installed as ruler of Mascara, his native place, fifty miles south-east of Oran on a slope of the Atlas mountains. He suffered defeats when he tried to lead his men against artillery fire, but when he relied on guerrilla tactics, and a war of rapid movement with camel-riders as the striking-force, he proved extremely hard to tackle, and beguiled the French into scattering their resources over too many outposts.

To shake off this incubus the French were willing at times to recognize him as ruler of Oran province and much of the west. But a permanent accommodation was scarcely possible, and critics objected that treaties with him helped him to build up his power, obtaining European stores and workmen and crushing those who stood in his way. Among these were tribal chiefs formerly auxiliaries of the Ottoman overlords and now equally ready to join the French.[5] From Mehemet Ali's Egypt Abd el Kader derived ideas of military organization which made him want to build the nucleus of a regular army; deserters from the Foreign Legion could be useful. He may have overdone this, and foregone some of the advantages of nimbleness. At some point guerrilla forces require to move forward to a higher level. But to sustain it they must have an adequate political comprehension and programme; and Abd el Kader and his following could not conceive anything more in accord with the needs of a new age than an old-fashioned theocracy, such as made brief appearances during the 19th century in corners of the Muslim world far apart.

In 1840 the soldier destined to wear him down, Marshal Bugeaud, became governor-general. His first task was to instil fresh spirit into his army, which was being raised to more than 60,000 men. The Comte de Castellane, who served in it, was conscious of how much the rigours of African warfare and climate were preying on the men's nerves, the horrid sight for instance of French heads stuck on Arab poles, the thought of their own heads meeting the same fate.[6] Other commanders tried to counteract this by a discipline far stricter than at home, and 'very energetic measures' including punishments 'not always in conformity with the military codes.'[7] Bugeaud understood, as Castellane did, that only complete confidence in their leaders could carry soldiers through Algerian ordeals, and he won his men's trust by his successful tactics and their affection by the blunt, frank manners that made them call him 'father Bugeaud'.

Bugeaud was a disciple of the Romans, and the book he wrote was 'a classic treatise on colonial warfare for later generations of French soldiers.'[8] He relied mainly on infantry, or mounted infantry. As he told a visitor, the later Argentine president Sarmiento, he thought poorly of the Arab horsemen who could be engaged, and was against the proposal advocated by some to transform the whole French army in Algeria into cavalry: it must remain a 'civilized' army.[9] Cavalry might by now be regarded, except by the blue-blooded, as rather primitive. Native riders or Spahis were all the same made use of, and not forbidden to follow native custom by collecting ears of dead foemen and carrying heads stuck on bayonets.

There was a moment, in a nocturnal surprise of a French camp, when Bugeaud had to come 'bursting out of his tent in scanty apparel and a night-cap' and save the situation with bayonet rushes.[10] But Abd el Kader's swift raids were being countered by a similar system of *razzias*, unexpected descents on encampments or settlements to destroy or carry off their food and flocks, a task in which friendly tribesmen were happy to co-operate. There were loud philippics in Europe against these operations, as naked robbery; but war is war, as Castellane replied, and in Africa it could not be won as in Europe by the capture of a capital.[11] Before the end of 1841 Abd el Kader was being pushed back out of Algiers province into Oran, and there a double line of French posts and magazines stretching along the coast was completed in 1843 by the building of Sidi-bel-Abbès. While the French were studying mobility their opponent, deprived of space and hankering for a regular army, was in some degree losing it. Compelled to remove further west, across the hazy border into Morocco, and seek fresh support among its tribes, he was followed up by Bugeaud, and at Isly in 1844 was drawn into a pitched battle ending in shattering defeat. Swarms of Arab horsemen rode close up, firing ragged volleys, while the French infantry fire was steady and deadly. Bugeaud was elevated to Duke of Isly; in 1847 Abd el Kader had at last to submit, not in time to save Louis Philippe from overthrow a year later. The European population was still no more than 113,000, less than half of it French, and to Sarmiento the colonists seemed to feel as if they were living in the crater of an inextinguishable volcano.[12]

Inland from the coastline were the scattered fragments of the Berber race, pressed back from the sea by the Arabs. As a diversion Abd el Kader had incited some of the Kabyle 'savages', as Castellane denominated them, and there were several brushes between them and the French before 1857 when Napoleon III, desirous of matching Orleanist achievement, set 25,000 men in motion, under Marshal Randon, against the Kabyle massif. A blockade was drawn round it, to cut the hillmen off from their brisk trade with the plains. Like Afghans and all such peoples they were divided by blood feuds, though they could rally together in a precarious union against the outsider, and here as elsewhere in northern Africa there were marabouts to infuse religious fervour into the cause. A British officer accompanying the French as observer had high praise for a resistance 'almost unparallelled for temerity and audacity', though Kabyle muskets and powder were obviously of poor quality.[13] Sack and destruction of captured villages was thorough. Old quarrels broke out again at once among the clans, and after the pacification Kabyle recruits were welcomed into the French ranks.

French success must have helped to put the thought of an African exploit into the head of Marshal O'Donnell, head of the Spanish government in 1859. The Moroccan war of that winter was a salient example of how such things were often embarked on for the sake of political advantage at home, especially by regimes as unstable as Spain's. O'Donnell had lately engineered a counter-revolution; Queen Isabel's reputation left much to be desired; the army would enjoy the unwonted sensation of fighting foreigners instead of its fellow-countrymen. Spain's credit and standing in Europe had sunk, and the best way to restore them would be a colonial war, a civilized equivalent of a head-hunt in other walks of life. As well as premier, O'Donnell was war minister and commander-in-chief, wielding a combination of powers not shared by any other colonial campaigner of modern times. By mid-December he was in the field, with an army of nearly 40,000 landing at the old Spanish enclave of Ceuta.

Frederick Hardman, *Times* special correspondent, thought that he was setting about his work without adequate preparation, and that many in the army expected a mere military promenade. Its rank and file were excellent material, the Spanish peasant soldier being inured to privation and toil, and 'temperate, patient, and docile'. Charity towards an enemy was not one of his virtues, and tales of Moorish cruelty inflamed his natural disposition; from the outset the war 'assumed the most sanguinary and ferocious character.'[14] Morocco's army consisted partly of 'regular' troops of the sultan, partly of tribal levies, and was hard to hold together for long. It was brave enough, and its long-barrelled muskets, though so cumbrous as to require a prop, could shoot straight. As to leadership and tactics, if the Spaniards were not very bright the Moors were in Hardman's view 'very stupid', in allowing the enemy to thread the arduous coastal defiles so nearly unmolested.[15] Still, it was painfully slowly that the invading army crept the short distance southward to its objective, Tetuan, even with the asset of a squadron at its elbow. On New Year's Day there was a clash at Castillejos where there may have been above a thousand Spanish casualties.

Tetuan, seven miles from the sea up a narrow river, was mastered by artillery and rocket-fire; the Jewish quarter was plundered by the routed Moors. But when the Spanish army moved on it had to fight a battle in which the Moors did better, Hardman considered, than ever before.[16] Fresh warriors were arriving from the wild interior, and zealotry was being aroused; the sultan at Fez was a semi-theocratic ruler. O'Donnell was ready to patch up terms of peace and go home to take part in the Te Deums and promote himself to Duke of Tetuan, adding one more to the bevy of exotic titles adorning Europe's military élite.

In 1881 the Egyptian army was at loggerheads with a degenerate and bankrupt monarchy. Its leader was a colonel, Arabi, an estimable if not brilliant character. Official Britain was watching uneasily because of the large sums lent to the khedive by the City. In July 1882 Gladstone pocketed his Liberal principles and sanctioned drastic action at Alexandria, ostensibly in the interests of law and order. With eight battleships and a dozen gunboats able to move close in, the fleet assigned to the task must have been the most powerful ever collected for such business. Bombardment of the forts was followed by the landing of an army of occupation, to which Britain, the Mediterranean garrisons, and India all contributed: Egypt was a point where the empire was well able to fasten its noose. In deference to the exalted financial interests concerned, those sent out from home numbered units from the Brigade of Guards and the Household Cavalry, rarely seen overseas.

Arabi's main corps at Tel el Kebir was protected by elaborate though uncompleted earthworks, planned on the latest lines with ditch, parapet, firing-pits. Wolseley's attack was delivered at dawn after a night march across the desert, a manoeuvre hailed as an instructive pointer to the future: firepower was now so formidable, ran the comment, that frontal assault by daylight was no longer feasible. By the testimony of men like Sir Archibald Alison, who was with the Highland brigade, and Sir Evelyn Wood, the Egyptian and especially the black Sudanese soldiers stood their ground and fought bravely, in spite of being taken by surprise, while their officers took to their heels.[17] Popular resistance was limited to the peasantry of the Sharqiya area in the northern Delta. Sedentary agricultural populations have everywhere been recruiting-grounds for regular armies far oftener than breeding-grounds of guerrillas, if only because they offer too easy a target.

During the 19th century Turk-Egyptian imperialism was spreading down into the Sudan and pushing southward along the Red Sea coast. Its villainies ended by goading the half-Arab tribes of the Sudan into a revolt which was aided by events in Egypt and by the advent of the Mahdi, the destined leader foretold by Islamic lore. Having been dragged into Egypt by the City, Gladstone's cabinet was now dragged into the Sudan by the feeble obstinacy of the khedivial government it had restored as its puppet. In 1883 Colonel Hicks, or Hicks Pasha, a Mutiny veteran now in Egyptian employment, straggled off from Khartoum with a disconsolate force of Egyptians. It was wiped out near El Obeid, the Mahdi's headquarters, after he and his lieutenants had skilfully lured them on into the desert until they were exhausted. Early in 1884 there was a similar check when General Baker's ragged little army was crushed by the redoubtable potentate of the eastern Sudan, Osman Digna. Excitement fanned by the Tory opposition bemused the cabinet into the contradictory plan of sending troops to Suakin on the Red Sea, and General Gordon to arrange evacuation of garrisons from the rest of the Sudan. Instead of discharging his mission he let himself be shut up in Khartoum.

In the hinterland of Suakin there was inconclusive sparring, with no clear aim. One lesson was that the enemy was adept at creeping into a camp at night and spearing unwary sentries, 'in a manner which was truly astounding, considering the precautions taken.'[18] Sometimes they were not taken, and an unforeseen attack on a zareba in March 1885 resulted in the rout of the 17th Bengal Infantry, sweeping away with it the camp-followers and imperilling the entire force. Meanwhile Wolseley was heading an expedition up the Nile to rescue Gordon. From the river Sir Henry Stewart was detached by a short cut across the desert. He had fewer than 2000 men, who needed 3000 camels to carry their supplies. They advanced in the square formation which had been part of regular warfare in Europe and now in Africa was frequently adopted on the march as well as on the battlefield, with baggage-animals and followers in the centre. At Abu Klea in January 1885 they were beset by a far bigger Mahdist host, and one side of the square was broken; yet after hand-to-hand fighting the assailants were repelled and suffered much heavier losses, at least 1500 killed it was reckoned in the less than half-hour of the fray.

Wolseley meanwhile continued more commodiously up the Nile, with strings of transports hauled by Thomas Cook's paddle-boats; but Khartoum fell and Gordon perished a couple of days before relief arrived, and in London the decision was for withdrawal.

In Egypt a new army was being forged, by Sir Francis Grenfell, Sirdar or commander-in-chief from 1885, with a fund of experience gained among Kaffirs and Zulus. It was of modest proportions, but far more efficient than the old one, under British officering on the lines so long rehearsed in India. Selective conscription fell on the peasantry, as before. Men were called up for four years, followed by four in the police. A swelling flow of deserters, or prisoners, came in from the Sudan, whose inhabitants were judged excellent fighting material. Among them there was always an admixture of black Africans from the far south, whose 'delight in flag-flying and military parade and drill' could be turned to good account.[19] There is something juvenile about any soldiering, after all.

In 1885 the Mahdi died; his successor the Khalifa was the architect of a crude State, despotic and military like all in Muslim history, and to some extent an example of desert dominating fertile land. Reliance was chiefly on the more nomadic western tribes, from which a strong body of irregulars was quartered at the capital, Omdurman, rather than on the more settled population along the Nile. A nucleus of regulars was mostly composed of black troops, more amenable to drill and discipline than the tribesmen. They had rifles, but replacements for these were hard to obtain, locally made powder was coarse, and there can have been little practice shooting. Like Shamyl and Abd el Kader, the Khalifa became a less effective military director as his political authority and ambition grew. Efforts to invade Egypt, the principal one in 1889, were a fiasco. Mahdism contained no message of social liberation, which might have appealed to the heavily taxed Egyptian peasantry, and they showed no sign of readiness to rise and welcome its gospel.

Some justification was thus furnished for the drive into the Sudan which would have come in any case, with Gordon's memory rekindling a glow of the righteous indignation of 1857. Planning was done at Cairo, not London, and with remorseless thoroughness; Omdurman was more than a thousand miles from the Mediterranean. Eventually, Kitchener moved southward up the Nile in a series of jumps and then pauses while another stretch of railway track was laid. Flood-waters carried gunboats over the cataracts, others were sent out in parts to be assembled. The Mahdists waited inertly, doing little to block the advance, until at the beginning of 1898 Berber was occupied. Distrust of the riverine population may have had something to do with the Khalifa's reluctance to quit his base. There were Arab auxiliaries, from tribes at enmity with him, in Kitchener's army of 17,000 Egyptians, including Sudanese, and about half that number of British troops. In part it was a civil war of the Sudan.

The first encounter came on the Atbara, near its confluence with the Nile above Berber. Under the command of Mahmud Ahmad, the Mahdist force was sheltered by a rampart of earthworks, logs, and thornbush, as well as by lines of trenches and rifle-pits, which Kitchener hesitated at first to tackle. With his army having to storm a strong position and the enemy standing on the defensive, the usual roles were reversed, and it cost nearly six hundred casualties. Cannon, some of Krupp manufacture, and rockets and Maxims, opened the way; but it demonstrated, a commentator wrote, that with British training the despised Egyptian and Negro could be among 'the very best troops in the world'.[20]

After a pause and reinforcement, Kitchener moved on unimpeded to Omdurman. Having allowed him to come so far the Khalifa would have done well to stay behind his redoubts and leave his opponent to do the attacking again. He had twice as many men, about half of them regular troops with rifles. Recent defensive action had not turned out well, however, and now there was a reversion to the infancy of Mahdism, the fanatical onrush. To make good his spiritual claims the Khalifa may have felt that he must act imperiously, and sweep the infidel out of his sight. He may have feared desertions in a long-drawn struggle. Perhaps an anachronistic kingdom, incapable of further development, could only end like this, in a sort of heroic suicide like that of the rajahs of Bali.

But the British may also have had some ground for believing that their bombardment of Omdurman brought the Mahdist host out from the town. In the combat, on 2 September, Kitchener showed himself no great tactician, and there were some anxious moments, but it ended in total victory, with losses enormous on one side, trivial on the other. In this massacre, rather than battle, 3500 shells and half a million bullets were fired by the invaders, in a culminating display of military technology. Not much resistance by ordinary people ensued, though there were disagreeable duties still in store for some of the winners. An officer detailed to accompany a force sent to catch the Khalifa set out expecting 'a poisonous show', and was not mistaken; he had to plod on foot through burning sand, while the 'good old pampered' 14th were allotted a hundred riding-camels. 'If they can't march they should be left behind.'[21]

Separated from the Sudan by Abyssinia, but sharing the same social and religious pattern, was Somalia, whose lack of any political identity brought on it partition among three countries, France taking the north and Italy the south, with Britain in the middle. It was the British who came in for most of the rough work, having to take on the celebrated 'Mad Mullah', another of those enigmatic personalities – he was a gifted writer as well as partisan – who led the rearguard action of the old Islamic world against European intrusion, but were at the same time harbingers of something new, national unification. His soubriquet, conferred on several individuals in other lands, reflected John Bull's conviction that anyone who rejected the blessings of British rule must be out of his mind. He led his opponents a very long dance, helped by their own uncertainties about whether they wanted to be in this arid wilderness at all. A protectorate was set up in 1887, partially abandoned after ten years of the Mullah and his adherents preying on caravans and keeping the country in turmoil. A dilemma faced here and often elsewhere was that withdrawal meant leaving friendly or 'pacified' clans to be punished by the others. It could provide an argument on many frontiers for permanent occupations not in themselves worthwhile.

In 1900 a Captain Swayne was brought in from India to raise and train a small local levy. In a land of chronic tribal warfare the number wanted could be collected with ease; they were licked into shape, mostly as infantry, by Indian NCOs from Aden and a score of officers from India and Britain. Their opponents' tactics alternated between regular engagements, always lost, and guerrilla skirmishes, frequently won. As everywhere in the Muslim world the instinct of the more enthusiastic or fanatical, the 'dervish' élite of the Mullah's following, was to rush on without counting the cost: any caution might betoken a niggardly trust in the protection of Heaven. Moreover it was hard to keep any big tribal force together for long. But the Mullah, whose forces were diminutive compared with the Khalifa's, and his religious claims less topheavy, always until late on kept his movement flexible and mobile, usually retaining the initiative; while his pursuers were always hampered by problems of supply, water above all.

It was proof of his hold over his followers, enforced when necessary as in Shamyl's Caucasus by horrific penalties against backsliders, that it was unshaken even when they had to be dispersed among the hills in small bands, as happened after the costly failure of an offensive in May 1901. One of their triumphs, at Gumburu in April 1903, they owed to a combination of surprise with reckless daring. A small British relieving force on the march was surrounded in thick bush, and charged by the dervishes in spite of its Maxims: it lost two hundred men, though they lost far more. More men had to be called in from India, with no less than a major-general to take over. At Jidbali in January 1904 the Somalis tried to break into a square. They came on more deliberately this time, in loose order, taking advantage of all the cover they could find. But few could get closer than a quarter-mile, and this worst of all their defeats cost them more than six hundred lives. Again the Mullah evaded capture, but in 1905 he had to draw off for a while and lie doggo.

In the later stages of his career there was a marked turn towards reliance on fortified strongholds, perhaps explainable by age and stiffening joints. He got masons from the Yemen to build forts, on the edge of an escarpment, which ought to have been able to bid defiance but were carried by storm fairly easily near the end of 1913. Here and in the Sudan it may have been easier to construct defences than to teach nomads how to man them. Driven further back, but given a respite by the Great War, the Mullah established a new headquarters at Taleh, with an astonishing ring of fortresses which must at least have had the value of impressing simple tribesmen.

In 1881 the French moved into Tunisia. As usual, mastering the interior took more than the effort anticipated, and 40,000 troops had to be set to work in the broiling summer heat. Many were young conscripts from France, which helped to make the whole affair unpopular. In 1885 a column suffered heavy loss in an ambush, but too often the Tunisians indulged in wild galloping charges, easily beaten off. Two decades later France was setting out to complete its conquest of the Maghrib, or north-west Africa, by snapping up Morocco. In 1914 German invasion of France halted, with some retributive justice, a full-scale offensive launched by France against Morocco in the spring. Meanwhile Spain had foolishly swallowed French bait and was trying to appropriate a portion of the country, round its old footholds of Ceuta and Melilla; Tetuan was part of it. Protest against a fresh draft of conscripts for Morocco set off the events of the 'Tragic week' at Barcelona in 1909; and while they were going on General Pintos, rashly pushing into the Riff mountain region, suffered a heavy defeat in the 'Wolf's ravine', with losses running into thousands. It was another of Europe's major reverses in Africa.

In September 1911 Italy went to war with Turkey in order to snatch its last African possession, Libya. So secretive had been the premier Giolitti and his much more aggressive foreign minister Giuliano, that the army as well as Europe was taken by surprise. Some weapons were in short supply, and there were delays in getting a corps of two infantry divisions ready. It was equipped with mountain guns, and the two Bersaglieri regiments had machine-gun sections; in all, 35,000 men, with 72 guns. With warships in support the coastal towns were seized, beginning with Tobruk; Benghazi gave most trouble. The Turkish garrison proved obstinate; still worse, the native population, counted on as usual to welcome the invaders as deliverers, showed no sign of doing so. Religion kept Arab and Turk together, and the soon unmistakable Arab hostility did much to turn European opinion against Italy. While Rome fretted over slow progress, General Caneva realized that any sweeping move into the trackless interior was impracticable. Every oasis harboured guerrillas, with weapons concealed in trees, even in tombs. By early 1912 it was clear that the war could not be won in Libya, and naval action had to be undertaken against Turkey, with a landing on Rhodes. Peace came in October, leaving Libya for Italy to digest.

There was a sharp collision at the Sciara al Schiat oasis just before the end, with 548 Italian casualties. In all 92 officers and 1391 men were killed, a proportion of one to fifteen. There were symptoms in the army of flagging ardour, and the government, overruling its commanders, judged it wise not to keep soldiers on duty for more than six months. When officers were allowed to apply for leave to return home, many did, and a shortage resulted.[22] Italy was deficient in the standard European type of officer; not for a very long time had there been a true military aristocracy. There were riots against conscription for colonial service, as there had been in 1896. Guerrilla activity smouldered on, finding a leader or spokesman in another sectary, Sayyid Ahmad al Sharif, who succeeded to the headship of the recently founded Senussi order of dervishes. In 1914 Italy still controlled not much more than the coast.

6

WARS IN BLACK AFRICA

i. Kingdoms and republics

Countries beyond the Sahara with a recognizable political structure formed a very diverse and widely scattered group. Oldest, and alone in maintaining its independence almost unbroken, was Abyssinia, a loose conglomeration or southward-expanding Amhara empire. Britain's incursion in 1868 had for aim no tangible gain, but the freeing of a consul and some missionaries held in durance vile by a ruler, Theodore, who seems to have been going out of his mind; true, there was much tactless British conduct to infuriate him.[1]

A base was found at Zula, south of Massawa on the Red Sea, with Egypt, its titular owner, more or less assenting. From there Theodore's mountain nest at Magdala was 400 miles south, through rugged country. It was chiefly as an exercise in logistics that the expedition was noteworthy, and as an effort to profit by Crimean lessons, medical and other. About 12,000 troops were collected, two thirds of them Indian and less well armed than the British; there was a multitude of followers as always. Transport would be the chief problem, though a railway was built for the short first stage, and tens of thousands of baggage-animals were mobilized. A break had to be made with old luxurious habits, and each officer was restricted to one servant and one baggage-mule: many dodged the rule, but as the march went on it was stiffened. Among the rank and file the hardships were felt acutely, and at one point there were symptoms of dissatisfaction in a British regiment. Things would have been worse if the overlord of Tigre province had not been willing to side with the British against Theodore. In the fighting at the approaches to Magdala the defenders were able to inflict pitifully few casualties. They had some cannon on the heights, but to direct fire accurately over a downward range of 3000 yards was beyond the gunners' skill; while the Snider breech-loaders of the British, in action for the first time, had a devastating effect on opponents who might have stayed behind cliff-top walls, but instead came rushing down from them to attack.

In 1885 Italy found a pretext of a well-worn sort for occupying Massawa as nucleus for a colony of Eritrea, which would deprive Abyssinia of a coastline. Hostilities broke out in 1887, and an Abyssinian army inflicted a reverse significant enough to bring down the Italian cabinet; but by 1893 there was an adequate body of well-trained native troops under Italian officers and NCOs to repel a Mahdist incursion. Against Abyssinians they would as Muslims show all the more alacrity. There was the familiar spectacle of military men eager to distinguish themselves; they were headed by General Baratieri, governor from 1892. He and the premier, the Sicilian Crispi, an eager expansionist, were old partisans of Garibaldi and liberty. Abyssinia under its new ruler Menelik was preparing to march into Eritrea: Baratieri, to forestall him, in 1894 made a demonstration in force into Tigre. After scoring one success he may have wanted to retire, but was said to have been overborne by his officers, some of them newcomers. Very likely soldiers of all flags making their colonial début were unrealistic about the chances of war, and all Europeans were coming to share the confidence inspired by one another's successes in Africa. In December a Major Toselli, leading the advance, was cut off and lost, with twenty officers and 1300 native troops.

Crispi sent reinforcements, and took King Umberto to Naples with him to see them off, but they were mostly raw volunteers. On paper Baratieri was being provided with a more than respectable figure of 30,000 Italians; fewer than half could be brought to bear at the front. He had besides 14,000 native troops, and 70 guns, mostly small mountain pieces. He was being prodded by the impatient Crispi, in need of trophies for political reasons. Menelik was an old and seasoned general, with a well-informed interest in modern weapons, and took the field in person, as not all African rulers did. He was at Adowa with an army said to number with its feudatory contingents 120,000 men, two-thirds of them with fairly up-to-date rifles. Forty thousand royal troops formed the core, with nearly all the guns; among these, a novelty for a non-European army, were Hotchkiss quick-firers, which were to prove valuable. His men were animated by a religious patriotism as ardent as any felt by their Muslim neighbours. In the battle, on 1 March 1896, some were like madmen, a survivor declared, with berserk fury.[2]

As so often with European armies, Baratieri's intelligence work was very faulty. Whether because some of his spies were enemy agents, as was said, and gave him false reports, or because of a dearth of cavalry for scouting, the Italians were quite in the dark about their position, and failed to co-ordinate their reaction to Menelik's enveloping tactics. In the worst of all European disasters they lost something like 6000 killed, more than half of them Italian, and 4000 wounded or captured. It would have gone harder still with them if enemy casualties, which may have reached 17,000, had not been crippling enough to deter pursuit. Menelik kept his head, and was ready for peace, leaving Eritrea with Italy; he must have doubted whether his army could break through its fortified lines. Adowa had repercussions further afield. It hastened the British conquest of the Sudan, by giving it the added motive of restoring the prestige of all white men. Africans beyond the seas could hail the battle as a triumph for Africa, as Asia a few years later hailed the Japanese victory over Russia. There were Indian nationalists too who 'secretly rejoiced'.[3]

As British power established itself little by little on the west African coast and then filtered inland, its most obdurate opponent was the Ashanti kingdom, built up largely on control of trade routes running inland and possession of more firearms than peoples of the interior could obtain. Its rulers did not enjoy undisputed control over the armed forces, and to compensate for this were setting up new units of their own, starting with royal slaves and a bodyguard of outsiders who seem to have been in the early 19th century Muslim horsemen.[4] Their soldiers were good practitioners of bush warfare, proficient in use of cover and surprise. In their first trial of strength with Britain, in 1821, the defeat and death of Sir Charles MacCarthy was a feather in their cap, though later the tide turned.

The real grapple came in 1874, when a punitive campaign as far as Kumasi, the capital, was ordered after Ashanti incursions into coastal territory. It was entrusted to Wolseley, who had with him engineers, light guns, and the ever-present naval party with rocket-tubes. Most of his troops were British; some good local material was being unearthed, particularly among the Hausa, a peasant people who had been overrun by the pastoral Muslim Fulani. Two native regiments with Wolseley were of partly Hausa composition; curiously, the Ashanti army too was enrolling a Hausa corps. In addition there was a West Indian Regiment stationed in west Africa.

The Ashantis lurked behind cover and harassed the invading force until at Amoafu, not far from the capital, they made their stand, with an army that may have totalled fifteen or twenty thousand, and may have suffered two thousand casualties. They gave a good account of themselves, but their muskets were mostly antiquated pieces firing lead slugs, and they were hard hit when guns were brought up to fire salvos at very close range into the undergrowth where they were massed. Not at all discomfited, they drew off, breaking up into small platoons which hung troublesomely about the supply lines. Kumasi was duly entered and burned; sickness among his men then obliged Wolseley to withdraw. In its last years the Ashanti monarchy kept up its endeavour to re-equip itself. Double pay was offered to deserters from the Gold Coast Constabulary, breechloaders were secured from French sources. But this was not forging a national army, and it may be that like many others in Afro-Asia the old political fabric was losing its vitality, wilting under the chill breath of the outer world, and lacked conviction to make use of its new means. When the sudden final stroke was delivered in 1896, by forces brought together from Gambia, the Cape, Malta, and Britain, there was no struggle. In Madagascar the Hova kingdom had lately crumpled up before the French in the same fashion, after long resistance earlier on.

Further east along the Guinea Coast, the kingdom of Dahomey was another conquest-state, enlarged during the century by able and aggressive rulers under whom an ethnically very mixed population was being fused into a kind of nation. Here too the armed forces were the last part of the state apparatus to be brought under firm central control, and bodies of royal slaves were the most reliable.[5] It was the king's celibate female battalions that gave Dahomey most of its fame or notoriety abroad. Burton on his mission to King Gelele was satirical about these Amazons, though he considered the male soldiery even worse: he saw none deserving to be called regulars, and only a third of them were armed with 'cheap trade guns'; these were kept in good order, and uniforms were neat.[6] In the later 19th century the army numbered about 14,000, three thousand of them women, with regulation costume, and drums and standards for each unit; there were a few horsemen, and some companies of archers with poisoned arrows.[7]

When Dahomey found itself in the path of French advance it did its best to get ready. Breech-loading rifles were bought, and even some cannon. These were a surprise to the French column in 1892, mostly African troops and Legionaries, and they inflicted some losses on it as it moved forward in square formation through bush less dense than in the Ashanti country. Guns were well handled, though their effect was reduced by shells failing to burst. Dahomey's army, with women-soldiers still in its ranks, was broken as it strove to bar the way to the capital; but irritating guerrilla activity followed. Perhaps because its first encounter with Europeans was also the last, Dahomey in its final phase preserved a stronger will to live than the Ashanti state.

Zululand was truly a nation in arms. On the map it looks a very minute corner of Africa, and if its population was really no more than about 300,000 it argues an extreme degree of militarization that in its last war in 1879 approximately 50,000 men were enrolled.[8] Of these about 40,000 were fit for action, half of them under thirty: young men were conscripted into camps and forbidden marriage until they had 'washed their spears'. They were banded in twenty-six regiments, each of which had a continuous existence, something very exceptional outside Europe, with shields painted in its own distinctive colours. It was a system forged under pressure of the drive southward in search of living-space, and perfected by the great conqueror Shaka; his broad-bladed stabbing spear, bringing with it a deadlier style of warfare, was an innovation comparable with the entry of the bayonet into Asia and Africa. If Zulu tradition can be relied on, he rejected firearms because of their slowness in loading, though he was clearly anxious to learn more about them. Posts of command were the reward of merit instead of birth.[9]

Zulu territory had its forests, hills, ravines, and use had been made of these. But the tendency of the expanding military machine was towards battles of encirclement on the open plains, and this would end by favouring the white man whose weapons were even better adapted to it than the assegai. Shaka's successor Dingane suffered a costly defeat by Boer trekkers in 1838, at the Blood River, where his army wasted thousands of lives by throwing itself in broad daylight against Andries Pretorius's well-prepared laager and three small cannon. Contact or collision with the whites was too intermittent to bring change; the Zulus were engaged in strife with African neighbours, as a rule easily quelled, or in civil broils. With prosperity the military system was lapsing, until restored by Cetshwayo. King from 1873, he might well think it time for his country to look to its defences, threatened by Natal on the south and Boer encroachments on the western and northern borders. But what was called for was a new plan of warfare, and he was going backward by reviving the regimental system and strengthening thereby the entire conservative pattern of life and belief.[10]

Sir Bartle Frere, governor of the Cape and formerly of Bombay, was a man of unquestioning annexationist faith. Disraeli's bungling and irresolute cabinet failed to hold him in check, and at the end of 1878 he forced Cetshwayo into war. Seven British infantry regiments were marshalled, with some mounted infantry, Colonial volunteers, the inevitable naval brigade, rockets, and Gatlings. Reinforcements brought in when the task proved a sterner one than Frere reckoned on included two cavalry regiments and a bevy of generals and colonels. Native forces were not easily organized in a region of white settlement and racialism. Even though it was the Natal settlers who would profit most by the conquest – the war itself was 'a superb financial windfall' for them and the Cape whites[11] – their mouthpiece Sir Henry Bulwer, the lieutenant-governor, was unwilling to let any Kaffirs be recruited. A Natal Native Contingent was got together, largely by the bait of cancelled tax-dues, but it was very poorly equipped, and many of the officers and NCOs were drawn from the 'less desirable' type of settler,[12] not always of British origin. Its record was understandably poor, and some of the men deserted; so did some white volunteers.

Zulus who had fallen foul of the despotic Cetshwayo were quite ready to collaborate with Lord Chelmsford's columns, and were helpful guides as they tried to converge on the capital, Ulundi, by five routes through unexplored country intersected by swollen rivers. Transport was soon in a chaotic state, as 700 ox-waggons and 10,000 native drivers and porters straggled along. Zulu armies were prodigiously mobile, and their commanders manoeuvred skilfully, appearing and disappearing and confusing Chelmsford as to the whereabouts of their main concentration. In January 1879 one British force, in an entrenched camp at Isandhlwana, was abruptly assaulted and overrun. It was one of Europe's dramatic defeats, like Maiwand eighteen months later. But the fortunes of war soon turned, and at Ulundi in July there was the familiar story of fire-power overwhelming courage, displayed by the Zulus as heroically as anywhere in the world as they tried to get to grips with their enemies. They were among the very few peoples for whom the bayonet would hold no terrors, but they could not get near enough to challenge it. 'The canister tore through them like a harrow through weeds', the war-correspondent Forbes wrote, 'the rockets ravaged their zigzag path through the masses.'[13] They had more than 1500 casualties, the British fewer than a hundred.

Britain had fought its recent Ashanti war with tried veterans, the Zulu war was a test of the 'Cardwell system' of linked battalions introduced in 1871, because, as in the Afghan war immediately following, it resulted in short-service recruits being sent to the front young and inexperienced. They incurred much criticism. Their firing it was said was often wild, a mere blazing away at nothing, instead of the controlled volley-firing that distinguished good European troops from Afro-Asians with firearms. 'These young soldiers are more bother than they are worth', was one intolerant verdict.[14] The Zulus, like other military societies in history too rigid to change, suffered from the opposite defect of being highly trained on lines no longer relevant. Individual warriors were not so unadaptable. In one of their attacks in force the British 'could not but admire the perfect manner in which these Zulus skirmished'. At Rorke's Drift 'they took advantage of every bit of cover there was, ant hills, a tract of bush'.[15] All the same, they were losing hundreds of men there and failing to wipe out a station made up of a few buildings held by scarcely more than a hundred men. Accounts of how many at Isandhlwana had firearms vary. After that victory they had captured rifles to add to their stock, but used them inexpertly, and the partial adoption left them in the same awkward unbalance between old and new as many other Afro-Asian peoples in that epoch. They could besides be thrown into confusion by cavalry pursuits. It was a grave deficiency in the Zulu army to have no mounted force of its own, after so many years of the horse in southern Africa, and various neighbours taking it into service.

By contrast, their neighbours the Boers had only the sketchiest organization, but were expert riders and marksmen. The British were to learn this painfully, but their first encounter gave little warning. It was in 1848, when trekkers who moved from the Cape to the Orange River showed that they considered themselves to have left British authority behind. A young cadet, William Fleming, was ordered off with his regiment on a 400-mile march, with officers allowed only one box each for their belongings.[16] Reaching the river in August, the force had to cross it on a couple of rafts, a risky business if the Boers had not for some reason fallen back from the other bank. Even so Sir Harry Smith, that 'most extraordinary man', had to put everyone on their metal: 'he is all life and engery', Fleming wrote, 'and works from daylight till dawn – swears most awfully at every one from his Aides de Camp down to the drummer boy.'[17] They marched to Bloemfontein, and on to Boomplaats where, on the 30th, 'the Dutch opened fire on us from a most beautiful position', but caused only a handful of injuries before being put to flight over the stony hills, cannon and horsemen expediting their retreat.[18] Shell-fire was something they were as little accustomed to as their African victims to rifle-fire.

The country between Orange and Vaal was turned loose in 1854 as the Orange Free State. Boers further on, in the Transvaal, were taken over in 1877 when their raw trekker republic was on the verge of collapse, and the British obligingly subdued some tribes for their behoof, but only earned the habitual ingratitude of settlers everywhere. In 1880 they rebelled, and had the best of three small affairs. In the last of these the impetuosity of Sir George Colley, an officer too much in a hurry for fame, played into their hands. He led his men to the top of Majuba hill, where he and two-thirds of them fell to sharpshooters. There were practically no Boer losses; for once the imperial biter was being bit, and for once discipline broke down and the force, losing most of its officers, dissolved into a mob.

This *lèse majesté* rankled, and as soon as the Sudan had been dealt with it was the turn of the Boers. Gold-mines, of course, were the *causa causans* of the Boer War. In 1899, unlike 1880, the Orange Free State joined the Transvaal. As much public fury was worked up against them as against any coloured opponents in the whole century, except in 1857. It did not need a black or brown skin to make John Bull see red. What soured British temper further was that these unprofessional soldiers, mere yokels, were soon scoring off their aristocratic assailants. Racial arrogance gave Boers something of the same fighting spirit as the poor whites in the Confederate army in America. British soldiers kept finding themselves peppered by marksmen they could not see, with no target to fire back at. Cavalrymen soon had to follow the ignominious Boer example and turn themselves into mounted infantry, looking for cover.

Britain went to war with 'extreme casualness', and a still firm faith in 'the traditional virtues of "amateurism"'.[19] It has been called the last of the 'gentlemanly wars', and officers brought with them valets, grooms, hampers of delicacies.[20] But before long the biggest forces ever employed in a colonial war before 1945 were having to be gathered. For the first time militiamen and Volunteers had to be sent overseas. Men from the Dominions took part, as if rehearsing for 1914. There were 8000, French-speakers among them, from Canada where the premier Sir Wilfrid Laurier tried vainly to restrain popular enthusiasm. A few years earlier there had been Canadian boatmen on the Nile, and 600 volunteers from New South Wales at Suakin. With its machinery recently overhauled the War Office did at least exhibit ability to mobilize and put in the field very large numbers. Otherwise, talent was displayed chiefly by contractors, in fleecing the public. When things came to an end public dissatisfaction was, for the first time, deep enough to make a searching enquiry unavoidable, and its report in 1903 'revealed an appalling picture of lack of preparedness'.[21]

British generals started with frontal attacks, as if to show that they were as good as Zulus or dervishes. In December 1899 General Wauchope, commanding the Highland brigade with a force sent out to relieve Kimberley, was killed in an impossible assault on a Boer position on a line of heights with two miles of trenches along its front protected by barbed wire. At Spion Kop Buller's attack was boldly conceived, but the staff work was 'criminally negligent and irresponsible', and the command 'utterly torpid and hidebound'.[22] Shortcomings displayed in this 'Black Week' were only partially remedied when Roberts was sent out to take charge. He was a man of 67; it was an era of venerable politicians, and reverence for grand old men spilled over into other fields. His chief of staff, Kitchener, 'was in no sense a staff officer and had no idea whatsoever of staff work';[23] he always insisted on doing everything himself. Kitchener's first essay was the battle of Paardeberg, in February 1900, the costliest day's work of the war; confusions and misunderstandings were largely to blame for the 1200 casualties.

A good many senior officers had to be relieved of their posts; they were sent to cool their heels at Stellenbosch, whence it became customary to say that a failed commander had been *Stellenbosched*,[24] as in the French army in the Great War he was *Limogé*. So many officers surrendered precipitately, Somerset Maugham heard, that 'it was not till some were shot and more cashiered that the majority nerved themselves to a stouter courage.'[25] In wars with Afro-Asians there was far less temptation to surrender: it would be jumping out of the frying-pan into the fire. In the later stages things were easier, and a barrister serving as sergeant in Paget's Horse, a retired officer's son, wrote to his family that as the war was dragging on he had better get himself promoted, 'because it is a picnic for an officer', and 'commissions are to be had almost for the asking if there is the slightest influence used at home.'[26] But in one way and another about 3700 officers were killed, or died, or were invalided out, leaving a serious shortage. As to the rank and file, men drawn from the auxiliary formations were even more inexperienced than short-term regulars. Of the two contingents of 'Imperial Yeomanry' from Britain the second proved no better than 'a vast number of untrained men lured by the pay of 5s a day.'[27]

Generalship did not scintillate on the Boer side either. Smuts held that the game could have been won early on, but for Piet Joubert and 'the age and decrepitude of this hoary old general'.[28] Adroit at small-scale tactics, Boers were products of a centrifugal society which could not rise to broad views of strategy or anything else. They tied up their forces by investing towns like Mafeking, while British reinforcements were poured into south Africa. Diehards who kept up the fight to the end, simply organized in commandos made up of squads of twenty-five men, excelled in harassing British columns and dodging pursuit. It seems strange that they could be so evasive, since they travelled with ox-waggons whose best speed was four miles an hour. Poor intelligence-work by the British army, a fault it was so commonly taxed with, must be part of the explanation. Boers sent out experienced men to reconnoitre, the British left it to callow juniors.[29] They fell back on the 'methods of barbarism' condemned by the Liberal leader Campbell-Bannerman, covering the veld with slaughtered cattle and, an ill omen for the future, rounding civilians up into concentration camps, where mortality was heavy.

'There is no denying', a British commentator wrote ' ... that war between white people in presence of the black has always been deprecated as a sort of treachery to a common bond.'[30] There was nagging fear of native uprisings, one reason why it was felt necessary to send out such bloated forces. Some did occur, though on a very limited scale. From the outset the combatants were in accord about keeping this a white man's war, and not bringing in soldiers of any other colour. Formerly they had been less squeamish. Boers as well as Britons made use of African troops; at Boomplaats there were some mounted Griquas with the British. Early in 1898 at the time of the Fashoda crisis it was heard in Paris that the British were thinking of bringing two thousand Zulus to the Sudan.[31] But as things were now in southern Africa it was felt that to put rifles into black hands might put dangerous ideas into black heads. The taboo extended to other races, and there was much comment in India on the absence of Indian troops from the scene, along with some satisfaction at British lickings.[32]

Each side accused the other of violating the code, and each had some limited justification, the Boers rather more: it was easier for the British, as far the stronger, to allow themselves a little latitude. At Mafeking Baden-Powell had a few hundred Africans, with obsolete rifles, as scouts or watchmen, who occasionally got a chance to use them. This 'Black Watch' was a medley of Zulus and others, and there was a contingent of 'Cape Boys' or Coloured, who had a special relish for firing at Boers.[33] That remarkable African Plaatje, who kept a diary of the siege in English, reproduced the native pronunciation of Maxim, *Makasono*, and compared the gun's sound to 'supernatural melodies in a paradise.'[34] It was rarely that Africans could take pleasure in the music of a machine-gun, but for once the bullets were flying the right way. In the long-drawn chase after the commandos Kitchener armed some ten thousand black messengers, drivers, and the like. Boers responded in their own fashion; when they caught a Kaffir scout during a night attack on a camp on the veld. They 'stripped him of everything and shot him as he went off.'[35] After the war they were soon able, in partnership with the English-speaking colonists, to put the black man back in his place. By holding out so long they forced an appeasement policy on the post-war Liberal government. It would never be feasible for Britain to mount such a ludicrously huge operation on south Africa again, especially when decks were being cleared for a war in Europe. In 1910 the African majority was abandoned to white domination. An 'armed peasantry', as Bernhardi correctly wrote, had made itself the leading people of southern Africa.[36]

ii. Tribes and villages

In black Africa only Britain and France collided with organized polities, and more often they like the Portuguese, Germans, Belgians, only had tribal peoples to deal with, though some of these had sharp enough claws. It was among them, in southern and then eastern Africa, that white settlers were pushing their way in. Cape Colony expanded briskly; with it came an inheritance of settler wars against native peoples, of the kind so frequent and so baneful in later southern African history. Of nine 'Kaffir wars' destined to stretch over a century, the first broke out in 1799. In 1812 Grahamstown, 500 miles east from Cape Town, was founded as a military base against the Kaffirs – a name covering native peoples, other than Hottentots, of various stocks. There was a still-moving frontier, along a coastal corridor flanked by the broken hill country at the edge of the plateau, where enemies could hide as they did, especially, in the Amatola mountains. Kaffirs were always accused of cattle-stealing, which no doubt was part of tribal life, as land-stealing was of settler life. Drought in their territories helped to drive them into hostilities in both 1834 and 1846; more continuously white encroachments were depriving them of more and more pasture-land.

A lone voice or two in the army could advocate conciliation.[37] Soldiers could at least appreciate warlike virtues in their foes, at times; settlers could never rise above what Winston Churchill, visiting Africa, called 'the harsh and selfish ideas which mark the jealous contact of races and the exploitation of the weaker.'[38] Livingstone wrote prophetically in 1847 of the danger of Africans further away coming to be filled with the same 'determined hatred' that most of those close to Cape Colony felt for all Europeans.[39] In the earlier days of empire the task of serving as bodyguard to flocks of plebeian settlers was not one that regular army men took kindly to. In Wolfe's eyes American colonists were 'cowardly dogs', Canadians 'vermin'.[40] To an officer in south Africa local volunteers, British or Boer, might appear not much more than cattle-reivers, who wanted Britain to do the serious fighting, and foot the bill.[41] When the governor during one emergency summoned all burghers, 'under the old commando system', to take up arms and join his soldiers, they made 'a most mean and pitiful response',[42] as American colonists often did when called on in frontier wars. Rather than do duty themselves they were willing at this stage to let natives be utilized. Hottentots were recruited to the Cape Mounted Rifles. Another army grievance was that 'winklers' or traders carrying stores to the camps in their 'winkel waggons' sponged up all the soldiers' savings by charging 'absurd and extravagant prices'.[43] According to Livingstone the Grahamstown storekeepers showed further smartness by selling muskets to Africans, and so making more likely the conflicts they were always looking forward to because war enriched them by inflating prices.[44]

Kaffir weapons were knobkerrie and shield and, by contrast with the Zulus, javelins instead of stabbing spears: each man carried half a dozen and could hurl them 'with incredible force', piercing a man's body, and killing at forty yards.[45] They were avid for muskets, which by the report of a witness often exposed to them they 'quickly learned to handle with considerable precision';[46] perhaps because accustomed to using missiles, and to taking aim from behind cover. They were adept besides at riding. Native deserters from British service could impart new tricks or flourishes. A leader came on horseback to a parley in a staff officer's uniform, 'attended by a mounted staff and a bugler'.[47] It was thanks to such adaptability that the Kaffirs were able to protract their resistance for so long, though different tribes or peoples were in the forefront at different times. On the other hand Kaffraria also supplied some auxiliaries to the British. It was not a simple democratic society; there were powerful chiefs, whom the wars must have strengthened, and there was a servile class of Fingos, 'wanderers', broken remnants of clans thrust down here by the Zulu avalanche. Fingos were hard to discipline, but fine skirmishers.

The sixth war, of 1834–5, began with an irruption by a Xhosa host, throwing the white population of the eastern Cape into panic. They were repelled with difficulty, a swingeing indemnity in cattle was collected, and all the territory up to the Kwei river annexed, to form British Kaffraria. Coming out as a new-fledged Ensign in 1846, Fleming was delighted to find another war in progress. He visited the scene of an engagement where the 7th Dragoons had cut up an enemy force and a river bank was strewn with corpses for five miles. 'I have got the jaw of a Kafir', he informed his family, 'which I took off a skeleton on the field as a relic'.[48] He was heartened too by the determination of a new governor, Sir Henry Pottinger, to have a real go at the 'treacherous and cowardly' foe. 'I think there is every chance of a good rattling war and no humbug'.[49]

Pottinger's strategy called for three divisions to penetrate the Amatola mountains from separate points and move towards a rendezvous. Fleming was disappointed by their failure to get to grips with the elusive foe. 'We burnt innumerable Kraals or villages consisting of from 6 to 12 huts', but when a scrimmage seemed in prospect 'the brutal cowards took refuge in a forest and were not game to fight'.[50] White men never outgrew their naive disgust at such unsoldierly conduct. Five officers who strayed out of the camp were found mutilated and beheaded, but William's juvenile ardour was not damped – 'the more I see of the army the more I love it'.[51] Some of his seniors had soon had enough of it: 'the old Hands don't like this work', and would like to retire.[52] By the time the 'harassing but inglorious' struggle ended he himself was tired of it, though he regretted the loss of eighteen pence a day of 'war pay'. He thought however that Sir Harry Smith, now in command, made peace over-hastily, instead of 'thoroughly breaking the enemy' as Pottinger would have done.[53]

Within three years Sir Harry was urgently asking for reinforcements from Europe, to make head against a fresh ebullition. It was stirred up, the whites perhaps with some reason believed, by chiefs and sorcerers fearful of losing their sway under the new order. Kaffir police, lately organised, joined in the outbreak, carrying their equipment with them. Hottentot converts on a mission station joined the rebels; so, in March 1851, did a body of Cape Rifles. 'What next?' exclaimed the delighted Livingstone. 'We may expect our cats to have a strike. Everywhere there is a strong feeling of independence springing up.' He derided the governor, Sir George Cathcart, 'this mighty man of valour', who would never forgive the Hottentots for foiling him or the missionaries for believing that they had souls.[54]

It was a hard bout, chiefly among steep and densely wooded hills, where cavalry was useless and the infantryman with his archaic uniform and cumbrous pack not much more at home. Captain King and his comrades of the 74th Highlanders, suddenly translated here from Cork, had a lot to put up with from cold, hunger, sandstorms, rainstorms, prickly scrub, and fatigue. Again there were regrets that 'attempts for a fair open fight were quite unsuccessful'.[55] Operations drifted on; a new commander appeared, but, Fleming wrote home, what they needed were ten new regiments.[56] England did at least send out several new-model rifles, and novel bullets like the Minié; Kaffirs were convenient subjects to experiment on. Rockets were useful for discharging into inaccessible gorges. But the enemy too was displaying ingenuity as well as tenacity. Small free-stone breast-works, cleverly constructed, sheltered snipers. With scanty impedi-menta, body greased, wrote King, the Kaffir 'works through the familiar bush with the stealth and agility of the tiger'; he quoted Sir Harry's description of these tribesmen as 'most formidable enemies, as much as I ever encountered', worthy peers of any Algerians or Caucasians.[57] Any jackal's lair or hollow trunk might conceal a foe; 'in an instant the silent forest is suddenly peopled as it were with a legion of naked savages'.[58]

Gradually their endurance was worn down, and they were left crippled by losses of life and then a vast confiscation of cattle, while the stubborn hill region was opened up by road-building, and small garrisons were planted in posts with stone wall and turret. There was an epilogue to this war in a march beyond the Orange river and a battle in Basutoland, whose resourceful chief Moshesh was fending off both Zulu and Boer. He came to palaver smartly attired in blue coat and gold-laced trousers, and his sons the 'princes' David and Nehemiah, educated at Cape Town, visited the camp and conversed in good English about the Peninsular War.[59] Africa was going through strange transformations.

In 1877–8 came the ninth and last war, with the Gaika and Galeka tribes this time; it too was partly provoked by famine. In the principal engagement the Kaffirs came on in close order, in the teeth of shrapnel and of Martini-Henry rifles making their first appearance. Frere described this as a 'very instructive action', from the point of view both of British fire-power and of 'Kaffir persistence in the new tactics of attacking us in the open in masses'.[60] There may be glimpsed in it an atavistic impulse provoked by despair, and the sealing off of their old hiding-places; it must have emboldened Frere to throw down his gauntlet to the Zulus.

Reversion to archaic modes of another sort could be seen in the setting up of Chartered companies, reviving the private-enterprise imperialism of early days. In 1889 the British South Africa Company was chartered; its master spirit was Cecil Rhodes, a not untypical empire man as one of seven sons of a vicar, most of them in the army. A year previously a mining concession had been secured, probably fraudulently, from Lobengula, successor to the Matabele conqueror Mzilikazi. He played for safety, but it was a weakness of his people's position that they were interlopers among the less warlike, and disunited, Mashona tribes. Some of these became their allies, but others, round the capital Bulawayo, were brought low, and the rest, in the north-eastern part of what was to become Southern Rhodesia, subjected to raiding.

At the end of 1889 Rhodes entered into a contract with a pair of buccaneers, Johnson and Heany, under which his company was to provide arms, and they were to collect men to occupy Mashonaland for it; if successful they would be given £150,000 and a spacious grant of land. A corps of 'Mashonaland Pioneers' was quickly raised, Englishmen and colonials and Boers, all expert with horse and gun, together with three hundred 'picked colonial natives'.[61] No impediments were met with; and then a Matabele raid supplied a pretext for swallowing up the rest of the country. The operation, in 1893, was organized very much as the conquistadors in America planned their forays. Each volunteer was promised a 6000-acre farm, a gold claim, and a share of the cattle to be seized, half of which would go to the company. Such spoils could attract men of good family and commensurate expectations. Some Border Police were lent by the governor of the Cape, Sir Henry Loch, an old cavalryman from India, who was easily satisfied that the Matabele were, as reported, 'blood-thirsty wretches'.[62] They had at any rate many African enemies, and another auxiliary force came from the Bechuana chief, Khama.

Most of the distance to Bulawayo was open grassland, giving smooth passage to cannon and horsemen. It was feared that the Matabele warriors, supposed to number about 15,000, would draw off into bush country, where they could hold out until the rains. Instead they exhibited what a British officer called an 'absolute want of generalship',[63] and came out, like so many other ill-starred armies, to offer themselves for execution. Their boldest attack, by about 5000 men, was made just before dawn, but they were trying to rush a well-planned laager, and it was on the watch. 'All the machine guns worked very well indeed'.[64] In another encounter the Imbezu regiment, forming the vanguard, suffered about 500 casualties out of its 700 men. 'For most of the troopers the war was almost without risk', more like hunting than fighting.[65] Bulawayo was occupied, Lobengula fled and next year died, on the Stock Exchange the company's shares soared.

In 1896 the Matabele took up arms again, and their new masters were taken aback to see them joined by the supposedly grateful and unwarlike Mashonas, who it seems did not take long to decide that if the Matabele had been bad, the white men were worse. A hundred settlers were killed, and help had to be called on from the army, which it was always taken for granted should be at the beck and call of any settlers in difficulties. Although the Matabele lost two fights, Rhodes felt compelled to make terms with their chiefs, in order to turn his attention to the Mashonas. They proved harder to put down, because more scattered, and perhaps also because a more democratic people. Hostilities went on into 1899, and 'bloody repression' marked their course.[66] Driven from their kraals, the people had their hills to take refuge in; a method was devised of setting off explosives at the mouth of the caves, to frighten the occupants, men and women, into giving themselves up.

In east Africa too British enterprise was set going by private venture. The East Africa Company had to rely very much on native soldiery; its employee Lugard incautiously took on some three thousand men from the Sudan, who broke out in 1897 in one of the most startling of colonial mutinies. In 1900, when Uganda was a protectorate, troops from outside had to be called in to suppress Nandi tribesmen, and India was the natural source. Only six officers were required to accompany a contingent of four hundred Punjabis, but with big game an additional lure 'practically every British officer in the Indian army', except married men, volunteered. One of the lucky, Henderson, left an account of the Nandis, who had both throwing and stabbing spears, unpleasantly barbed arrows, short swords, clubs, shields; it was borne in on the party that 'these gallant savages were not to be despised'. Masai spearmen with the expedition were worth having. 'These young warriors are beautiful animals', thought Henderson.[67]

In 1900 the sweeping acquisitions of the Royal Niger Company were taken over and turned into a Protectorate of Northern Nigeria, with Lugard, who had joined the company, put in charge. Son of an army chaplain in India, he had served in the second Afghan war and in the Sudan and Burma. A potentate with a good deal in common with Kitchener, he at once sent a party under military escort into the

Tiv country of middle Nigeria to construct a telegraph line, leaving it to instinct or Providence to apprise the Tivs of their new status. His men were viewed as trespassers, and set upon. Tivs were an acephalous people, and their villages often fell out, but they were toughened by long exposure to Muslim holy-war slave-raiders from the north; they had their own style of warfare, abandoning their settlements and taking to the thick bush, along with their poison-tipped arrows. Lugard sent a strong detachment to educate them with a rocket tube and five machine-guns, the equivalent for such a people of an atomic raid on a modern country. Reporting the 'chastisement' to London, he professed regret for 'the very great loss of life among these ignorant savages and the burning of scores of villages with their food'.[68] After a similar episode in 1906 the Colonial Office, to its credit, wrote later that year prohibiting acts of aggression, and warning that it could not sanction expeditions merely for the purpose of 'teaching the natives the efficacy of the maxim'.[69]

French power was being enlarged during the Second Empire from its foothold at the mouth of the Senegal river. Here its leading spirit was Faidherbe, an engineer officer who after duty in Algeria was made governor in 1854. One of the names his provident parents gave him was Caesar, and unlike Paris at that stage he was aiming not simply at trade but at annexations. French distractions in other parts of the world, and then the 1870 debacle, thwarted his more high-flying schemes, but they were renewed by a fresh generation of enthusiasts, and from 1880 'the era of military expansion' was under way.[70] Economic greeds and illusions in France dovetailed with the personal ambitions of army men who were often a law unto themselves. Between 1888 and 1893 the conquest of the western Sudan was carried out. A tough combatant was met with in Samori, a Muslim convert with dreams of founding an extensive kingdom. It did not take him long to learn the futility of facing the French in the open, and to turn to guerrilla tactics; his men 'used their modern weapons with devastating effect.'[71]

This did not disturb French opinion unduly, because the occupation was frugal of French manpower, and this was drawn not from the army but from the *infanterie de marine*, desert-plodding marines incongruously far from their native element. Good military material had been found in Senegal, whose *tirailleurs* soon won an excellent professional if not moral reputation. In 1890 a battalion of *tirailleurs soudanais* was added. African porters were equally indispensable, and were sometimes chained together in gangs to keep them from absconding. But a bad impression was made by an incident in 1894 when a detachment after passing through Timbuctoo was overrun in its camp by warlike Tuaregs, and 11 officers, 2 French NCOs, and 68 native soldiers lost their lives. A reaction set in against the way France was being dragged in the wake of colonial soldiers and their 'dashing strategies',[72] and barbarities leaked out which made their talk of a civilizing mission grotesque. At the end of the century a discredited military administration was wound up.

Kipling's picture of a Portuguese naval officer in Africa may have been a caricature,[73] but proud as Portuguese at home might be of their long imperial tradition it was clearly not now drawing the best talents into its service. Expansion was discouraged by scattered revolts, like one in Angola in 1860 against taxation. 'The war followed a customary pattern, with the Portuguese backing a usurper leader.'[74] African partition kindled emulation and even dreams – brought to nothing by Portugal's ally Britain – of joining Angola and Mozambique by a belt stretching across the continent. Between the lethargy of the oldest empire and the drive and efficiency of the newest, the contrast was striking. German empire-building may be said to have had a pre-history of participation in other countries' undertakings, by Germans in the Foreign Leigon, or in tsarist or British service, or as adventurers on their own. In New Zealand the most admired exponent of bush warfare, until his death in a skirmish, was an erstwhile Prussian officer, Gustavus von Tempsky, who had picked up his craft in the jungles of central America.

A company set up in 1890 to exploit Tanganyika had to be superseded almost at once by the government, which announced its presence by a long train of what might be called shooting-excursions. Revolt flared up on a broader scale in the south in 1905, when Muslim and pagan, and feuding tribes, combined against the white man, though there were others he could still make use of. Taken by surprise, many Europeans were killed, and it was more than a year before repression was complete. German methods were always robust, and in this obscure struggle more than a hundred thousand Africans were said to have perished, many from starvation: like Lugard and others, the Germans went in for confiscation of food supplies. All the empires were copying from one another.

What the Germans were carefully noting about their subjects' ways of fighting was summed up in a textbook on field service in 1911.[75] A good many old muzzle-loaders were knocking about; they were of little use except to bolster their owners' confidence. Their arrows were often more effective; they were highly reliable up to 55 yards, and could kill at up to 100 or more, if poisoned at 220: native shields were good for warding them off. Masai warriors did not bother with guns, and left poisoned arrows to their old folk, but with spear, sword and club they were very proficient, and, when tamed, made 'excellent auxiliaries'. Africans too were learning, and it was essential to be ready for 'surprising changes' from one campaign to the next. Here was an example of how small, self-managing peoples could find it easier to experiment than big muscle-bound armies like the Zulu.

In the Cameroons it was deemed politic to enrol police recruits from outside, Nigeria and Togo and Dahomey and the Sudan. Mutinies and other contretemps compelled the setting up in 1895 of a regular military force or *Schutztruppe*.[76] A law of 1896 limited native troops to the number required for policing each territory, but in East Africa at any rate Germany was soon taking into account the possibility of having to fight European rivals, and as a newcomer had less prejudice than others against using native manpower, within Africa, for the purpose. Officers were carefully picked; all had done three years in the army with an 'excellent record', and they and German NCOs were expected to acquire a good knowledge of the lingua franca, Swahili.[77] For native troops they began with some Sudanese, on whom they set a high value. Suitable martial stocks were then found among their own subjects. There was an effort, evidently successful, to attach askaris or soldiers to the government by treating them, and encouraging them to regard themselves, as a privileged caste, much as the Kaiser's army was in the Fatherland. A penalty was that the conceited askaris wanted servants, women, camp-followers, like their European betters. With a mobile company of five Europeans and about 150 askaris there might be four times the number of non-combatants. Routes were guarded by simple stone forts, with two bastions or towers diagonally opposite, and looped walls or, oftener, a firing platform.

'Everyone agrees that punitive expeditions ... are things which cannot be avoided', a German apologia after the Great War declared, citing a long tally of British precedents.[78] In South-West Africa as in Tanganyika rebellion followed closely on German occupation. In 1904 the Herreros took up arms in the northern region, others in the south. An Englishman who had some curious glimpses of events was the later General Ironside, then a very young man in the artillery. 'He had loved every minute of the South African War', and when it ended panted for more action. 'The Army was meant for war and how much war was he likely to have in his life?'[79] He was to live through two world wars. A good linguist, he joined the Germans in the guise of a Boer with waggons for hire. At the outset their forces were minute, with no officer higher than captain; it was months before Lt-Gen. von Trotha arrived to earn his sinister reputation. The navy had no troop transports. Like the British early in the Boer War, they failed to see the need for mounted infantry. With a strength built up to about 2500 men and 30 guns, divided into small columns, they tried to surround the main body of rebels in the Waterburg, but moved too slowly. The Herreros got away, but only from German bullets to the hunger and thirst of the desert.

7

WARS OF
TWO OCEANS

i. The British in the Pacific

Only in New Zealand had the Pacific peoples a homeland where they could multiply sufficiently to make a fight against the white man. To prepare them for the test they had a long history of fighting one another. Maoris were a warrior race for whom bravery in battle was the supreme virtue. Their wars were customarily brief and not too destructive, with only rudimentary organization; their hilltop villages were protected by ring above ring of stockades and trenches.[1] Yet when the white Prometheus appeared on the scene with his gift of firearms, they were eagerly snatched at, and made the old limited warfare so much more deadly as to threaten the race with suicide. It was a change occurring in many lands, like the leap from native beer to fire-water.

Here the stiffest resistance did not come early on, because the first stages were of gradual infiltration by settlers instead of conquest; it came later, as the land-hunger of colonists and speculators intensified. By then westernization and conversion to Christianity were well advanced. Sporadic clashes led to the government stepping in and annexing the country in 1840, by the so-called treaty of Waitangi. Four years later a chief named Heke collected about a thousand men, ready for a stand. Extra troops had to be summoned from Australia; with them came Surgeon Pine, not long since afloat on the Yangtze, in the course of the first Opium War. A brush took place in April 1845 in the Bay of Islands, where Maoris refused to give up their arms and sought refuge in the bush. 'The 96th and Marines', says Pine's diary, 'were *disorderly* and *plundering* nearly all day,' winding up with a massacre of pigs and fowls. 'Oh! the noble art of war!'[2]

A friendly chief joined them, with 'a straggling beggarly band of uncouth-looking natives', with 'guns of all shapes and sizes', and they set off to look for Heke and another leader who had raided and burned the township of Kororareka. They were confronted by a *pah* or stockade on 'an elevated glacis, sloping outwards towards a swamp', and hung round with thick flax matting which seemed to be bullet-proof.[3] Lt-Col. Hulme was for retiring and waiting for a cannon, but a council of war at dawn came down in favour of assault. Rockets were discharged from three hundred yards, but all missed or did no damage. Meanwhile the soldiers crossed a hollow, under brisk fire, and mounted the slope to a breastwork, where a mêlée broke out. Hulme had to withdraw his men, leaving the enemy triumphant, though believed to have had much heavier losses than the British, 13 killed and 38 wounded.[4] In June they made another sortie, over very disagreeable country and across the Waimate; they mustered about 500, with bullock-carts carrying guns and stores. Pine was given plenty of work, and he and his colleague Dr Galbraith had the satisfaction of being commended in brigade orders. Sporadic skirmishing spluttered on, while Pine occupied his leisure hours botanizing. He left Auckland for Sydney in May 1846 in charge of wounded; the total losses suffered by his own 58th regiment were not trifling, 65 killed and 440 wounded.

Sir George Grey, governor from 1845 to 1853 and a soldier by origin, called the Maoris in later days 'his favourite native race', warriors chivalrous as well as intrepid, and talked of the perils of storming a forest *pah* defended by firearms.[5] Even artillery could fail to smash a barrier of logs lashed together, and soldiers and marines approaching in close order after such a failure lost a third of their number. Another way had to be devised, patient digging of covered trenches to allow attackers to reach their objective. By mid-1847 Grey was able to report all quiet. But soon after his departure a movement to stop the transfer of tribal lands began, and in 1858 an elderly chieftain was chosen as 'King', or symbol of a nascent Maori nationalism. Hostilities were resumed in 1860 in protest against the purchase of a large tract round the estuary of the Waitara river, and it was in this Taranaki region on the western side of the North Island that most of the fighting of 1860–1 took place.

Experience was teaching the Maoris some improvements, and the warrior chief Titkowaru was a virtuoso at designing defences. One *pah* met with in 1860 was a regular 'bush fortress with palisades, a moat, underground galleries, elevated firing platforms', and a garrison of a hundred.[6] A truce in 1861 was followed by renewed exchanges in 1863. This time a wider area of the North Island took part, including the central uplands where the 'King movement' was strongest. In a battle at Rangiriri on the Waikato river a hundred

British were killed, though twice the number of Maoris were captured. They had no master-plan, but there was some resort to mobile guerrilla warfare, which a corps of Forest Rangers was formed to counter. One side had only flintlocks or sporting guns, with clubs and spears, the other was using Enfield rifles, grenades, howitzers, and gunboats. There was a heroic last stand at a *pah* bombarded and assaulted by 2000 troops; refusing to yield, the defenders broke out, and some escaped.

Maoris were being expropriated for the benefit of settlers and land-dealers, but as in the Kaffir wars most of the fighting was left to the Queen's soldiers. New Zealand has no legendary Buffalo Bill. In the wars of the 1860s militia and volunteers swelled the numbers available to three thousand, but between them and the regulars feeling was always strained. One feature of forest fighting was that loss of officers was likely to be exceptionally heavy; they had to be at the front, and could be picked off at short range. Maoris knew quite enough about the army to prize them as targets. This and dislike of the clamorous colonists must have helped to make the troops prefer sticking to coastal routes. General Sir D.A.Cameron showed less and less ardour for his task; in the end, disgusted by the bloodshed, he resigned and went home. There must have been occasional Highlanders who remembered how their own people had been dispossessed to make room for sheep, like the Maoris now. His replacement Sir T.Chute had every desire to get at the 'niggers', as he called them.[7] But in spite of an outcry by the colonists, most British troops were withdrawn in 1865–6, the last in 1870. They left behind in a church near a battlefield a memorial tablet in honour of the men they had been fighting, a rare act of chivalry such as no settlers were ever capable of. Between whites and Maoris fighting dragged on until 1872, more embittered and savage now, although there never ceased to be some clansmen willing to join the aliens.

A strange last chapter of the wars was the endeavour of a semi-Christian religious leader or prophet, Te Whiti, to turn tribal lands in Taranaki into a sort of Tolstoyan commune.[8] Steps were soon being taken to break it up. Te Whiti was able to persuade his followers to oppose them with peaceful disobedience alone; the suspicious government took laborious precautions, roads were built, blockhouses constructed, earthworks thrown up. There was some loss of life, Te Whiti was imprisoned, the land seized. In 1926 a royal commission belatedly censured an 'unjust and unholy war', but the money compensation it proposed was nugatory. Armed or unarmed, the Maoris' long struggle earned for them a degree of respect, a status less degraded than that of most subject races.

Elsewhere in the Pacific one island that tried to resist its fate was Viti Levu, biggest of the Fijis.[9] There the coastal tribes had been Christianised, and settlers were flocking in to prey on them; in 1875 pressure was put on the still pagan tribes of the mountainous interior, or 'Devil-country', to submit. They were deterred by fear of losing their lands, and by reliance on their rocky strongholds. Two intransigent chiefs forced the issue by attacking Christian villages. Sir A.H.Gordon, the well-meaning governor, was unwilling to call in British troops, both because the terrain would not suit them and because he disliked the thought of a conflict of races, and preferred as he said to let bad natives be brought to book by good ones. He ordered a *levée en masse* in the adjoining districts, and instructed each chief elsewhere to send thirty men, as a kind of 'feudal service'. A couple of thousand men were quickly assembled, a picturesque concourse with forbiddingly painted faces. To arm them was less simple; most could only be given an assortment of old muskets from England, Russia, America. A good many Civil War weapons from the USA may have trickled into outlandish markets. Columns moved into the highlands from different points, caves where many of the people hid were rushed, defiance soon faded. In earlier cases of this kind the government behaved fiercely, burning townships and deporting all the people, whose labour was sold for shorter or longer terms to the planters. Gordon eschewed any such reprisals, but insisted on the execution, after civil trial, of ringleaders convicted of murder; the result he believed was 'most salutary'.[10]

ii. The Dutch in the Archipelago

In a neighbouring ocean the Dutch empire was spasmodically growing. Disputed claims brought friction at a number of points with the British, and with a third party, the Spaniards in the Philippines, whom both were inclined to think very unreasonable. Spanish naval and other officers 'fomented trouble to gain distinction', it seemed to Britons,[11] never slow to detect motes in other eyes. Some official observers in 1874 condemned Spain's efforts to subdue the Sulu islands as bringing discredit on all Europeans; it was a case of 'a Christian Power murdering, pillaging and burning', and individuals picking quarrels in the hope of plunder and reward.[12] Apart from such competition, there were disagreements among the Dutch, like those in British India early on, between those in favour of expansion and others who judged it better to draw the line.

One compelling argument of the party of action was the need to put down piracy. A typical mid-century episode was a combined military and naval expedition to the island of Billiton, between Borneo and eastern Sumatra. Pirates were found in a bay guarded by two forts. Their ships came out to attack, but were worsted, while the troops disembarked to attack the forts. These proved to be merely earthworks with a dry ditch and thorn-hedge, and in spite of the 'terrible kris' in the miscreants' hands the operation was speedily completed. It cost 50 killed and 100 wounded; of the enemy six or seven hundred were polished off, and the rest captured.[13]

Another affair described by a participant in both took place in 1859 in Bali, just off the eastern tip of Java, where local rulers were accused of molesting shipping in breach of treaties. A strong force of 3500, under Maj.-Gen. van der Wijck, made an unopposed landing, but next day had to tackle a rajah's stronghold consisting of two redoubts encircled by a wall twelve feet high and a ditch thirty feet deep as well as a bamboo hedge, and garnished with cannon. One was captured after stern fighting, the other beat off all attempts, and at the end of six hours the assailants had suffered 246 casualties, a polyglot list with 12 officers and 104 other Europeans among the names, 25 Africans, and 103 men of the Archipelago.[14] It was many years before the whole island was added to the Dutch empire. In 1906 the time-honoured rite of a rajah and his entourage choosing death rather than dishonour, and coming out to perish in a hopeless charge, was enacted for the last time.

Sumatra, twelve hundred miles long, was the main theatre of Dutch expansion. The once powerful Muslim sultanate of Achin, or Atjeh, had dwindled since the 17th century, and was now limited to the northern corner, where its proximity to the Straits Settlements gave it an importance for British commercial interests; they were suspected of egging it on to defy the Dutch. With numerous fits and starts, conquest was spread over more than a quarter-century, and its long duration stirred more public interest in Holland than any previous colonial contest.[15] A commencement was made in 1873, with too few troops because the Dutch, like Europeans on so many occasions, underrated their opponents. Achinese were warlike, and relatively well armed, and knew how to make themselves invisible in the thick bush covering most of their country. For want of cannon the Dutch suffered severely when trying to take jungle stockades.

In the second expedition in 1874 they made use of the Achin river, but their two columns, missing their rendezvous, blundered about in the labyrinth. Defeat of the sultan and occupation of his petty capital did not mean the end. His authority was more nominal than real, and the congregational principle so much a part of Islam everywhere accustomed people to local co-operation. They carried on the struggle here and there, led by chiefs and preachers. There were frequent pauses and shifts of Dutch tactics, and wrangles between moderates and whole-hog annexationists.[16] In 1896 reinforcements enabled a large-scale 'pacification' (the favourite European term) to be undertaken, and in the next few years the Dutch – whose long-lost kinsmen in south Africa were just being pacified by the British – broke the back of the resistance. Not until as late as 1908 was it all over.

iii. The French in Indochina

When the allied sovereigns exchanged New Year greetings in 1861 Queen Victoria trusted that amity between Britain and France would be cemented by their 'glorieux succès' in the second China war just concluded, and that the war would benefit not themselves alone but also 'ce peuple bizarre', the Chinese.[17] So far as rejuvenating the Chinese government and army were concerned, it had no such happy outcome; they were past praying for. When the next blow came, from France, it was again only the common soldier who was ready to meet it.

Ideas of a French niche in Indochina, fired by British example in the Far East, began in the 1840s, and were taken up by the Second Empire. In February 1859 Saigon was occupied; in 1862 Annam (Vietnam) was compelled to cede it and Cochin, the three southern provinces. Military men were the keenest on further moves, and sometimes took the bit between their teeth, especially after 1870 when the army wanted to restore its name but defeat in Europe turned public opinion against overseas adventures. Resistance was met chiefly in the northernmost province, Tonking, often up in arms against its own government and now infested by 'Black Flags', irregulars who seem to have begun as remnants of the Taiping rebellion from over the Chinese border. In August 1883 the fire-eating Admiral Courbet bombarded the forts at the mouth of the Hue river, close to the capital, inflicting 'fearful loss of life';[18] a treaty was extorted, providing for a protectorate over the whole country.

This was followed by a more determined French drive in the north,

109

but this in turn brought China into the contest. Peking claimed a loose suzerainty over all Indochina; it could not desire to see its late enemies the French on its border; and a new national feeling was dawning in China. Regulars with some perfunctory training on Western lines were sent, and in 1884 Tso Tsung-tang, the general who had recently carried out a remarkable reconquest of Sinkiang, was put in charge of planning. Courbet was eager for an ultimatum and full-scale hostilities, but France was too insecure in Europe to spare adequate resources. As a diversion troops were landed in Formosa (Taiwan), and in August 1884 there was a violent bombardment of the port of Fuchow and its arsenal from the sea.

Meanwhile fighting went on in Tonking. Guerrilla action was taking toll of the French; in a three-day battle in June Chinese troops took part in a defeat of the French near Baclé. Chinese gunnery was ineffective, and tactics were unsophisticated, but at constructing entrenchments, and fighting hand to hand, the soldiers showed their worth. General Négrier's method was to push forward and envelop one isolated strong-point after another, obliging the defenders to retire. To strike terror, all prisoners, not excluding wounded soldiers and civilians, were executed.[19] The game had to be played and won rapidly, for fear of opinion at home turning against it. Labour was forcibly requisitioned, and harshly treated. Mass flight of coolies, and consequent shortage of provisions and ammunition, were one cause of Négrier's worst setback, at Langson near the frontier in March 1885; he was wounded, and there was a helter-skelter withdrawal. Jules Ferry, the imperialistic premier, fell from power.

A more vigorous Chinese government could have followed up the success, but the French were allowed to regain lost ground, and in June the treaty of Tientsin gave them most of what they wanted. It had not been won cheaply. For one thing, an English journalist in Paris was told, the notion of General Boulanger trying to invade England if he came to office was absurd, if only because France after its recent exertions in the Far East was no longer strong enough at sea. 'The wear and tear of the Chinese campaign played havoc with the material of the French navy.'[20]

110

8

REBELLIONS

i. European settlers

After the toils of conquest came the fears of rebellion, more acute in some colonies than in others, but never slumbering. Anxiety about malcontents at home helped to keep them awake. Many of these belonged to national movements, like the Polish or Irish or Catalan, but most disturbing of all was the spectre of social revolt. During the Mutiny an officer was enraged to see British soldiers allowed, because of the heat, to march in shirt sleeves 'like a lot of insurrectionary haymakers!'[1] It was not many years since England's helots, the farm labourers, had mutinied, and the association of ideas is significant.

Military power had always to be ready for use, though the frequency of its use varied greatly. By comparison with most other empires, the British seldom invoked martial law.[2] Sundry legal difficulties or obscurities stood in the way. Self-esteem could make administrators reluctant to turn to the army for help – 'Such pangs', an experienced Anglo-Indian wrote, 'does it cost a civil officer to acknowledge that his people are in revolt, and that the authority has passed out of his hands.'[3] In Spanish possessions things were very different, not surprisingly when provinces of Spain were so often under martial law or some variant of it. India however had special units of armed police, which might be billeted on refractory districts, in the manner of Louis XIV's *dragonnades*.[4] Military settlements were sometimes planted as a reserve of strength in case of need, for example on the troublous eastern borders of Cape Colony. Four 'military villages' fell victim to Xhosa fury in 1850. Sir George Grey set up new ones, with army pensioners from England. Many New Zealand towns started as garrison posts, like the capital Auckland; 1700 discharged soldiers were brought in to form colonies near it in 1842. In central Asia small Russian populations gathered round the forts, and time-expired soldiers were encouraged to stay there.

In April 1810 the first independent government in Spanish America was proclaimed at Caracas, while Spain was fighting to regain its independence from Napoleon; in December 1824 Spanish power was finally extinguished, except in Cuba and Puerto Rico, by the battle of Ayacucho, in Peru, 9000 feet above the sea. Only limited numbers of troops could be sent out from Spain, even after 1815; more had to be found in America. In every region the long-drawn struggle was in part a fierce civil war.[5] Much of Spain's strength was worn away on the *llanos*, the vast rolling plains of Venezuela, and the pampas of Argentina. Here dwelt a scanty but fiery race of herdsmen, not unlike the Cossacks of old, horsemen wielding long lances, who might erupt on their own, or be drawn in by either side, but more readily on the rebel side when there was a man of their own kind to lead them, as Antonio Páez did on the *llanos*.[6]

Like the gauchos of the pampas his men were often of mixed blood. But it was seldom that the non-white races, though all were brought into the conflict, could strike a blow on their own account. Only in Mexico did some of the Indians play a distinct part. Some Negro plantation slaves were liberated and enrolled by Bolívar, who had been helped in exile by Pétion, president of the black republic of Haiti. Chile's warships were manned a good deal by ex-slaves, or slaves, sometimes presented to the navy by their patriotic masters, as well as by pressed men and criminals.[7] Very little democracy or equality, either racial or social, emerged from the years of bloodshed; Spanish-speaking America belonged to landowners and merchants.

Cuba was much later in rising. One cause must have been Creole fear of the mass of black slaves; the élite consisted largely of owners of sugar plantations. Even when a section of it began to aspire to end the Spanish connection, most of the militants were confined to the 'Oriente', the poorer eastern region. With the relative smallness of the country, its whole population at mid-century under half a million, and all its coasts exposed to Spanish sea-power, this made the support of the masses, not excluding the Negroes, indispensable from the outset. Revolution and the fall of the Bourbon dynasty in 1868 plunged Spain into half a dozen years of turmoil, and gave Cubans their opportunity. Soon much of the Oriente was under rebel control. In the insurgent ranks were many blacks, and one of them, Antonio Maceo, was before long a leader. The rebels were poorly armed, most of them only with machetes, though a Cuban committee in the USA was able to send some weapons bought with subscriptions from Cuban workers there. Tactics had to be mainly on guerrilla lines, designed to create chaos by destroying sugar-mills, cutting telegraph wires, blocking routes. Remarkable skill was displayed by small detachments, constantly on the move, with rough field hospitals, workshops, family quarters, established in hide-outs in the forests and hills.

Two linked hesitations haunted the political leadership, and fomented dissensions. One was about how quickly and fully emancipation of the slaves should be carried out, to mobilize their support; towards this Céspedes, leader until 1873, moved as haltingly as Lincoln towards emancipation in the Civil War. The second question was whether to risk a drive into the western part of the island, where the bogey of a Cuba in the hands of black men like Maceo was easily raised. At length, early in 1875, the daring guerrilla chief Gómez crossed the boundary, marked by a Spanish line of ditch, embankment and barbed wire, studded with forts and watch-towers. But discords continued, and next year, following the Bourbon restoration in Spain, strong reinforcements reached the government. It was able to take the offensive; in 1878 the rising collapsed.

By the time the struggle was resumed, slavery had disappeared, and a newer middle class was coming into the lead, capable of better organization. In 1892 the Cuban Revolutionary Party was founded in exile. Its chief inspiration, Martí, was a radical who belonged to the threshold of an epoch of socialist-led revolt. Awareness of expansionist sentiment in the USA, and the danger of Cuba being swallowed up, led him to hurry on a fresh uprising early in 1895.[8] He returned to Cuba in April to take part in it, and next month was killed. Again the Spaniards were committed to an endless wrestling-match with a half-invisible adversary. A British officer on the scene noticed how they were paralysed by lack of roads and the hostility of the people, which meant that they could get no word of their opponents' whereabouts, while their own were always known; and all the time they were being exhausted by tropical diseases as well as by enemy action. He was critical of them for letting themselves be reduced to the defensive; and he remarked that 'the frequent executions and the stern reprisals threw a darker shade' on all their operations.[9] Like various colonial regimes in years to come they were trying to cut the roots of rebellion by the *reconcentrado* system of rounding the people up into locations where they could be kept under watch and ward. It stirred up more hatred.

In Spain backing for the war was diminishing. The well-to-do could buy themselves off from army service; they were sending the poor to Cuba, not their own sons, the republican Costa Martínez said, just as they skulked while common folk were fighting Napoleon.[10]

Colonial service did at least hold out more opportunity of promotion from the ranks, especially during the grind of a long war when some officers would be less eager to go out. British views of foreign officer corps were coloured by the fact of some of them being less socially exclusive than Britain's; the critic in Cuba explained Spanish failure to act in small energetic detachments as due to 'most officers having risen from the ranks and therefore lacking the self-reliance and initiative which are indispensable qualifications.'[11] At any rate, from the more mountainous east revolt spread gradually westward. Spanish defeat was foreseeable by the time the USA went to war with Spain, nominally to rescue the Cubans, really to safeguard American investments. After Spain's defeat and three years of American occupation the upper classes were prepared to accept control by Washington as an insurance against social reform.

French Canada was a morsel more easily swallowed than digested by the British empire. Late in 1837 some Québecquois took up arms. Their political spokesman Papineau held aloof; and instead of relying on mobility the rebels gathered in stationary camps here and there, with little sign of any common purpose. During the winter there was some harassing of army posts, and next year another effort, the work of a secret society of *Frères chasseurs*; it came to nothing within a week. Rather more threatening was a rising of the *métis* or mixed French-Indian community, the biggest element in the sparse frontier population along the Red River in Manitoba. This had a prelude in a minor outburst in 1870, and the setting up of a 'provisional government', quickly disposed of when Colonel Wolseley appeared on the scene, in between his Chinese and African exploits, with a few troops.

Its leader Riel, who was nearly pure French by ancestry, was recalled in 1885 from a long exile to head another rising, caused by what Denison, a militia officer in the force mobilized to deal with it, called bureaucratic meddling and muddling; he considered that the métis were 'practically goaded into rebellion'.[12] Riel had been drifting into a half-crazy religious exaltation, a symptom perhaps of his people's hopeless position. He wanted métis and Indians to make common cause, but this ensured that all white settlers would be against him. Not many Indians joined in, though younger men tried to prod their more cautious chiefs; and both they and the métis were poorly armed.

Volunteers flocked to the colours, from as far away as Nova Scotia. This was Canada's first military enterprise of its own, with Britain represented only by a few officers, mostly retired. One of these was

General Middleton, who had settled in Canada and been given command of the militia. He felt sorry, he wrote to the Duke of Cambridge, for his men, mostly 'well-to-do tradesmen's sons or in business and who thought they were going out for a picnic', with little inkling of the unpleasantnesses awaiting them. They for their part did not enjoy being ordered about by men like a veteran of the Madras Fusiliers with a 'thoroughly old-time British officer manner of damning Militiamen in general and Frenchmen in particular.'[13] There was a fight in April at Fish Creek, where neither party displayed much science. As a prophet Riel could inspire, as a tactician he was ill-qualified. His men began to melt away. A last stand was made at Batoche, his headquarters, ringed with concealed rifle-pits. It would have been better to stay out in the open, and harry the approaching enemy; but the inclination to remain under cover, on the defensive, was a very widespread one on the weaker side in many such confrontations. There was ill-feeling in French Canada when Riel, despite a jury's recommendation of mercy, was hanged.

ii. Non-European peoples

India under the British was for a complex variety of reasons remarkably free from rebellions. The grand exception was that of the army, their own creation. Another, coming just before it, was a rising not really against their rule, but against oppression by other Indians. The Santal aborigines of the borderland between Bengal and Orissa were another people, like the métis and Red Indians, off the highroad of history. Their discontent flared up in June 1855 under the nose of the government at Calcutta, greatly to the astonishment of the latter which had scarcely ever troubled its head about them since the time of their heavy-handed subjugation by Warren Hastings. They had come to be thought a 'most peaceable, quiet, timid people'.[14] But some of them had been straggling out of their hills, seeking land or work, and falling easy prey to Hindu landlords and usurers underpinned by British lawcourts. At first the multitude which poured down now on to the plains was pacific enough, but violence soon broke out; it was chiefly directed at Bengali moneylenders, who were said to be undergoing 'fiendish outrages'; villages were burned, cattle driven off.

Some kind of leadership seems to have been thrown up, but the Santals' armament did not go beyond bows and arrows, and it

115

scarcely seems that they were capable of a real combat. Many had lost touch with the old forest life, and by coming down from the hills they were letting themselves be caught in the open. Simple peoples were not seldom stranded like this between an older and a newer existence, unable to defend themselves effectively in terms of either. What remained to them was tribal unity and the courage it fed. They were 'brave to infatuation', wrote an officer who had to exterminate a band shut up in a mud house, when they refused to surrender.[15] In November martial law was promulgated, and by the end of the cold season the work of suppression was complete. There was a howl for blood, as always on such occasions, but the authorities kept reasonably cool. Santals were no life and death challenge like the sepoys two years later. Road-building was put in hand, to give work to those in danger of starvation, and the causes of the tragedy were investigated. Some improvements were made, and the debt-slavery in which many Santals were held was, in legal theory at least, abolished.

'There was not a Sepoy in the war who did not feel ashamed of himself.'[16] Writing its history a dozen years later Hunter found that officers concerned with the repression were still reluctant to talk of it. Evil memories must have been left behind by many colonial wars, to haunt solitary hours and sleepless nights. A great part of the record must never have been written down. 'The details of border warfare', he concluded, 'in which disciplined troops mow down half-armed peasants ... afford neither glory to the conquerors nor lessons in the military art.'[17]

On the surface as far removed in character from the Santal rebellion as in space and time, but with some underlying kinship, was that of the Philippine Islands. There Spanish settlers were always few, and the élite which took the lead was a native one, though westernized in culture and religion, and as in India composed of many ethnic groups. A middle stratum of landowners gave birth to many of the Young Filipinos, while the greater landlords remained loyal to Church and State. In 1872 a rising of native soldiery at Cavite was put down, and its instigators fled to Hong Kong. A more plebeian and militant movement was taking shape, the underground Katipunan, with a following of land-hungry peasants for whom national revolution would be at the same time agrarian revolution.[18] The government tried to suppress it; in 1896 revolt broke out; José Rizal, the youthful patriot, writer, and exile, was caught, tried by military court at Manila, and shot. Leadership fell to Emilio Aguinaldo, who came from the middle-landlord and official stratum. Before the end

116

of 1897 he was induced to give up and retire to Hong Kong, while the more resolute men of the Katipunan went on fighting. In the Philippines even more than in Cuba it was always the army's habit to try to crush disaffection quickly, by unsparing severity. A British businessman left a description of a General Villamar whom he met, a soft-spoken invalid living on milk, but merciless with captured rebels.[19] In 1898 the Americans brought Aguinaldo back, to make use of him against the Spaniards, but then shouldered him aside and annexed the islands. Revolt against Spain went on as revolt against America.

To kindle revolt in a country only lately conquered was as a rule much easier than in older colonies. Links with the past were still intact, and among common people memories of independence, the reassuringly familiar sensation of being exploited by men like themselves instead of by strangers. Equally, such revolts were likely to be no more than repetitions of the previous resistance, and condemned in advance to failure. An instance is the rising in Khokand in 1875–6, against Russian exactions, taking the time-honoured form of a call to holy war, and crushed promptly and ruthlessly by Skobelev. Another example is the 'Great Rebellion' of 1817–18 in Kandy, the hilly interior of Ceylon, only a couple of years after the overthrow of the old kingdom. This had been accomplished without much difficulty except in getting guns and stores up through the trackless hills, though an attempt in 1803–5 had failed. It was marked by two miscalculations that Britons frequently fell into: they expected to be welcomed by a people groaning under a hated yoke, and they tried to set up an unwanted pretender to the throne as a puppet.

Only some sections of the population were drawn into the rebellion, but among them were both chiefs and priests whose status suffered with the fall of the monarchy, and commoners perturbed by an influx of Muslim and other traders from the lowlands. It is thought of today in Ceylon as 'a truly "national" uprising'.[20] It was all the harder to put down for being unguided and sporadic; government forces were spread thin, and as in so many similar cases had to have recourse to intimidation, by such methods as depriving suspect villages of food. Sinhalese were not a martial race, but they had bows and arrows, some muskets, and plenty of spirit, as Major De Latre, at the head of a marching detachment of the 1st Ceylon Regiment and a few British soldiers, early in 1818, found to his cost. His men were subjected, he reported, to 'constant and persevering attempts of the enemy', who lay low behind rocks and 'took deliberate aim through

117

small openings in the jungle'. He himself had a musket-ball through the arm, and though he reached his objective, Nalanda, on the northern fringe of the highlands, he was soon compelled to withdraw.[21] But it was a sign of how backward-looking this movement was that it was punctured by British seizure of the Buddha's Tooth.

Of the British soldiers, some of whom had lately fought at Waterloo, only forty-four were killed, but they were ravaged by disease.[22] Kandyans were to figure for many years in the British mind as embodiments of 'artfulness, perfidy, treachery and sullen unregeneracy.'[23] This may explain the over-readiness of the authorities more than once later on to react massively to slight affronts. This happened in 1848, when what was really no more than an effervescence of peasant discontent at tax burdens was mistaken for insurrection. Martial law was declared, dwellings burned down, cattle impounded, and suspects shot in batches of four; all this was kept up irrationally long, in spite of protests by the chief justice. Something similar recurred in 1915.

Very soon after the Kandy outbreak there was an analogous but far graver conflict in Java, going on from 1820 to 1825, with the principality of Jogjakarta as the focal point. It was an old vassal of the Dutch, but their recent ousting by the British (as by the Japanese long after) must have undermined respect for them; and their government, restored in 1815, was impelled by financial needs to make drastic changes. Feudal rights were tampered with, but, whatever may have been intended, the peasantry got no benefit. When Dipa Negara raised his standard the people flocked to join him; Europeans and Chinese traders were massacred. But though he and his nephew gave proof of high talent for irregular warfare, he was in essence a man of the past, a prince of the reigning house and an Islamic devotee or seer. A sword was reported to have dropped from heaven at his feet. Asia was dreaming of magical weapons, Europe was making them. It was a 'blind, instinctive protest against the disintegration of a traditional society'.[24] General de Kock worked out effective though costly measures, setting up strong-points, linked by roads, from which his flying columns could scour the countryside. It was a war of attrition for the ordinary people as well as rebels, with immense devastation. Total loss of life from war, famine, and disease has been estimated at 200,000,[25] vastly more than in Britain's worst colonial revolt, 1857

All conquered Africa was smouldering. In the north, expropriation of Algerians from their land to make room for settlers ensured that bitterness would not die down.[26] Apart from Russia in 1856 and Holland's loss of Belgium, France was the only colonialist country to suffer a defeat in Europe during the 19th century, and the shock was felt by its nearest dependency. Widespread rebellion in Algeria followed, and 'a dirty war, marked by extreme cruelties on both sides'.[27] As after 1945, French professional soldiers wanted to regain self-esteem by showing that they were still more than a match for any Africans. Further seizures of land were carried out, to attract more immigrants, French or other. Further risings ensued.

Far to the south, in the early 1880s there was an attempt by the Usutu or nationalist party in strife-torn Zululand to try conclusions again with the British, but it was soon quashed, and in 1887 full British sovereignty was proclaimed. When fresh disorder broke out in 1906 it marked the chaotic beginnings of a new era. Here too colonists and speculators were allowed to take over the best land; a poll-tax imposed in 1905 was the last straw. Payment was refused, and some disorders broke out; the Natal authorities flew into a panic and declared martial law, with public executions to advertise it. The sequel, the 'Zulu rebellion', was mostly a chase through hills and forests of insurgents led by a chief named Bambata. Finally they were trapped in a deep gorge, and butchered by artillery fire and then infantry action. 'No prisoners were taken ... dum-dum bullets were extensively used.'[28] It was one of the most ghoulish episodes in all the annals of the empires. During the campaign Gandhi, then living in Africa with a simple faith that 'the British Empire existed for the benefit of the world', offered to raise an Indian ambulance unit. The governor of Natal accepted, and bestowed on the future Mahatma the rank of sergeant-major. He and his companions were chiefly employed to nurse Zulus, suffering not from wounds but from festering sores caused by flogging.[29]

iii. European solidarity and the Boxer Rebellion

Among Europeans there were clashing ambitions, and mutual suspicions, as in 1859–60 when Spaniards were convinced that Britain, with Gibraltar in mind, was secretly aiding Morocco. Nevertheless, as a rule they were ready to endorse, and sometimes assist, one another's colonial activities. Before the fall of the legitimate monarchy in 1830 Nicholas I was taking a benevolent interest in France's Algerian venture, and Colonel Filosoff, an expert at breaking in Muslims, was being sent with good advice. In 1857 there were mixed feelings in France, which had not forgotten how it was bundled out of India by the British, and the press was disposed to dwell on British cruelties. In Italy moderate opinion was firmly Anglophile, though left-wing democrats were disapproving. Discordant views were more loudly expressed in Russia; the Crimean War was only just over.[30] But by and large there was a prevalent European sympathy for Britain, and it was warmly shared by Americans as liberal-minded as Oliver Wendell Holmes, who was convinced that Delhi, like Carthage, merited annihilation.

In 1891 Italy was given leave to land forces at the British port of Zeila, as a second point of access to Abyssinia; a British force was allowed to disembark at the Italian port of Obbia during the wild goose chase in Somaliland. German troops dealing with stiff-necked tribes in east Africa were permitted to bring in stores through adjacent colonial territories. During the Boer War the Kaiser, by his own story, drew up with his staff a strategic plan which he presented to Britain. He felt entitled in return to ask Britain in 1907 to 'compel' the Cape government to help in catching a rebel band which had crossed into South-West Africa – in terms felt by Edward VII to be too peremptory.[31]

To the non-white world it might well seem that all Europeans were as thick as thieves. In China during the French aggression the others were ruefully conscious that it was harming trade, but in their philosophy Chinese victory would be even worse. Their solidarity, and its limits, found strident expression in their single grand combination, joined by the two new imperialists outside Europe, Japan and America, to put down the Boxer rebellion of 1900. This got under way, in a very complex situation, as a revolt of north China peasants against a government oppressive to its own people and feebly compliant with foreign demands. The empress Tzu Hsi's government had to fall back on diverting the movement against the foreigners, and half-heartedly sharing its patriotic stand.[32] 'Boxers' were a hybrid between the old village militia, now restored, and the secret societies in existence for centuries. They owed their name to a drill or gymnastic training part of whose function was to work them up into a state of frenzied excitement, like a war dance. Mostly very young, they had grown up on popular romances and dramas about heroes, warriors, adventures. An unfriendly mandarin derided their fondness for theatrical phrases and gestures.[33] They were in a way playing at making events, as children learn by playing; they were stumbling on to the stage of history, self-conscious and in need of reassurance.

In north China there had been fewer peasant revolts than further south to impart practical lessons, and they made scant use of firearms, the weapons of the foreign devils, choosing to rely on swords and spears like their forefathers. They showed the instinct of so many peasant rebels to flock together in masses, to fortify their confidence as well as to strike alarm into the enemy. The most dedicated of them were ready for mass charges, like so many fanatics in other lands, and like many others believed that they could make themselves invulnerable. 'Tales of massacres and torture kept pouring in', a foreigner wrote,[34] and the diplomatic quarter at Peking was beleaguered. Early in June foreign warships gathered at Taku, whose forts at the mouth of the Pei-ho river leading towards Peking had been more than once bombarded in the Opium wars. On the 10th Admiral Sir Edward Seymour set off with a scratch force of seamen, and a Russian colonel as chief of staff, to relieve the legations. He was attacked first by Boxers, then by regular troops, the railway line was cut, and he had to beat a retreat. His report made it plain that some at least of the Chinese could improvise shrewd methods of obstruction; they kept up a 'galling fire' from 'well-selected positions', and had to be driven at bayonet-point from village to village.[35]

At Tientsin on the river the foreign settlements were under siege, and it was there that the severest fighting took place before the invaders, covered by fire from warships, managed to gain possession of the whole city at the end of June. Clearly Chinese determination was impressing the allies. Not until 4 August did they set forth again, when their strength had grown to about 20,000 men, with 8000 Japanese the most numerous, followed by the Russians with nearly 5000. They were met with a courage which seemed to verge on the superhuman. A German officer's diary, parts of which got into print, commented admiringly, as many witnesses did, on the Boxers' 'magnificent contempt of death'.[36] General Stewart thought the regulars brave enough – 'But how can you expect troops to fight who are invariably deserted by their officers the moment danger approaches?'[37] A decaying society like old China decays from the top down.

In pursuit of fugitives, and later in punitive raids, the allies were able to make full use of their cavalry. Chinese bravery might be praised, but all prisoners were executed out of hand, and memories of 1857 were stirring as the army drew near to Peking. Stewart expected an indiscriminate revenge to be taken if the legations fell.[38]

Ironically, most of the British contingent, apart from the Welch Fusiliers, was Indian, because the army was busy in south Africa. Stewart may have wondered whether his Indians knew anything about the Mutiny, and the sack of Delhi and Lucknow; but he was quite proud of them, and felt that they were unfairly blamed for many outrages committed by other soldiers. Happily the diplomats had been more frightened than hurt, and a wholesale bloodbath in Peking was avoided, although the city was very thoroughly looted. Soon Indian regimental bands were discoursing music in the parks.

Even in 1900 it was possible for foreigners to make some use of Chinese recruits. Britons were highly pleased with their Chinese regiment, Germans were setting on foot a similar force. But striking progress towards a new China could be seen between the first Opium war in 1840–2, a British contest with the government leaving the masses largely indifferent, and 1900, a foreign onslaught on the people of north China with the government not much more than a spectator. Among the allies there were ominous symptoms of division. Stewart saw them watching each other 'with intense suspicion, if not hatred'; at Tientsin there was continual quarrelling and scuffling, French and German soldiers threw stones at British officers.[39] Beaten though they were, the Boxers accomplished something by convincing Europe that China would not be easy to master; and something else by drawing the aliens into a situation certain to worsen their jealousies. It was at once the climax of an era of European fellow-feeling against the outside world, and a milestone in the slide towards the European civil war of 1914.

9

A CENTURY
OF WAR

i. Advance of military technology

An officer's diary at Multan at the end of 1848 hailed yet another triumph of 'that true weapon the bayonet, which never yet failed to bring success to the British soldier.'[1] With the same trusty companion a quarter-century later Wolseley's men stormed the lines of Tel el Kebir, not deigning to answer the shower of bullets they were met with. But even with bayonet in hand no one cared to wait for a torrent of charging 'fanatics' to reach him; and guerrillas, lurking snipers, equally unknown to the classic wars of India, could not be hit without far more accurate, long-range fire than Brown Bess and her contemporaries were capable of. Armaments especially of the heavier type were advancing for another reason too: they were coming to form a growing sector of big business. In Britain's case conservatism was still potent; yet it can be maintained that the Victorian army was learning to be 'a highly effective and economical instrument of imperialism', well up with other armies in technical innovations.[2]

By about 1850 Britain and France were exchanging musket for rifle, and adopting the elongated instead of round bullet designed by the French officer Minié (a soldier from the ranks) for his rifle and tested in the late Kaffir war. In 1855 both improvements were welcomed by the American army, hitherto in a country still only on the way towards industrialism conducting its Indian wars with nothing better than the old smoothbore: with 'minnie ball' and rifle 'at last the frontier soldier had a weapon long deserved.'[3] An improved Enfield rifle was just in time to play an eloquent part in the Mutiny, as well as in the Crimea, and it could be adapted to breech-loading. By the end of the century it evolved into the Lee-Enfield, long to remain a standard model, with smokeless powder adding to its virtues.

For his Scinde Horse, Jacob designed a useful carbine. But

cavalrymen's minds usually moved as much more slowly as their horses moved quicker, and late in the century in India they still trusted to the sabre and ignored the short cavalry firearm which had 'brilliant achievements' to its credit in the USA, many of them against Red Indians.[4] Another fruit of Yankee ingenuity was the Colt revolver. In European armies this was an officer's weapon, and so lent itself to greater variety. Men going to Burma in the 1880s could take any sort; they had to find their own ammunition.

It was specifically for colonial purposes that the celebrated dum-dum bullet was invented, by Captain Clay at the Dum Dum arsenal near Calcutta, to meet a demand for something to stop a charging 'savage' or 'fanatic' in his tracks. Soft-nosed, it expanded on impact and made a large gaping wound instead of drilling a narrow hole. At El Teb in 1884 some of the British soldiers, fearful of being overwhelmed by a dervish avalanche, converted their bullets into soft-nosed ones by slicing off the head of the nickel case.[5]

That early colonist Robinson Crusoe rigged up a contraption for firing a number of muskets simultaneously from his dwelling. America had magazine rifles in use as early as the Civil War, but it was only after the Russo-Turkish carnage in 1887 that European governments hastened to lay in a supply. They could soon fire 25 or 30 shots a minute, with a flat trajectory. The great leap forward however was the machine-gun, again an American product but directed very much towards a European market and an African field of action. Without Africa for a target, indeed, the machine-gun might have evolved far more slowly; their destinies were interwoven. It was an invention that ought in logic to have come from Britain, whose failure to hit on it is one of many symptoms of the industrial stagnation the country was relapsing into.

For a number of years the machine-gun was too unreliable for soldiers in the wilds to pin their safety to. Wolseley omitted Gatlings when stocking up for his Ashanti campaign, because of their habit of jamming, like the one in Newbolt's poem. The Maxim proved more trustworthy. Someone on the way into Matabeleland in 1893, writing home about 'black devils' and 'worthless Mashonas', expected the operation to be 'watched with great interest by the outside world', as the first full test of the gun.[6] By 1900 it could be bought in parts, for carriage on the heads of porters. A similar American offering to progress was the Hotchkiss, soon adopted as standard equipment by half a dozen colonial armies.

Callwell in 1906 gave a mere couple of pages to machine-guns; he considered their place 'fairly well established',[7] which sounds like damning with faint praise. He did go on to acknowledge their 'tremendous' effect, as a weapon for the backwoods, against waves of attackers, like the Zulu impis, and their value in circumstances where the best-trained infantry fire might waver. Sluggish Russia was not slow to appreciate them, and used them for example in Central Asia in 1870. Russians had been borrowing from the West for centuries as the Japanese were now doing. A machine-gun, it has been pointed out, was an economical weapon, enabling small forces to subdue and then hold down large populations.[8] It belonged to the labour-saving technology of the USA, and the colonial settlements too were short of labour and had to economize on it. Africans were coming to see Maxim-guns as 'magical gifts of the gods to the white man'.[9] To others they might look like gifts to capitalists and policemen at home. A socialist with army experience, H. H. Champion, warned his colleagues in 1886 that if they went in for street-fighting and barricades now they would be 'just like savages, who, with their arrows and bows, array themselves against Gatling and Nordenfeldt guns.'[10]

Heavy guns, required at one time for sieges in and about India, were not much needed for colonial warfare now, except for naval bombardments. These were found useful by the Dutch in the Archipelago, and Italian shelling of Somali coastal towns 'had a salutory effect'.[11] Kagoshima, Alexandria, Fuchow, Bangkok, were among other chosen targets. On land the premium was coming to be on light, portable cannon, to accompany troops through desert, jungle, or mountain. Here great advances were made; a commander no longer had to object to taking guns with him, as Bugeaud did in Algeria, for fear of their retarding his movements overmuch. Americans made use of light field-pieces in hunting down Apaches. In many kinds of country any gun on wheels was impracticable. Evolution was towards such a weapon as the 3.7 'mountain pack howitzer' developed for the Indian army at the Eskmeals gun range in Cumbria, which could be drawn by a horse but could also be broken up into six loads and packed on to mules. Projectiles were improving at the same time. Picric acid as an explosive was discovered in 1885, and gave birth to a new brood of monsters whose testing-grounds were the empires. Melinite was tried out by the French in Madagascar, where it had an unnerving effect, though Callwell observed curtly that Hovas were always ready to run away.[12] At Omdurman the big guns fired lyddite shells, already a legend for their destructive power.

The West was no less well equipped for defence than for the

offensive. Improvised field works took many shapes. In hot dry lands temporary shelter could be provided by a zareba, one of various borrowings from local practice, a thorn-bush barricade round a camp to which breastworks of sand might be added. Soldiers roaming from frontier to frontier carried such exotic names with them, and in Canada a 'zareba' could be a square camp with waggons drawn up on the four sides in Boer fashion, with shallow trenches added. Thorn-hedges were a primitive anticipation of barbed wire. Once more this item came from America, where it was manufactured in bulk in the late 19th century for cattle enclosures on the prairies. Semi-permanent defences could utilize local materials and styles, as the *Manual of Field Works* pointed out: free-stone breastworks, like the *sangars* of the north-west frontier and Himalayas, blockhouses of shingle and corrugated iron, surrounded by barbed wire, in south Africa. In north Africa the Legion had a standard type of fort, a hundred yards square with a firing platform under the parapet of its nine-foot-high walls and a fifteen-foot tower at each corner; it could be held by fifty or sixty men. Not unlike it was the isolated British fort evolving on the north-west frontier, a rectangle with the men's quarters built against the crenellated walls, a platform above them, a tower at each corner looped for machine-guns.[13]

In one way and another plenty of scope was being afforded to the engineers, who for a long time had reason to feel undervalued. One writing from a fortified post in Zululand where he had thrown a drawbridge across the ditch was 'glad to say we have been able to be of great use in many ways here, and quite demonstrated the necessity of Royal Engineers in the field.'[14] A wire-rope bridge over the Indus constructed by Captain Aylmer high up in the Himalayas moved Durand to the reflection: 'A good Royal Engineer officer on the frontier is worth his weight in gold.'[15] Technical progress in civil life supplied fresh expedients. Napier's army in Abyssinia had with it the latest well-boring equipment.

Before mid-century there were macadamized road surfaces in Algeria. Railways were a British speciality, and the first field railway was laid by civilian contractors in the Crimea in 1855. In India the army had a railway department from the 1860s, well ahead of Britain, thanks to the stimulus of the Mutiny. For the second Afghan war vast quantities of supplies, as well as troops and animals, were carried to the frontier by the Sind, Punjab and Delhi Railway, which in November 1878 alone ran eighty-one special trains.[16] Experience in Egypt in 1883 led to the forming of a railway division within the engineering corps, and in 1897 the building of a line to Abu Hamed in only six months could be extolled as 'an engineering miracle.'[17] In the Boer War steam traction-engines hauled eight-inch guns, and an armoured train helped in the defence of Mafeking. More than in most of Europe, colonial railway systems were governed by military wants, as in India after the Mutiny. Witte found his plans for Russian Asia interfered with by 'monomaniacs' like Kuropatkin badgering him for 'strategic railways' that were often pure fantasy.[18] Steam-boats on the Ganges were valuable in 1857, and Nile and Niger followed Indus and Irawaddy as their highways. On the Nile Kitchener had armoured steamers. Ocean-going troopships were slower to evolve. In 1895 the British military attaché in Paris pointed with relief to French failure to collect in six months enough shipping for the transport of 15,000 men to Madagascar, without heavy equipment; it seemed to rule out any possibility of a French invasion of Britain.[19]

Ultimately the revolution in carriage by steam and then petrol would make colonial warfare more humane in one way, by reducing the need for legions of often unwilling porters, and of baggage-animals, another unfortunate species of conscript, which suffered and perished in untold numbers on every campaign. They might be as cosmopolitan an assemblage as the armies frequently were; for the march to Magdala thousand of mules were got together from Spain, Italy, Asia Minor, as well as camels from Arabia and Egypt. A soldier in the Zulu war noticed how quickly he got used to the continual thrashing, of mules and their drivers alike, necessary to keep the ponderous convoys moving.[20] Mountainous areas were especially fatal. San Martín the patriot leader crossing the Andes to Chile in 1817 lost a third of his horses, nearly half his mules. Every Afghan march meant countless creatures worked or starved to death. Deserts could swallow nearly as many, as they did in Central Asia, or in the Sudan where someone on a march noted: 'a lot of camels had to be shot, and were instantly torn to pieces by the Arabs coming along with us.'[21] In Somaliland camel mortality in 1902–3 was 'enormous', reaching nearly half the number employed. In the East Africa campaign during the Great War the British alone lost 50,000 horses.

Colonial wars, often fought over extended theatres, required good signalling, and accelerated its development. It was in an engagement in 1879 in Afghanistan that the heliograph was first used. African sunshine favoured it, and signals in Morse could be picked up from seventy miles away. But co-operation between Kitchener and French at Paardeberg was impeded by a cloudy sky. In Tanganyika the Germans organized heliographic communication over nearly 900 miles, and it was used in South-West Africa by columns in pursuit of the Herrero rebels. At night signal-lamps with shutters could be brought into play, as they were in Abyssinia in 1863 and near Suakin in 1885. In both these operations field telegraphs were also laid. During the Moroccan war in 1859–60 Ceuta was linked with Spain by submarine cable. In 1883 when Suakin was threatened the Eastern Telegraph Company was commissioned to lay a cable to it from Suez, down the Red Sea, as a task of 'very urgent necessity'.[22] In Somaliland in 1903 every method had to be tried, including wireless. Radio transmitters accompanied the Italians to Libya. German East Africa had three or four wireless stations by 1914, and the army was pressing for more. Another use of electricity was to power searchlights. At Suakin one was perched on the town wall, to keep a look out for snipers; the 1885 campaign in that area was fertile in technical novelties. Another was used in Mashonaland in 1890, as a precaution against night attacks. Searchlights were mounted on the gunboats going up the Nile to Omdurman. The dark continent was being illuminated, though its own peoples could only grope like blind men.

Ballooning made slow, fitful progress after its start in the late 18th. century, but imperial requirements made themselves felt here too. In 1884 Hartington as Secretary for War was asked about French trials of balloons in Tonking, and whether Britain meant to follow suit; he assured the Commons that the matter was being considered.[23] Next year a marching square near Suakin had an observation balloon tethered to a waggon, and messages fluttered down on sheets of paper from a height of four hundred feet. The effect on the minds of any watching inhabitants must have been as much a gain to the invaders as any information they were getting. Observation balloons gazed down on the Boer War, and on China in 1900. More ambitiously, an aeroplane took part in Indian army manoeuvres at Aurangabad in 1910, possibly with some eye to a chastening impression on Indian nationalism. It was quite in the logic of history that war-planes should be tried out first in a colonial war. On 23 October 1911, an Italian Blériot plane reconnoitred the Turkish lines near Azisia, and a week later a pilot dropped grenades on two Libyan towns, tiny heralds of thunderous skies of a not distant future. Bombings were also carried out by dirigible airships. Enough was accomplished to galvanize the military mind of Europe, and ensure unanimous rejection of any ban on air bombardment at the Aviation Conference at Paris in 1912.

ii. Food, drink, health

From Tibetan heights to Nigerian heats the gamut was very wide. Campaign needs threw up multifarious items of paraphernalia, though fewer improvements than could have been found if more careful thought had been bestowed on them. Eye ailments were a besetting risk; in Egypt in 1882 soldiers were given sun-glasses with wire meshing at the corners to keep out sand. Food came first, and it was often impossible to live off the country. Canned food was invaluable. Devised in Europe under stress of the Napoleonic wars, it was first issued to the British navy in 1813. At Cawnpore in 1857 officers facing a siege were busy collecting 'large contributions of liquor and hermetically sealed tins from their mess-stores'.[24] Some of the tinned meat taken to Morocco two years later proved unwholesome, however.[25]

Alcohol was almost as indispensable as food. It supplied some nutrition, mollified hardships, and sharpened appetite for battle: there must have been a dash of Dutch courage in all Western armies in action. At daylight before a battle in the Punjab men foodless since the previous morning were given a pound of bread and a dram of grog. One trooper got through a hungry night in the Punjab by mixing water with what liquor he had and sharing it with his horse.[26] Sepoy Sita Ram never saw white men backward when it came to blows except when baulked of their tot. 'They would fight ten battles in succession for one bowl of spirits.'[27] Tolstoy heard of the creature comfort put to a more sinister use, from a cadet who came to him with religious doubts: he said that at Geok Tepe the soldiers shrank from carrying out in cold blood Skobelev's order for a massacre of the inhabitants, until they were given enough drink to blot out any scruples.[28] Among Britain's native troops there were a few who enjoyed a noggin. Gurkhas, a writer on them reported, 'cheerfully accept any alcoholic drink available, good rum being their favourite.'[29] Before a fight on the pampas Páez plied a band of naked Indian archers he had enlisted with brandy, to keep them from being scared by the sound of firing, and they fought furiously.[30]

Without this solace the empire could not have been won. But its ministrations were too often vitiated by abuse. Lord Roberts became chairman of a Royal Army Temperance Association, which sought to wean the soldiery away from chronic drunkenness. When the 32nd Foot were relaxing after their exertions in the Punjab the colonel threw the canteen open for three days, 'rum passed from hand to hand in gallons', and most of the men's hard-won gold pieces were garnered by the women of the 61st, quartered near by.[31] Sordid conditions, and boredom, made drinking the only escape, apart from desertion, far less easy overseas than in Britain, or the more drastic one of suicide, which was far from rare. From other armies too Bacchus exacted tribute. Thomas Campbell came to the conclusion that drinking was worse still among the French in Algeria, and a doctor assured him that more than a quarter of the annual loss of 3000 men was due to it.[32] An English soldier in Africa later on associated French troops overseas with an 'immediate demand for "pinard"', or army ration wine, as an antidote to 'Cafard, that legendary disease' of boredom which 'seemed to chase all volatile Frenchmen wherever they went'.[33]

British soldiers carried cholera with them from Bengal to Nepal. Throughout history germs have been invisible skirmishers, not seldom deciding the outcome of wars. In many areas sickness was the great leveller, redressing the balance against the white man's weapons. In the decade 1819–28 the British army mustered on average 47,000 men at home, 53,000 overseas: the former had an annual mortality of 1.5 per cent, the latter of 5.7 per cent, and the average of the two was three times as high as for men of comparable age in civil life.[34] There was always in colonial wars a desire for speedy victory to curtail losses from disease. One death-haunted place had always been the West Indies; soldiers as well as slaves paid with their lives for planters' profits and Europe's sweet tooth. Marryatt's nervous officer was feverishly anxious to exchange into another ship when his own was under orders for the West Indian station.[35] Other graveyards were joining it. Both the Opium Wars were medically harrowing, and in ten years after the second the original roll of the 58th Foot at Hong Kong was practically eliminated by disease, chiefly dysentery; a major and a woman were said to be the sole survivors. During the 1850s there was marked reluctance to go to Burma – 'and no wonder, for Burma was then a veritable death trap.' It brought the 47th N.I. down from a thousand men to under five hundred in four years.[36] Sepoys fell victim no less than Europeans.

Efforts to insure soldiers against such war-risks came belatedly and haltingly. An officer bound for the first Burma war wrote bitterly of 'the disgraceful negligence of a miserable government' in sending them off without medical supplies.[37] Wolseley represented a new, scientific spirit; for the British soldiers in his Ashanti campaign he provided pocket water-filters, and prescribed a daily dose of quinine; even this failed to keep a good many from falling ill. His precautions were noted by the French, and adopted in their invasion of Dahomey.

Yet of 1050 Legionaries only 450 survived, most of the others falling to fever. Radama I of Madagascar is supposed to have said, as many other rulers might have, that a certain disease was 'one of his best generals'; his words were borne out in 1895 when the French loss of 3400 out of 15,000 men was due almost entirely to sickness. Half a century after the Spanish army owed two-thirds of its 7000 deaths in the Moroccan war of 1859–60 to cholera, the Italians in their Libyan war lost nearly 2000 from sickness, far more than their battle losses. Napoleon's lost army in San Domingo had spurred some French doctors into a study of tropical diseases,[38] but research did not begin in earnest until late in the century, chiefly in British possessions and in the USA, where the Panama Canal became an incentive.

Wastage of life in peacetime on colonial duty – and at home, in a country as backward as Spain – had for one of its causes insanitary barracks. In 1842 the 28th landed at Bombay from Australia hale and hearty, only to begin dying of cholera in hot, crowded, airless barracks. On the march the camp reproduced the same atmosphere. 'I never saw anything like the filth', wrote one sufferer in the Punjab, with carcasses strewn all round.[39] Droves of camp-followers added to the mess. Altogether the story of British troops in the empire is 'a record of callous indifference to human suffering'.[40] In India, Florence Nightingale discovered in 1862, the annual death-rate was 6.9 per cent, which meant that one company out of each regiment was sacrificed every twenty months. This in spite of perpetual worries over recruiting, which frustrated the aim of the Cardwell reforms in 1871 to keep an equal number of battalions at home and abroad. In 1879 there were 59 at home, 82 abroad; in 1905, 71 and 85.

Even after the Crimean War gave its impetus to reform, Florence Nightingale's efforts to improve army health at home and in India were an uphill struggle against the dead weight of military and bureaucratic inertia and stupidity. 'It is this desperate guerrilla warfare ending in so little which makes me impatient of life', she wrote,[41] in a metaphor reflecting times when a small war was always going on somewhere. British military hospitals were still horribly insanitary in the Boer War, not much less perilous than the battlefield. Imperial needs were producing a special type of field hospital, the hospital ship. In the first China war the *Victoria* did duty; for Abyssinia the Admiralty provided three. They were only too likely to be even more deplorably managed than shore establishments, with drunken orderlies to do the nursing. For the Egyptian and Sudan expeditions of 1882 and 1884 parties of nurses trained on Florence Nightingale's lines were asked for, and earned gratitude. In 1885 there was a well-appointed hospital barge on the Red River, and Nurse Miller became known as Canada's Miss Nightingale. No such amenities were coming the way of Europe's opponents. Without her intending it, Florence Nightingale's teachings facilitated colonial conquests of all types, as they would help to prolong the Great War.

Army doctors through most of the 19th century cannot be credited with very high professional standards. There were some engaging characters among them, like Dr Martin of the 14th Madras N.I. who prepared for the third Burma war by smuggling his darling piano over from India, disguised as a crate of 'medical comforts'. At Rangoon it was detected, and 'a Tartar of a Surgeon-General' made him leave it behind. He sought consolation in a banjo, and practised assiduously, 'much to the annoyance of his neighbours'.[42] It was a vital part of Florence Nightingale's mission to get the status and quality of army doctors improved. As technicians they, like engineers, were apt to be looked down on by genuine officers, as the fighting men deemed themselves. Surgeon Pine, who graduated from Edinburgh in 1832, trudged about the world wondering when his luck was going to turn. Back in 1843 from China, he got a step up next year, into the 58th, but this meant setting out with it at once for New South Wales. 'I cannot avoid the conclusion that I have been hardly used. ...'[43] Doctors were not given full officer status until 1898, the year when the Medical Corps founded in 1873 became the Royal Army Medical Corps.

iii. The soldier's vocation

In Persia in 1857 first General Stalker and then Commodore Ethersey shot themselves. Responsibility sometimes weighed heavily on men so far away from their moorings. Others shielded themselves by bold posturing, a habit encouraged by the increasing glare of publicity. Real professional skill was not common. Victorian standards of education for the army were 'appallingly low'; character was honoured in preference to knowledge.[44] Small wars fostered improvisation, but allowed planning to be let slip. A staff college, set up in 1858 after lengthy debate, was one of the post-Crimea reforms, and in 1902 Kitchener opened another in India. But Wolseley's fruitless navigation of the Nile was retarded by 'major errors and incompetence in staff work',[45] and the Boer War revealed how little had still been achieved. From 1885 to 1904 there was a Colonial Defence

Committee in London, doing no more than gather and circulate data about such matters as training. Co-ordination was poor: a Supply and Transport Department, reorganized in 1888, busied itself with elaborate plans which Kitchener when sent to south Africa as chief of staff knew nothing about. In the French army too, at least before 1870, staff work was notoriously poor.

Apart from chances of prize-money,[46] for the men at the top there were titles and emoluments in store which might put them on a level with quite affluent businessmen. Napier of Magdala got a peerage and £2000 a year for himself and one more life, but lump sums were coming to be the convention. Wolseley was given £25,000 for his Ashanti work, Kitchener £30,000 after the Sudan, £50,000 after the Boer War which netted Roberts, as commander-in-chief, £100,000, not less than Haig was considered worth at the end of the Great War. Fortune helps those who help themselves, and Kitchener and a group of associates got a handsome grant of land in Kenya, confiscated from the Nandi tribe, by a 'somewhat irregular transaction' sanctioned by his friend the governor.[47] In other armies rewards and refreshers might be no less generous. Paskievich's defeat of Persia in 1828 brought him a liberal donative. Land in conquered territory might be another nest-egg for a Russian. When the sudden Persian attack came in 1827 commanders floundered because, it was said, they had 'diverted troops to work on their newly acquired estates'.[48] With the march of progress General Lazarev, captor of Kars in Asia minor in 1878, was one of a number of lucky Russians who came in for ten acres each of oil-bearing land. Between acquisitive capitalism in Europe and rolling back of frontiers in Afro-Asia was a labyrinth of intermediary impulses.

But the way to the top was narrow, crowded, sometimes tortuous; one consequence was that commanders were often too old to benefit by advice or new ideas. This was so not least in the British army, where jeremiads about poor pay, slow promotion, favouritism, were never-ending. The Pearson who started in India in 1825 at the age of nineteen became a captain in 1831, and sixteen years later was writing to his wife: 'I am very much disgusted with my bad fortune.' Still a mere captain, he was mortified by the sight of men junior to him drawing ahead. 'I am standing still and wearing out my constitution on Indian service to be looked down upon at last as an Indian officer. . . .'[49] It is hard to share the impression of an excellent judge that 'very few brooded over these grievances',[50] though there were as he says gaieties and enlivenments to take some of the sting out of them. An easy-going man in south India in the 1860s found

133

life, with its abundance of leisure and servants, 'truly delightful';[51] but he soon quitted the army, to seek repose still more unruffled, or brighter prospects, in the Church. 'On board this vessel nothing but discontent with their lot from Indian officers', wrote Gordon on his way to India in 1880.[52] 'You don't get your bread till you have no teeth left to eat it with', one such lamented.[53] A dodge for speeding promotion was known as 'purchasing-out', a practice not officially sanctioned, but winked at. On reaching the rank of major a man became entitled to a slender pension, and might agree to retire if those next in line offered him a sum to supplement it.

During the first Afghan war a Company officer wrote sourly in his journal about how the public was always being bamboozled by 'the flaming despatches of a Queen's General on service, in the East', which painted the royal regiments in gorgeous colours, while publicity never failed to be given to 'whatever may be said in disparagement of the Company's Army'.[54] Roberts had kindred feelings during the Mutiny, when he thought Queen's men were getting too many of the plums left by so many Company men being killed. 'This does not suit our Royal Brethren', he commented when Sir A. Wilson, a Company man like himself, was given the artillery command.[55] After the EIC and its army gave up the ghost there was a parallel estrangement between regiments at home and the socially less glamorous ones overseas. India attracted poorer men, and thus relieved the army of discontent which at home might have been more troublesome.[56] Overseas there was a similar snobbery on the part of officers in British units who looked down on those attached to native troops.

Among those who put on uniform for the sake of a career, instead of for a few years' lounging in or near London, there was always behind the scenes much jostling and jockeying. General Sir Norman Stewart's account of the ladder of promotion is the more convincing because he suceeded in reaching the top, like his father before him. 'Jealousy! what a curse this is in our Army', he exclaims, over a malicious rumour set afloat about the conduct of one unit in a tight corner during the second Afghan war. He saw officers on the march there already scheming for good jobs, and 'the Cabul heroes', Roberts and his lieutenants, 'are quite satisfied they are going to get all the plums.'[57] Staff officers he regarded as 'one of the abominations of our service', obsequious to their superiors, supercilious with the regimental officers who did the real work. Influential relatives, a pretty wife, frequent visits to Simla were the right cards to play. Anyone content to drudge at regimental duty would be 'a beast of burden' to the end of his days, unless a chance of distinction on active service came his way. If so he could count on prompt promotion, 'for to give the devil his due, merit in the field is speedily rewarded'.[58]

All this helps to explain why officers were always avid for a smell of powder, and would nearly always deem the most unjust war better than the most just peace. Pearson in 1847 was hoping that the Sikh war would rescue his career from the doldrums, though careful to build 'no airy castles for a wandering imagination to inhabit'. At Aliwal he led the charge of his regiment, which had severe losses, and was the first across the enemy entrenchments, under the eye of Sir Harry Smith who immediately promised him his majority.[59] Half a century later Winston Churchill in India, a typical young man in a hurry, was pestering his mother to pull strings and get transfers for him to places in the limelight. He burned to be in the Sudan with Kitchener, and Lady Randolph did her best, but warned him that 'The chances of being taken are extremely remote as the competition is tremendous.'[60] The Boer War offered opportunity on a grander scale than any previous colonial shindy, and all who could seized it. In India the authorities were dismayed at so many officers disappearing on one pretext or another to south Africa. 'They're all busting for glory', a private there said disapprovingly.[61] Older ones, in a position to shape events, might do so wrong-headedly. Baring in Egypt told the prime minister that he could not trust the judgment of any of his military men, because of their craving for action.[62]

'I shall miss any chance of a show now', someone in Nigeria grumbled after failing to get into the Sokoto expedition.[63] The British army was very fond of amateur theatricals; there is a theatricality about an army's whole existence, and the slang term *show* for a military operation of any sort is revealing. So is the passion shared by all the armies for dressing up. Officers collected a row of medals as women did jewels, and while waiting for them found a substitute in dazzling raiment. None the less, yawning or fretting occupied more time than anything else. Boredom and daily frictions made duelling, down to the middle of the century, a common occurrence in British garrisons overseas. Drinking helped to promote it; officers as well as privates sought refuge in the bottle from isolation and frustration. 'Life up-country was incredibly dull', a survivor pointed out.[64] At the siege of Multan an officer was court-martialled for being drunk on duty, and died of drink before being sentenced. Such anecdotes are numerous, and more men may have broken down under stress of their ordinary lives than on the battlefield. Much nearer our day a youthful commandant in a lonely fort on the north-west frontier, sitting in his room with nothing to do, kept finding the bottle floating down towards him from its shelf, as it were, of its own accord.[65]

The majority kept going by filling up their time with trivial occupations, above all with Sport, the killing of animals and birds. A life like the one revealed in General Sir Peter Strickland's diaries was a life of routine duty, perpetual shooting and fishing, polo, golf, bridge. He never read a book, and took no interest in any of the countries through which he peregrinated. To individuals of any mental alertness the army atmosphere was hard to breathe. One who started in India in 1895 made up his mind thirty years later that it was time to retire, because of failing health but also because 'I confess I am tired of the intellectual and artistic barrenness of life in the army in India. ... The ordinary talk of the mess, dear good things though they all are, perfect sahibs to the backbone ... exasperates me by its unvarying sameness.'[66] Much more an intellectual, John Morris felt the tedium still more acutely, and drew a graphic picture of the narrow enclosed world of a regimental mess in India and its artificial rituals.[67]

It was not to be wondered at, an enlightened critic wrote in 1846, that there should be so much talk in the British army of a lack of good NCOs, when it took no pains to give men the means of qualifying themselves by education. He contrasted this neglect with the state of things in some other countries. 'Great attention has been paid to the diffusion of useful scholarship in the French army....'[68] In Algeria in the 1840s every outpost was furnished with some four hundred books, though they may have been read more by officers than by privates. How uninstructed the typical British soldier was came home to an officer in charge of three hundred raw hands, mostly from the slums of Manchester and Liverpool, going out to India during the Mutiny. 'Some of them were so ignorant that they were actually not aware of the name of the reigning Sovereign.'[69] 'He is a perfect Yahoo', the 'Subaltern' wrote of one of his men, '– just caught from the wilds of Ireland, and can speak very little English ... but as we only want hands, not heads, it's no matter.'[70]

This philosophy changed by very slow degrees. By the end of the 1870s every regiment in India had its library, of a thousand books or so (it would be interesting to know how carefully they were chosen as pabulum for loyal soldiers of the Queen); in the 1880s magic lanterns and slides were being added, to enliven lectures. But technology was far outstripping any improvement in human material, at the bottom as well as at the top. To Roberts the Boer War was a demonstration that recruits with more capability and initiative were needed. A sharp-witted youth who a few years later commenced a quarter-century in the Rifle Brigade, mostly served abroad, got to know the ins and outs of an army still fixed in old grooves. Down to 1914 mechanical drilling was still the alpha and omega; 'the powers that be did not consider that any member of the Forces had any brains to think for themselves, that is, any member below a commissioned rank. ...' He soon got a step up, but not to a bed of roses, because 'all NCOs were detested by the men', whom they were expected to bully. 'The whole trouble about the pre-war army was fear, Privates for Corporals and Corporals for Sergeants and so on.'[71]

If privates good enough to be made NCOs were not plentiful, those who could be thought entitled to commissions were exceedingly few, so that army prejudice against promotion from the ranks was seldom challenged. Here again outstanding merit in the field was the best passport. After one Indian battle four men of an Irish regiment were awarded commissions. Even when the offer was made it might have to be declined for financial reasons, as it was by Sergeant-Major Gowing in India in 1862,[72] or, at first, also in India, by the later field-marshal, Sir William Robertson.

In the Spanish army Isidro Alaix rose from the ranks during the South American wars and reached the rank of general. In the Russian army, by comparison with western European practice, there was a certain blurring of the line between NCOs and officers, because of the category of 'under-officers' who started as NCOs but were eligible for a commission after six months.[73] An individual who began on this footing was D.A. Milyutin, who rose to be War Minister in 1861, the year of the abolition of serfdom, and initiated the reorganization which preceded the grand change of 1874 from selective long-term conscription to universal short-term service. He laid great stress on better professional education for officers, whose incompetence the Crimean War had shown up. What is interesting from the imperial point of view is that Milyutin served as a young man in the Caucasus, and in 1856 was chosen by Prince Baryatinski as his chief of staff there. They worked out a more flexible structure of command and organization, and in the 1860s this model was extended to the whole country. Central Asian experience was a further leaven. After 1874 regular schools for NCOs were set up. All nobles now had to serve, and in 1895 about half the officer corps were still nobles by birth; but the privileged Guards, trained in the Military Schools, were gradually being overtaken by lower-class entrants from the 'Junker' cadet schools. In China in 1900, when armies had an opportunity for a critical inspection of one another, General Stewart thought the ordinary Russian soldiers splendid, their officers very unworthy of them.[74] War with Japan soon confirmed this, at least so far as staff work and the higher command were concerned. Tsarist Russia was capable of changes, but not of a true rebirth.

iv. Native troops, and the cost of conquest

As in the Roman empire, more and more fresh peoples were being drawn or dragged into service; and Europe could claim better success at turning Afro-Asians into regular soldiers than almost any of their own rulers. Various Western nations preened themselves on superior ability, particularly Britain which had the widest experience and, in its Indian army, the most resplendent achievement. Extolling the new British-trained army in Egypt, Auckland Colvin affirmed that 'The spirit which animated their officers had communicated itself to the men', and that the lack of sympathy with other races frequently alleged against Englishmen was less marked in military than in civil life;[75] by that date a not unjustifiable claim. Fraternizing between British and other units, when they shared danger in the field, was occasionally observable, as it had been in India. When a brigade was entering Berber in 1898 Sudanese battalions lined the road 'and their bands played their British comrades in, amidst enthusiastic cheers for the Queen'.[76] All the same, the qualities displayed by the Egyptian army in 1898 would make it all the more to be feared, if one day the nationalist spirit of 1882 infected it again. Most of its units were kept in the Sudan, while British troops garrisoned Cairo.

France was steadily building its own sepoy army. In 1878 the 19th Corps, stationed in Algeria, was made up largely of Arab *tirailleurs* and light infantry, along with Zouaves and Legionaries. By 1914 there were seven regiments of Spahis, besides the *tirailleurs algériens*. Men were invited to enlist, but any shortage was made good by compulsion. Selective conscription for four years was imposed on Tunisia at once; on Algeria in 1912, with substitution allowed. In west Africa quotas were fixed, and headmen were responsible for seeing them met; four years was again the term for the *appelés*, or men compelled to serve. Similar regulations were applied to Indochina and Madagascar. Before the Great War the totals mobilized were modest; but among the 76,000 men engaged in the occupation of Morocco at the end of 1913 there were 12,000 from Senegal and 14,000 other Africans.[77] A book on the battle history of France's black troops, published in 1940, held that aptitude for war was hereditary in the Negro race, because in Africa a state of war had been normal, and cited General Weygand's dictum that every officer who commanded these soldiers loved them: their leading characteristic was ready obedience.[78] In Eritrea 'native troops, well cared for, became devoted to their Italian officers'. Later on Somalis were made much use of by Italy as soldiers and policemen, in the Fascist era chiefly nomads from northern districts, prized as natural warriors.[79]

Gruff talk of 'indiscipline and inefficiency' among western and southern African troops was often heard from the Horse Guards.[80] But at Nice in 1847 Cobden was assured by Sir George Napier, a soldier and former governor of the Cape, that a regiment of Hottentot dragoons commanded by his son were very small men but better fighters, when under British officers, than either Kaffirs or Boers, and so full of spirit that they had to be held in leash rather than egged on. 'This confirms my opinion', Cobden reflected, 'that all races of men are equal in value when placed under like circumstances. ... '[81] This opinion has been borne out by later history, but it was not shared by the military men of his day, who examined the material passing through their hands with a very discriminating eye.

How close they came to gauging the real dispositions of Afro-Asian peoples, as these have unfolded themselves subsequently, would make a curious subject of enquiry. A Somali was 'an attractive rogue', in a British officer's view, 'too light-hearted and almost frivolous' to be a first-rater, but brave enough when well led.[82] A War Office estimate gave him higher marks, though with the caveat that 'as is the case with all natives, much depends on personal influence and handling', the Somali being vain and temperamental.[83] In Tanganyika the warlike capabilities of each tribe were scrutinized with Germanic thoroughness. Many were dismissed as 'timid' and 'cowardly', passively submitting to the stronger.[84] Everywhere the white man's impulse was to denounce pugnacious peoples and to despise peaceful ones as poltroons; it was very marked among Americans in contact with Red Indians. Skobelev had Kirghiz fighting-men with him at Tekke in 1881 as auxiliaries; they were at first enrolled as regular troops, but he reduced them to irregulars, thinking it unwise to place native and European units on the same level. Georgians and Armenians were liable to the same conscription as Russians; their soldiers, like those of other minorities, were usually posted far away from their homes, so as to have less temptation to run away, and, no doubt, less compunction about firing on the people when required to do so. Georgians often rose high in the army, as in other walks of Russian life. They had a feudal and warlike tradition, but Armenians, much more a commercial people, did not lag far behind.

How to reckon the costs of imperial wars is a problem bristling with difficulties, but some points stand out. Russia's ambitions were all the more expensive because they helped to involve it in wars with Turkey, and finally involved it in war with Japan. France had to pay the whole military budget of its colonies. Some book-keeper's sleight of hand must have been possible, but annual colonial expenses rose by 1885 to 238 million francs, and, after some decrease, rose again before 1914, with the Moroccan venture, to 637 million. Here was one good reason for the mixed feelings of the French taxpayer about his burgeoning empire. Still, it would have cost him far more if he had not had the use of cheap native soldiery. Holland had the twofold asset of cheap soldiers from other islands, and Java to pay for them.

Possession of India gave Britain the same felicity on a grander scale. About the same time in 1880 as the altercation in the Commons about who should pay for the second Afghan war, the House had several discussions about military costs in south Africa. John Bull viewed such matters very differently when the boot was on the other leg. Forcible objections were raised, and endorsed by Gladstone, to the colonists being allowed to provoke Kaffir wars and then apply for British troops paid for by the British taxpayer.[85] This was precisely how Indians were objecting to Britain provoking wars and making India pay for them and help to fight them. Thanks to this juggling, an Indian historian declares, Britain acquired much of its territory in Asia 'at absolutely no cost to the British exchequer. ...'[86] At least the empire was being got at bargain prices, especially by contrast with the enormous sums squandered on the French wars of 1793-1815. Conquest of the Sudan cost a mere £2,400,000, of which Britain paid only a third. Yet steady refusal to give more money to the army ruled out the idea advocated by Roberts and many others of two separate establishments, one of short-term men for home defence, the other of long-service men, who would have to be paid more, for the empire.

Some reckoned the first Burma war to have cost up to £15 million: the first Afghan war has lately been calculated at £8 million,[87] with no compensating gain. In 1902 the War Office compiled a schedule of official returns of costs of seventeen principal conflicts between the Crimean War and the Boer War, and of the numbers of men engaged. The heaviest item in the bill was £28.7 million, for the Mutiny, followed by £23.4 million for the second Afghan war, with 71,700 men at work. Abyssinia came next, far behind, with 12,000 men and a cost of £9 million, and the Sudan in 1884–5, with far more men, 26,000, but a rather lower cost, £7.3 million. The second China war, the Zulu war, the occupation of Egypt, were all computed at between four and five millions, though the manpower in these three cases was 14,000, 17,000, and 31,000. In various others the investment was far more modest: £700,000 for the two Maori wars of the 1860s, £661,000 for the Ashanti campaign of 1873–4.[88] For the seventeen items in the list the total comes to £98.5 million. The Boer War cost more than double this, a sudden huge escalation. There were always overhead expenses on training, troop movements, pensions, and so on. If the cost to the British Isles of rearing young men, year by year for two or three centuries, to be sent out to die of disease or in battle around the world, could be added up, it would represent a very heavy debit entry in the balance-sheet.

v. The resistance

In the Great War archers were among the local material drawn on in west Africa, and proved quite useful. Native weapons as well as men were sometimes utilized or imitated by Westerners. About 1850 a British officer designed a cylindrical bullet 'on the inspiration of lotus pith arrows which he had seen blown in India.'[89] There may have been some interplay of eastern and western genius in the 'stink-ball' or 'stink-pot' which before dwindling to a schoolboy's practical joke was in use by western navies and eastern pirates. It was cited as a Chinese invention by a writer in 1869 who seemed to regard it as the source of a current project to make 'shells charged with noxious gases'.[90] Tomahawks were carried by the American navy, and made their mark sufficiently for their name to be attached today to a class of nuclear missiles. Hussars at El Teb used Arab spears by way of lances, pursuing cavalry elsewhere used Zulu assegais. In the trench fighting of the Great War axes came back to life, and clubs, some of them known from their shape as 'knobkerries'. There was some experimental use, which might have been carried further, of shields and armour. Soldiers tackling stockades in the second Burma war wore breastplates. Rider Haggard's three heroes setting off for fresh adventures in Africa took with them shirts of chain mail, made in Birmingham, and he thought lives could have been saved in Zululand had the War Office been equally provident.[91]

In Asia and Africa few real advances were being made, though in China a long dormant ingenuity was beginning to stir once more. In

141

the second Opium War there were attempts to destroy British ships by means of what Admiral Seymour called 'floating explosive machines', one of 'very ingenious construction' containing 3000 pounds of gunpowder.[92] Elsewhere for the most part old equipment continued to be produced, with old shortcomings unremedied. Burma's gunpowder even at the end of the kingdom's independence was 'afflicted by a curious apathy', while some of its iron swords could be bent double.[93] True, such defects were not unknown in Western camps. Wolseley in Egypt was choleric about poor ammunition and defective bayonets, as well as breakdowns in supply; they led to a committee of enquiry on the government arsenals. Old-style cannon seldom made much of a dent on Western forces. During a long pause in the Himalayan expedition of 1893 the Gurkhas greatly enjoyed their games of football on a piece of ground under fire from guns on the mountain ledges above, whose aim was so absurdly inaccurate that no one bothered about it.[94] On the Nile in 1898 gunboats were able to steam unscathed past well-constructed Mahdist batteries.

Western weapons became steadily more impossible for any non-industrial country to match; but Afro-Asia could buy them from the West as readily as the West could hire soldiers from Afro-Asia. Abd el Kader was getting English arms, an Englishman admitted, but not from the government as Frenchmen suspected. 'Traders of all nations, in seeking the best markets for their goods, notoriously disregard patriotic, and international considerations.'[95] This fact was usually taken for granted as part of what Ukridge would call 'the big, broad, flexible outlook' proper to the businessman. Sir Stamford Raffles at Singapore kept a wary eye on Americans, as commercial interlopers and salesmen of guns for which there was a brisk demand in his neighbourhood.

Their prices might be higher than their quality; but many Afridis encountered in the Tirah campaign of 1897 had good magazine rifles. In the early years of the 20th century there was known to be taking place 'a very large illicit importation of firearms into almost every part of Somaliland. ...'[96] Where there was any State organization, cannon too could be added. In the second Afghan war British light field-pieces were sometimes outranged by enemy guns. But these were simpler to acquire than to master, and it was not easy now, with the expansion of empires and hardening of racial attitudes, to hire European mercenaries, as in India in old days. In their place a trickle of former members of Europe's native forces might bring expertise with them. Osman Digna had several, among them mechanics familiar enough with electric wiring to defuse a mine carefully planted to blow up snipers near Suakin. But such talents had little chance of being appreciated and fostered under the sway of the Khalifa.

Enemy artillery only really mattered in the Boer War. There at the outset 41 Boer guns confronted 173 British, with 37 machine-guns against 65, but the Boers had a surprising lead in quick-firing cannon, 28 to virtually none.[97] In Afro-Asian hands even muskets or rifles were seldom effective. That there was ordinarily little to fear from enemy shooting was one of Callwell's oftenest repeated maxims. Men with little discipline or firing drill were very liable to lose their heads, as western troops did at times, in the flurry of combat, and blaze away at random. Somali dervishes were 'most inaccurate and excitable Marksmen'; one opinion was that they would have been 'infinitely more dangerous' if they had gone on using spears as well. Instead, all over north-east Africa adoption of firearms had made spearmanship 'a lost art'.[98] A failing reported from almost everywhere was a habit, seemingly ineradicable, of firing too high. It may be conjectured that it was due to an instinctive expectation that the bullet would sink earthward quickly, like a javelin or arrow. Kaffirs firing from cover were among the few savage sharpshooters who appear to have become good shots. Pathans were another exception.

Baffled opponents may have been driven to fancy that the white man was safeguarded by talismans such as Asia and Africa were always in search of. He too had wished for them in earlier, more credulous days. Rabelais's swashbuckling Friar John feared nothing in war except artillery, and he had a special prayer to ward off cannon-balls. Some white men ages later may have picked up primitive superstitions; at the time of the Boer War some Afrikaners were said to rely on native charms to make their jackets impenetrable.[99] It is very striking to find how much of the magic lore of the borderlands in the 19th century was conjured up by fear of shells and bullets. Spells to deflect them were being added to those long in use against plague, accident, death; and Zulu warriors had always undergone elaborate 'doctoring' before battle.

European invasion brought fresh and profitable business to witch-doctors, medicine-men, shamans of every persuasion. In Kaffraria a magician undertook to turn bullets in flight into water. Matabele insurgents in 1896 thought they knew how to do this with Maxim bullets, and the same recurrent idea was spread by the Maji-Maji cults in the 1905 revolt in Tanganyika. Founders of new cults could have no better means of advertising them. No hard experience seems to have shaken the astounding courage of adherents of the 'Hau Hau' sect started in 1862 by a Maori leader who saw visions and promised immunity to bullets. Higher religions, or their devotees, could not afford to lag behind. A band of 'Invulnerables' fought in the first Burma war, tattooed with tigers and elephants, and incurred heavy losses by exposing themselves recklessly. Tibetans in 1904 were firm believers in spells purveyed by the lamas. In Somaliland the Mullah was another who told his men that he could turn bullets fired at them to water. Presumably the faithful were convinced that a great many fired at them failed to arrive because disposed of by his agency on the way.

Magical protection could do as much as any faith in heavenly rewards to inspire hopeless headlong attacks, like those of the Boxers, infatuated by beliefs woven out of old village superstition and vulgar Taoism by ages of secret-society ritual. Delusion of another kind may perhaps explain another weakness in the resistance to Europe. A British manual of 1921 stressed the need for an outer line of pickets round camps, and other precautions, in hill country where night attacks might be expected.[100] By then times were changing; earlier, as Callwell remarked, night attacks were surprisingly rare.[101] Fear of darkness and the powers of evil may have been the cause. In east Africa the Germans found it difficult to execute night marches because their native soldiers and porters might be terrified at any moment by ghosts.

It was guerrilla resistance that usually put Europe to most annoyance, and as practised by its most gifted exponents it could foreshadow at times what it was to become in our era, one of the most sophisticated branches of the art of war. Afghans and Pathans were recognized proficients in irregular warfare, and on the north-west frontier generations of contact with the white man gave them time to learn. In the Tirah war there was only one charge of swordsmen, 'a mode of fighting for which Pathans were formerly noted'.[102] The official report on the third Afghan war of 1919 noted both stronger and weaker points of the enemy. They knew how to evade a blow, and to 'follow up a retirement relentlessly and with the utmost boldness.' On the other hand they lacked 'steadfastness in adversity', and lost heart when kept under continuous pressure.[103] Even success was not always pressed home by such fighting-men. Lure of plunder was often the cause. After Maiwand the Afghans only pursued the retiring British for a mile or two, during which they inflicted severe losses, before returning to ransack the battlefield. It was much the same after Adowa; Italian stragglers were cut off by villagers, but there was little organized chase, and it was not from any lack of cavalry. Only political ideas and organisation of a later day would rectify these deficiencies.

Irregular wars were 'people's wars', and, more than other kinds, might rouse the concern and even enlist the aid of women. They often urged on their men, who had taught them in many lands to honour and obey the male sex for its fighting prowess above all. Dervishes in Somaliland hurling themselves against machine-guns were 'encouraged by the shrill cries of their womenkind in the rear'.[104] It was the same among the Kabyles, whose women were always ready to set the brand of disgrace on a coward; and in the Kabyle war of 1857 all the tribes revered a prophetess, Lalla Fathma, old and ugly yet dignified as the French found when they at last captured her. Women occasionally took a hand as combatants, though nowhere else in the organized fashion of Dahomey, or as auxiliaries. There were episodes in the Caucasus of women in men's attire fighting bravely against the Russians, and there were women among the Ghilzai insurgents captured by Outram in Afghanistan, and in the Mad Mullah's following. During the Mutiny, when the city of Jhansi was being defended by its Ranee, women carried ammunition to the batteries. Ashanti women were sometimes seen reloading muskets for their men. It was a foreshadowing of women's emancipation in revolutionary China that the Boxers had companies of girl helpers, the 'Red Lanterns'.

To the most untutored or atavistic level belonged the torturing of prisoners or mutilation of corpses by women. Pathan women – like Glendower's Welshwomen – were very often accused of such doings, and similar allegations turn up in various corners of the globe. Women themselves all through history were a sort of subjugated race. They may have found an outlet for smothered resentments against their own masters in this licensed violence against men of alien blood, as Europe's common soldiers may have done in battle against other races.

10

CIVILIZATION AND BARBARISM

i. The civilizing mission, and religion

In 1903 the French were building a monument at Cairo to honour the 'heroic martyrs of Civilization' who fell in Bonaparte's invasion of Egypt. It was a rooted conviction of all Europeans that their armies represented civilization, confronting the barbarism of outer darkness. It inspired the general readiness to applaud any European gain as a gain for all Europe, and for progress. Campbell saw the French in Algeria 'opening, as it were, the northern gate of civilization' into that 'large space of the globe,' Africa.[1] To such views the most liberal could subscribe. 'Volunteers of the Charter' who fought on the Paris barricades in 1830 went on to fight the Algerians; the new government was happy to see their backs. Each empire took pride in some outstanding service. For Russia this was the putting down of Turcoman slave-raiders in Central Asia. It was universally commended, and might be classed with the suppression of Pindaris and Thugs in India. British, Dutch, and other warships added to the common treasury of merit by their exertions against piracy.

A British field-marshal's baton bore a small gilt effigy of St George dealing faithfully with his dragon. Napier's march to Magdala could be ranked as a splendid dragon-hunt, an ethical showpiece. A Victorian moralist of war could count on the assent of all readers to his proposition that 'no War was ever commenced with purer motive ... and carried through with a stricter regard to the highest principles of Christian morality'.[2] Usually territory was going to be appropriated; but there was a strong inclination to believe, if in some cases to pretend, that this was in accordance with the inhabitants' interests, and even wishes. Quite often the countries being taken into custody were themselves imperialistic, and weakened by minority discontents. When British troops were entering Assam in 1824 David Scott, commissioner on the north-east frontier, issued a call to the people to rise against the tyrannical Burmese, most of them, he reported, showed delight at the British coming.[3] As a rule a passive welcome was preferred; rebels against an old authority might not make docile subjects of a new one. In 1853 Dalhousie rejoiced to hear of his troops in Burma advancing unopposed, and received by the people with 'music and applause' and jars of cool water.[4] Aeroplanes could be used for propaganda as well as bombing, and leaflets were dropped on the Libyans to reassure them that Italy was coming as their friend and ally against the common Turkish foe.

'O God, thy arm was here' – Henry's cry at Agincourt was echoed by a long line of his compatriots as they contemplated victories with heavy loss to their opponents and little to themselves. 'There never was a series of events in which the hand of God was more sensibly present', Dalhousie wrote after his Punjab success.[5] Clergymen in India, or anywhere in the empire, would say Amen. An eccentric Thomas Bombay presented Outram with a bible and prayerbook, feeling unable to contribute to a sword of honour for him because, he explained, 'it is the object of my office and ministry to keep the sword in its scabbard';[6] but the sentiment would have occurred to few of his brethren. In a fort in Kaffraria his fellow-Anglican the Rev. J. Wilson took his share of duty, and did sentry-go with musket at the ready. Cannon rolling into Matabeleland were escorted by the bishop of Mashonaland: Church as well as chartered company was carving out a fresh province. In the Philippines, Sinibaldo de Mas reminded his countrymen, religious Orders and priests stayed permanently while officials came and went, and in times of crisis marched at the head of their flocks: 'a friar is worth more than a squadron of cavalry'.[7] In 1854 the bishop of Angola was acting-governor of the province.

Missionaries were often, and no doubt well-meaningly, advocates of forward policies. A Rev. H. Soltau submitted a lengthy memorandum in favour of annexation of Upper Burma. He foresaw only trifling resistance from the soldiery, 'a cowardly set of ruffians', three thousand of whom he had seen routed by three hundred Chinese.[8] During the guerrilla struggle in Burma an officer fell in with a pistol-carrying Catholic missionary from Alsace who on the strength of twelve years' knowledge of the country told him that the enemy were 'fiends in human shape' and that 'it was waste of powder and shot shooting them as hanging was more economical.'[9] In New Zealand the German Lutheran missionary Riemenschneider served the government for long as an intelligence agent. American missionaries in Angola helped a Portuguese force to capture Chindunduma. Clearly men like these were not narrowly national in their allegiances; all the same they could be as patriotic as anyone when Europeans fell out. According to a British naval commander, an ingenious contraption used against his ship off German west Africa in 1914, with two torpedoes attached to a motorboat, was designed by a missionary, who offered to guide it to its target under a white flag.[10] Two Germans captured in east Africa in the same war turned out to be 'fighting missionaries'.

Converts might represent something like a fifth column, as the Boxers accused them of being in China. In 1857 Christian sepoys sided with the British; they were not many, but one is said to have given away a plot for a rising in the Bombay army. In the Zulu war the Natal Native Horse were largely Zulu or Swazi converts, who owned their ponies and excelled at scouting. In the Dutch East Indies nearly all the Amboinese who provided most of the native soldiers and police were Christian. Frenchmen in Indochina made no bones about the usefulness of the numerous Catholic converts during the conquest.

Churches in Britain, draped with regimental flags, were filling with inscriptions and epitaphs commemorating fallen heroes of empire. On a wall of the Anglican cathedral at Edinburgh a tribute to a Lt Bradbury of the Gordon Highlanders, who was born at Calcutta in 1877 and died of wounds at Elandslaagte in 1899, leads to the text: 'The souls of the righteous are in the hands of God.' The righteousness of empire was becoming a new Justification, of faith and works combined. In the churchyard at Kinross in Fife the memorial of another brief existence, that of the son of a governor of Mauritius, killed in action in Somaliland in 1903, ends: 'I have fought the good fight.'

In earlier years particularly, the quantum of real religious concern among officers overseas was far smaller than words like these imply. There was always much individual variation. Distance and danger might make the average man more careless about his spiritual condition, the serious man more serious. One factor was that family links between Church and officer corps were so close. Born at Cawnpore in 1832, Roberts was the son of an officer whose father at Waterford was a clergyman with a large family, out of which two sons entered the army, two the navy. Jacob of Sind, born in 1812 of small-squire ancestry, had for father a vicar with eight sons, whose younger brother had five; of these thirteen young hopefuls eight joined the armed forces. From the parsonage some men at least carried with them a faith which could sustain them in the hour of trial. The Punjab 'Subaltern', son of a vicar, grandson of a bishop, closed one of his diary-letters home with the words: 'Do not be uneasy about me; I am under the protection of Him who ordereth all for the best.'[11] A few weeks later he was dead of exhaustion, aged twenty-one.

Piety was sometimes strongest in young men, not long removed from early surroundings. Michael Dawes was twenty-seven when he began keeping his diary of the first Afghan war, in a handwriting perhaps indicative of spiritual turmoil as well as camp discomfort. He felt it 'very disturbing' for the army to have to march on the Lord's day – most of its members found it unpleasant enough on any day – worse still to be fighting on the Sabbath. He was consoled by the prospect of distributing copies of the scriptures to the Afghan people, and delighted to find no ban placed on this.[12] On bigoted tribesmen they might be expected to have an effect more inflammatory than edifying. John Mills, surgeon in Persia in 1857, was another sabbatarian. February 15 with its religious observances was for him 'a most blessed contrast to the dreadful day last Sunday was ... a day of battle and bloodshed, man's hand raised against his brother man.'[13] Europe's creed gave soldiers all that a faith can, without in any way impeding their operations; other armies, like the Zulu (or the Roman) might let chances slip while their soothsayers awaited auspicious hours. Pearson was disclosing a more unusual scruple, which might be viewed in more than one light, when he told his wife that he always prayed to have no blood on his hands, and that heading the charge at Aliwal he did not 'injure or wish to destroy the life of one opposed to me ... the lancers did their work, as an officer 'tis my opinion should lead and direct and not save under particular circumstances be cutting and slaying'.[14]

William Fleming's thoughts began turning to serious subjects after five years in south Africa, when he was still only 23. He left the army presently, and became vicar of peaceful Chislehurst. At first he had envisaged a mission to the soldiers, 'whom the world looks upon as the offscourings of society', but of whose moral welfare it seemed to him a 'National Sin' that government should be 'so totally careless and thoughtless'. 'None except those who have served in it', he wrote to his mother, 'can form any idea of the total want of Religion' in the army.[15] The lumpen-proletariat from which so many of the rank and file came had no religion. Peasant soldiers had a lively if crude sense of a commerce between heaven and earth, and most Irish or Spanish or Russian soldiers were peasants, as were most French recruits before universal service came in late in the century. It must have impressed English officers during the siege of Cawnpore to see a Catholic priest, Joseph Moones, 'well fed by Irish soldiers who gave him tasty bits from their scanty rations'.[16] 'Danger softens the heart' and inclines it to prayer, said Castellane of soldiers in Algeria voluntarily attending mass.[17]

For the first time the Boer War brought something like a cross-section of Britain into the field. Wesleyan soldiers gave each other the password '494', the number, in the Sankey hymnbook used in their worship, of 'God be with you till we meet again'.[18] Nonconformist thinking about wars of empire was less monolithic than Anglican. 'I do not believe in gunpowder Christianity', a Methodist minister on a visit to a threatened Maori settlement declared.[19] But Methodist hymns were not without some martial flavour and imagery, like the well-loved 'Hold the fort', reminiscent of soldiers manning defences on perilous frontiers.

In the first Burma War, Doveton looking back regretted, the British army scarcely affected even an 'outward semblance of religion'.[20] As the century wore on, religion was in a sense being displaced from the empire's heart to its extremities. While insidious doubts crept in to undermine faith at home, on the frontiers where simpler thinking sufficed it grew, in the guise very often of 'muscular Christianity'. It may never have spread very wide or deep in the army. A young man's reason for attending an Anglican service in India in 1919 with a pal was 'Not that we had turned religious all at once, but it passed the time along till dinner-time.'[21] At least, there was a service for them to attend, as a result of the provision of chaplains, in earlier days a very scanty band even by comparison with the surgeons whose spiritual partners they might be considered.

Doveton thought that there should be chaplains accompanying the troops just as doctors did.[22] That to the ordinary soldier such a notion was in his day outlandish is suggested by the term 'Padre', picked up in India from the Portuguese. They like the Spaniards had always had priests with their forces. In 1860 the vicar-general of the armed forces and titular patriarch of the Indies wrote in praise of the noble performance of their duties by Spanish chaplains in Morocco.[23] In 1911, when numbers of Italian priests vied in offering to go with the army to Libya the government gratified the long estranged Church by consenting.

Britain by comparison had an obstacle in the multiplicity of its creeds. For long the Church of England was able to keep a monopoly, but too many soldiers were Scots or Irish, and in 1839 a general order laid down that each was free to adhere to his own faith. However, in 1829 the office of chaplain-general had been allowed to lapse, and the number of chaplains declined to an exiguous handful. It may be supposed that clergymen overseas in those days, like medicos, were there because unable to find openings at home. Dalhousie dismissed several, one (in jail for debt at the time) for refusing to visit soldiers suffering from venereal disease or anything else that was their own fault.[24] A regiment in the Punjab wars had a 'parson' with a pretty wife, with whom he attended all the dances at the officers' mess; frequently he had to be carried home, to the amusement of the sepoys.[25] In the West Indies, by a Captain Stuart's account, 'some very "rum clargy", as they say in Ireland' were to be met with, and at least one chaplain of his acquaintance was 'a very queer fellow' indeed.[26] When the summer palace at Peking was being plundered in 1860 a chaplain cut short his service to take a hand, returned with a loaded mule-cart, and next Sunday preached what a hearer called 'an admirable sermon against covetousness'.[27]

The Crimean War quickened army interest in religion, as well as medicine, as a useful tonic. In 1858 twenty-two Anglicans, with thirty-four assistants, were appointed, and a due proportion of Presbyterians and Catholics was soon added. They were awarded commissions in 1858, standard pay in 1859, uniforms in 1860. Religion was being given a firmly official status. Some chaplains were ex-officers, many from military families; one of their functions, from the army's point of view, was 'keeping the Other Ranks under watchful surveillance'.[28] Individuals might undertake secular duties as well, like a Mr Badger in Persia in 1857 who doubled as chaplain to headquarters and Arabic interpreter. At Peiwar Kotal the Rev. J. Adams insisted on acting as extra aide-de-camp to Roberts, and later in the Afghan war he won a VC. As chaplains grew more respectable, they gained more influence over their flocks, or their fellow-officers, at any rate so far as outward decorum was concerned. After the Mutiny Sita Ram noticed that officers of sepoy regiments were giving up the Indian women most of them formerly lived with; he shared a common view that in such ways chaplains were pushing British officers and Indian soldiers further apart.[29]

Catholic chaplains won Captain Stuart's approval as 'brave gallant fellows', undaunted either by cholera or by battle.[30] On the Ridge before the storming of Delhi an old French priest, co-opted as chaplain, added his prayer to a lengthy Protestant sermon. At Tel el Kebir the Catholic chaplain of the Guards was wounded, though he lived to be bishop of Gibraltar. The honest Anglican chaplain in *Kim* detested popery, but had a high respect for his colleague Father Victor's insight into human problems. In fact the overseas army may be looked upon as one of the starting-points of ecumenicalism. Such collaboration was another facet also of Europe's united feeling against the lesser breeds.

Christianity was sometimes on the other side, not only in the Americas. Three Filipino priests were among those executed after the Cavite mutiny. In Menelik's camp before Adowa there was imposing religious ceremonial, and priests were busy hearing confessions and giving communion. It was as pious bible-readers that the Boers gained much of their German sympathy in 1899. One of their leaders, Koos de la Rey, was under the influence of a 'prophet', Nicholas van Rensburg, whose visions helped later on to push him, when old and muddled, into the rebellion of 1914.

On the whole religion was a far less potent force in the conquests than in the resistance to them. A European army marched on its stomach, not its soul, and looked to alcohol for most of its higher flights. Islam, as ever since its birth, was Europe's arch-enemy. It provided a substitute, fiery but erratic, for the staider discipline instilled in Western troops by centuries of training and of national feeling. When it broke loose from rational calculation it provoked the futile grandeur of the dervish charge, much as Kirk exaltation brought the Scots army down from its hill to be crushed at Dunbar. Mahdism inherited in the fullest measure the Islamic tradition of blind faith in leadership by a single God-sent man, which could not make for sensible planning. The Sudan was the classic spectacle of an invading army moving on like a steam-roller, and infatuated defenders throwing themselves under it like devotees under the car of Juggernaut.

In remote corners paganism, more fluid than the higher religions, took on novel shapes, often borrowing ingredients from Christianity. The ghost dance of the Sioux, Hau Hau in New Zealand, Mau Mau later in Kenya, were cults filling the blank left by breakdown of old patterns of faith. Kaffir militancy in 1819 was instigated by the prophesyings of a new leader. Another like him preached war in 1851, in the wake of drought and hunger. Two brothers who saw visions of the gods precipitated the Santal rebellion. But in the end all these worshippers, higher or lower, were looking up to heaven for aid when aeroplanes began descending from the skies to bomb them.

1857 was in one aspect a war of religions; rebels destroyed churches, temples and mosques were desecrated. Muscular Christianity never had such an afflatus before or after. The most pious army men were among the most ruthless. One was Neill, who denied any biblical warrant for 'the modern tenderness for human life'.[31] Britain was the home of *The Messiah*, which like much of Handel's religious music strikes at times the note of triumphalism, of Jehovah-wrath, a spirit closely akin to Mahdism; and these men of 1857, facing the enemies of God and flag, were obeying the injunction to break them with a rod of iron, or dash them to pieces like a potter's vessel. Any blow struck at false creeds and their false priests was a blow for civilization. 'Our enemies are the monks', Curzon wrote to Younghusband in 1904.[32] 'The Dalai Lama,' Younghusband wrote to a political ally in India, 'is at the bottom of all this trouble and deserves to be well kicked. The *people* are friendly enough to us.'[33] In Africa such axioms were held still more firmly. Bartle Frere, author of the Zulu war, was a keen churchman. In west Africa human sacrifice was the evil most loudly denounced. Benin was anathematized as 'one of the foulest dens of slaughter in one of the worst regions in Africa.'[34]

Yet zeal might have to be tempered by expediency, and compromises made with false gods, as with bad rulers and ruling classes who could be useful puppets. While Christianity and Islam sparred, paradoxically more and more Muslim soldiers were entering European service. There was always some risk of their religion affecting their reliability. In Somaliland there were times when the Mullah's reputation filled Britain's local recruits with a kind of 'superstitious awe ... a growing belief that the Mullah was immortal.'[35] In Upper Burma many monks took part in the popular struggle; when Roberts paid a visit later on he went out of his way to conciliate influential divines. Early in British India a Hindu priest might be seen blessing regimental colours, with British officers looking on, as they continued to do at religious ceremonies, including animal sacrifices, in Gurkha regiments. If popish chaplains were acceptable, Brahmins and mullahs must be accepted too. One of Germany's reproaches against British use of Indian troops in the first World War was that they were brought to Europe with Hindu, Muslim and Sikh holy men to fan their ardour and promise paradises to those who fell for the empire.[36]

ii. Doctrines of colonial war

On the battlefield, where civilization and barbarism came face to face, the contrast was more clearly visible in weaponry than in spirit or intent. When Canton fell at the end of 1857 Sir John Bowring, the plenipotentiary, was contemptuous of the hopeless Chinese struggle, 'the strategy and the weapons of barbarism against consummate naval and military tactics with all the appliances which science has brought to experience'.[37] Europe was fond of parading its concept of 'civilized warfare', but in contests overseas it was 'scientific warfare' that was being talked of more and more. Even within Europe progress towards an explicit code of conduct was very halting. International law, remarks the Shepherd in one of the *Noctes Ambrosianae*, in 1834, 'seems to me nae better than a systematized and legalized scheme o' rape, robbery, piracy, incendiarism, and murder.' To which the Professor rejoins: 'Quite correct.'[38]

It would have been more accurate, then and later, to paint the colonial scene, where no international law obtained, in these gloomy colours. At odd moments an agreement on the spot might be some remedy. In 1820 Bolívar and the Spanish general Morillo, after years of enormities and reprisals, met and took a pledge to treat prisoners humanely and not shoot deserters caught fighting on the other side. They at least spoke the same language. But from their earliest days colonists in North America and their promoters in England maintained that no restrictions were binding in warfare against enemies like Red Indians; in New Zealand in 1869 Prendergast, attorney-general and later chief justice, argued that laws of war among civilized nations could not apply to a contest with Maoris.[39] A better man, Sir Harry Smith, for whom Christianity, progress and the British empire were all one and the same, inveighed against 'canting ultra philanthropists' in England who were finding fault with the treatment of black men in the Kaffir wars. His view was that 'war against savages cannot be carried out according to acknowledged rules but to common sense'.[40] Probably most soldiers would have endorsed this; some would have added a reference to the voice of conscience. Kitchener had little to fear from his own conscience, but in 1885 during a withdrawal in the Sudan he had a tussle with his superior, Sir Redvers Buller, who doubted whether filling in wells to baffle dervish pursuit could be squared with the usages of war.

Bombardment of towns and civil populations was repugnant to European opinion, some in Britain protested when Kagoshima was mauled by the navy in 1863. Britain's bad eminence in this sphere can be ascribed to the temptations of naval power. 'The lives and property of the entire city population are at my mercy,' Admiral Seymour warned the governor at Canton in 1856, 'and could be destroyed by me at any moment'. When Baden-Powell objected to Cronje's threat of further shelling of Mafeking, on the ground that women and children could be hit, it might appear that Britons were not fond of taking their own medicine. By that time war even outside

Europe had to be conducted in a stronger glare of publicity, and in 1911 care was taken to reassure Italy's friends that Admiral Faravelli's bombardment of Tripoli must, as one of them wrote, 'be considered a most humane one', avoiding mosques and hospitals and injuring only seven civilians. [41]

From time to time the issue arose in Europe, urgently in 1870, of whether combatants not in uniform could claim any rights. Outside Europe it came up most distinctly in the case of Boer irregulars, who as white men could be expected to understand what penalties they were incurring. Against derailing of trains, sniping at passengers, and so on, Roberts ordered punitive measures 'in accordance with the recognised rules of warfare'; some of his officers were over-zealous, it was admitted. German military opinion, anti-British though it was, held that the circumstances 'made many of the severities practised by the English necessary.'[42] With opponents like the mysterious Celestials it was harder to feel solid ground. Notwithstanding their own threat at Canton, the British thought it showed a most 'savage disposition' on the governor Yeh's part when he called on the citizenry to help in extirpating them, and offered rewards.[43] Engels writing on this China war poured scorn on 'civilization-mongers who throw hot shells on a defenceless city', but cry out at the other side's rejoinder as 'cowardly, barbarous, atrocious'.[44] Still, China had more or less recognizable soldiers, forts to assail, and a capital to pounce on. It was otherwise when no such clearly defined targets presented themselves, and the enemy were ordinary people defending their homeland. Then, Callwell confessed, 'war assumes an aspect which may shock the humanitarian'.[45] In New Zealand in the 1860s rewards were offered for 'rebel' heads, as in America in earlier days for Red Indian scalps; sackfuls were collected.

Appreciation of enemy qualities was not always lacking. It was more readily felt about enemies of other countries. An Englishman considered Abd el Kader entitled 'to rank with the most honoured patriots of more civilized states.'[46] But another, who began by dismissing the Somali resistance as a mere travesty of patriotism, was constrained to admit in the end that a man like the Mullah, looked up to by his people as the embodiment of a struggle for freedom, could not deserve total condemnation.[47] Such a feeling might find expression even on the morrow of a battle like Isandhlwana, when the *Natal Witness* deprecated the inevitable howl for revenge. 'There are qualities, undoubtedly, in the Zulu nation which we are bound to respect'; in courage they resembled the untamed Highlanders of old, and Britain might look forward to enrolling them 'among the bravest soldiers of the Empire.'[48]

Dismissive verdicts were far commoner. From Englishmen they were apt to be tinctured by Victorian attitudes to sexuality, which the lower races indulged in so uninhibitedly. Rebel Hottentots were reported to be wallowing in 'the most disgraceful licentiousness and depravity'.[49] A catalogue of Baggara villainies in the Khalifa's Sudan wound up: 'Bestial immorality and consequent disease are rampant.' Yet even Baggaras were left behind by other, more sedentary tribes there 'in cunning, in the more degrading forms of vice, and in restless spirit of intrigue.'[50] Among headlines in the Edinburgh press in 1899 were 'Barbarity of the Boers'; 'Savage Treatment of Women'; 'Boer Inhumanity to Women'; 'Bloodthirsty Boer Women'. They recall many denunciations of the sepoys in 1857; and to some jaundiced eyes the Boers were not merely rude yokels, but even their title to pass as white men might appear questionable. 'Too many Dutch people here', an officer on leave near Bloemfontein soon after the war scribbled in his diary; 'they talk and gass [sic] together, d – d rebels', and some look 'rather dusky, would be looked on with suspicion in India.'[51]

'Treacherous natives, waiting in ambush' in Kaffraria,[52] represent what may have been the commonest stereotype of all. A monument in St Mungo's cathedral at Glasgow commemorates an officer, formerly of Hodson's Horse in India, buried in 1860 in the Russian cemetery at Peking. 'Treacherously taken prisoner by the Chinese, when in command of an escort, and under the protection of a flag of truce, he died a victim to the cruelty of a barbarous Foe.' All the mutineers of 1857 were traitors, and this was of a piece with the rest of their wickedness. At Sciara el Schiatt in 1911 the Arab guerrilla attack justified, in the view of an English apologist, 'an extraordinary energy in the repression of treachery and of the savage instincts of the natives'. After the rising in Tripoli which followed he brushed aside 'another outcry from the sentimentalists': the soldiers were only defending themselves against 'treasonable aggression'.[53]

Identical reasoning could be applied to many other cases, for example that of the Burmese guerrillas or dacoits encountered by Kipling's young officer, monsters who crucified captives and set them alight.[54] In 1911 Italy compiled a propaganda volume in which the Libyans were accused of a long list of crimes, crucifixion of prisoners among them.[55] It was an index of hardening attitudes that before the Hague Conference of 1899 the British War Office and Admiralty protested against any abandonment of an asset like the dum-dum bullet, on the ground that it 'would favour the interests of savage nations and be against those of the more civilized'.[56] The Hague Convention banned the dum-dum from civilized warfare, but left it to be used against wild animals or wild men. Even so, a British army writer was irked by the resolutions moved, as unwarrantably aimed at Britain.[57]

Again, a widening gap between what men on the spot thought permissible, and what at home was still judged infamous, is suggested by a Conan Doyle tale[58] about a young officer in an outpost on the edge of the Mahdist Sudan who, having arrested a taciturn Arab on suspicion, feels reluctantly compelled to reject his Egyptian aide's hint at torture. 'No, no. It's all very well here, but it would sound just awful if ever it got as far as Fleet Street.' He sees no harm in threatening the prisoner with a red-hot horseshoe, or in promising him a flogging. Nor does his captive, who turns out to be the commander-in-chief in disguise – often worn by Kitchener in younger days. In his panegyric on war as the fountain of civilization, Ruskin told his listeners at the Royal Military Academy that 'the great veteran soldiers of England are now men every way so thoughtful, so noble, and so good', that the army scarcely needed any moral guidance beyond theirs.[59] Kitchener's guidance, or at least his talk among intimates, was 'brutally and startlingly cynical'; and there was disquiet over his treatment of forced labour in the Sudan, as 'stories of constant floggings and occasional hangings trickled through to Cairo.'[60] Illusion and reality could not be much further apart.

Everything, or almost everything, could be tolerated if it was deemed necessary for the upholding of prestige. This curious word, signifying an entity almost apotheosized as tutelary deity of empire, came into English in the 17th century, through French, from a Low Latin term for a deception, or conjuring-trick, and for some time kept the same meaning. Its later sense was not really so far removed from it, for imperial authority always had to weave spells round its subjects' minds. Prestige was guarded most jealously of all in India, whose people were supposed to be preternaturally responsive to any failures or indignities that might befall their white masters anywhere. In the East, one pundit wrote, 'A defeat – and everyone deserts'.[61] In 1847 the governor-general Hardinge was nervous of any setback as likely to 'vibrate throughout India, aye through Asia.... Every skirmish against our arms with the Caffres is joyfully proclaimed in the Native press; the same of New Zealand.'[62] It seems an astonishingly early date for such reactions. Similarly a reverse in the Sudan had to be promptly expunged because it was said to have set

Muslims crowing 'in every bazaar from Cairo to Calcutta and Central Asia'.[63] There must have been a tinge of exaggeration in such alarms; Britons were too far self-isolated from their subjects to read their thoughts. Still, bazaar gossip was a staple of Indian life, and as Sita Ram said there were always idle folk inventing tales, greedily swallowed if they were to the government's discredit.[64]

Those not hypnotized into accepting white superiority had to be made to do so, by processes for which *cowing* was an expression often in English mouths. Overjoyed by the capture of Ghazni in 1839 Palmerston wrote that it would 'cow all Asia and make everything more easy for us';[65] a bad guess. Dalhousie commended Hodson and Nicholson by saying that 'Their very name cowed whole provinces'.[66] Callwell – Anglo-Irish on both sides, an artillery-man in India, in the second Afghan war, the Boer war – uses the word habitually. The right way to handle Asiatics is 'to go for them and to cow them by sheer force of will',[67] he writes, very much in the tone of an animal-trainer; indeed breaking in horses, as well as keeping Irish peasants and the rest of the lower classes in their place, must have helped to form this mentality. His book can be taken as the distilled wisdom of a century of imperial soldiering. He cannot be taxed with any taste for 'frightfulness', or bloodshed for its own sake: his approach is as detached and professional as a clinical diagnosis. It takes for granted an immense, unbridgeable chasm between civilized man and barbarian. It abounds in myopic generalizations and clumsy pigeon-holings. 'Irregular warriors individually possess the cunning which their mode of life engenders. ... All orientals have an inborn love of trickery and deception'.[68] *Fanatics* were in Callwell's mind a separate, not fully human species, like communists in Cold War nightmares. But non-whites of all shades merge in his thinking into haphazard conglomerations: 'bands of fanatics, of cut-throat mountaineers or African savages' – 'Savages, Asiatics, and adversaries of that character.... '[69] On all and sundry it was essential to impose 'a moral inferiority' by always keeping the initiative. 'The lower races ... are greatly influenced by a resolute bearing'.[70]

Thirty years after the Mutiny a Viceroy of India reproved an Amir of Afghanistan for his 'shocking barbarities' in putting down rebels.[71] British and other authorities were frequently on record as anxious to avoid any like blemishes. 'HMG deprecate any needless injury to life and property', the Foreign Office cautioned the Admiralty when Canton was under attack in 1857. 'They are anxious at all times that War should be carried on with as much regard as possible to the dictates of humanity'.[72] Baron Gros, French plenipotentiary out there, chimed in: to destroy Canton would be both purposeless and 'an act of barbarism which would stamp the two flags of France and England with an indelible stain.'[73] Despite his blood-curdling threats to Yeh, Admiral Seymour stated that before an assault he admonished his officers verbally and in writing, and was happy to bear testimony 'to the forbearance and good conduct of the seamen and marines.'[74] Some accounts of what was happening are in a different key. Force was requisite to introduce China to civilization, a British officer on the spot wrote, but it should never be 'unjustly or cruelly applied', and he regretted to see his countrymen 'perpetrating all sorts of violence'.[75]

Authority far from the scene too readily assumed that its humane injunctions (when seriously intended) were being heeded. Portuguese conduct in Africa always tended to be worse than what Lisbon prescribed. Occasionally a real effort was made to ensure that word and deed were in harmony. In 1854, finding that the army command was not going to take any steps, Dalhousie fulminated a general order about two Burmans killed unwarrantably as suspected spies by a lieutenant; its purpose was 'to prevent the same savage conduct by other young officers, conduct calculated to irritate and alienate our new subjects'. [76] Such scrupulosity the men of action may be supposed to have received with the same impatience they felt at humanitarian twaddle at home, among goody-goodies like the Aborigines Protection Society. Callwell asserted that in the third Burma war great care was exercised to punish only dacoits, and destroy only those villages which harboured them willingly;[77] but harassed men beating the jungle could not decipher the village mind, and cannot have drawn the line with pedantic nicety. Sir Arthur Gordon in Fiji in 1876 was distressed to hear of indiscriminate burning of villages, and Captain Knollys was reminded that such action was forbidden – though how else pacification was to be effected, the officer conveying the order confessed he did not know.[78]

Military philosophy emerges in the words of the commander-in-chief in *Kim* explaining the need for a full-scale operation on the Frontier: 'This comes of not smashing them thoroughly the first time.' In a school-story of that date an experienced prefect points the same moral, warning a novice against the mistake of being too mild. 'If you hit, hit hard; then you won't have to hit often.'[79] Algeria was for decades a caution against involvement in long-drawn struggles. In favour of the gospel of the knock-out blow commanders could argue too that the most vigorous measures were really the most humane, because they put a term to the bloodshed. On untutored peoples 'a heavy blow struck without hesitation' always had weight, Callwell wrote, and he dwelt complacently on the 'rigorous treatment' of disaffected tribes in southern Africa. 'Uncivilized races attribute leniency to timidity'; 'fanatics and savages ... must be thoroughly brought to book and cowed or they will rise again.'[80] It was repeated ad nauseam that Asiatics and Africans understood only the language of force. What else there was for them to understand, when invaders marched into their countries, no one explained.

General Macdonald in Tibet seems to have vastly overestimated enemy strength, and nervousness may have made him feel that a good bloodletting would be the shortest way to break it. 'I got so sick of the slaughter', a machine-gunner wrote home after the fight at Guru, 'that I ceased to fire, though the General's order was to make as big a bag as possible.'[81] Englishmen might be readier to condone such tactics when practised by other armies than their own. Russian methods in the Caucasus, one reflected, might be 'morally indefensible, but possessed of undoubted advantages in dealing with Oriental peoples.' Fire and sword, sacked villages, ravished women, gave the tribesmen 'a lesson they thoroughly understood and fully appreciated', since this was how wars were conducted among themselves.[82] Sir Harry Johnston, one of the founders of British power in Africa, considered the Dutch and Germans 'on first contact with native races apt to be harsh and even brutal', but this won them the respect of Asians and Africans, 'who admire rude strength'.[83]

iii. Realities of colonial war

All theorizing of this sort was in part an effort to rationalize blind passion let loose by the turmoil of battle. At the storming of Nilt fort in the Himalayas in 1893 British officers were said to have prevented their Gurkha, Dogra, Pathan soldiers from killing all the defenders in revenge for lost comrades. On many other occasions there was no such intervention, or it was made in vain. Long, exhausting sieges always aroused vindictive fury, as that of Multan did with none of the excuses the British could make for themselves in 1857. Russian military annals often spoke of soldiers running amuck at the end of them, killing all who came in their way; this was treated as a matter of course.[84] Street fighting was more inflammatory than any other ordeal; three days of it at Bougie in Algeria in 1832 ended in 'indiscriminate slaughter' by the French. But similar excesses might take place in the open field as well. At Miani, Waddington recorded,

'Quarter was not asked or given. The wounded were shot or bayoneted by our exasperated soldiers.... '[85] At Chilianwala, the 'Subaltern' wrote, some British wounded were heard to have been killed, 'and fearful was the retaliation the Europeans took for it'. After the battle there were sights that would 'poison an angel's dreams'[86] – a phrase a poet might envy, but they may have poisoned his own, and helped to cut his life short. After Gujarat he could only fall back on the reflection that 'after all, it is a war of extermination.' Sergeant Pearman tells how Sikhs in flight from the battlefield were hunted down and killed. 'I never saw such butchery and murder!'[87]

When prisoners were being massacred after the battle of the Atbara 'Tommy was just as bad as the blacks', Kitchener's brother wrote.[88] It may be, as was sometimes said, that native troops more habitually indulged in brutality; but they were sometimes intended by their employers to indulge in it. Auxiliaries, still more, could be used at times for work that Europeans might feel squeamish about, or that it was undesirable for Europe to hear about. In 1857 Sikhs were given the congenial task of 'making an example' of Fatehpur. In 1886 local partisans, along with some regulars, were sent into two provinces of Vietnam, to expedite the process of subjugation by a 'merciless repression' which was long remembered,[89] never perhaps forgotten.

When men from one community were used against another they were at feud with, more than ordinary zeal could be counted on. Fingos employed against the Kaffirs who oppressed them had ground for revengefulness. Efforts were made to keep it within limits, but it gave rise to incidents like one when officers could not stop them from murdering prisoners, a woman among them, until some of the 'half-tamed savages' were knocked down and put under arrest.[90] There was an analogous situation in Vietnam where the French learned to make use of primitive hillmen against the dominant people of the plains who preyed on them, a *politique des races* which was a special version of divide-and-rule. In many other cases it was a simple matter of playing on tribal enmities, as the Russians sometimes did in the Caucasus, the British in 1894–5 in Uganda, or the Americans in the Philippines. Gilbert Murray was not the only one to feel misgivings about what he called the 'continual employment' of 'uniformed savages', liable 'to lead British warfare in various unmentionable details rather too close to that of savages without uniform.'[91]

Conduct towards wounded enemies might be very different once the frenzy was over. Half a dozen Sikh survivors of Chilianwala were admitted to the British hospital and 'treated with the greatest care'.[92]

161

After the storm of Bharatpur in 1825 some hundreds of enemy wounded were given medical aid. At the capture of Chapo in 1842 there was heavy bloodshed, and riding down of fleeing Chinese, but next day dismay was felt at 'most distressing sights' inside the town, 'mothers drowning themselves and their children; husbands drowning their wives, and whole families dying from poison'. All that could be done to reassure the people was done, 'the wounded were dressed and fed, and on our departure were liberated and presented with money.' 'The Chinese cannot understand', Surgeon Pine wrote '... and say "Yours is a curious kind of warfare; you come and fire upon us and wound us and then pet and cure us"'.[93] They might well be puzzled; amid such erratic shifts a new age was painfully struggling into life. An improvement seems visible between the first two Burma wars. Doveton looked back with remorse on the little humanity shown in the first, and deplored the demoralizing effect of long-drawn fighting with barbarians; in the other it could be said that enemy wounded were regularly succoured instead of being shot.[94]

It was another advance that colonial conquests in the later 18th and 19th centuries were virtually the first wars ever fought outside Europe where women were not one of the chief prizes. But if not now regarded as legitimate spoils of war, they did not always escape the attentions, frivolous or criminal, of invaders. Revolt in Georgia in 1812 was set off by a rape said to have been committed by a Russian officer; in the Caucasus officers in winter quarters passed the time with local women, who may not all have been there of their own free will. It was acknowledged after the first Afghan war that British officers at Kabul and Kandahar compromised themselves deplorably with women, not always it seems of the courtesan class.[95] This was remembered, and in the next Afghan war an interdict was laid on relations with women. At Tripoli in 1911 the Italians made a great point of assuring their new subjects that their females, like their religion, would be respected. In Tibet there was no need for such circumspection, if we can trust a reminiscence of 1904: 'People very dirty and primitive and women far from beauties. Never any case of venereal among the troops!'[96] But all accounts of the growth of anti-foreign bitterness in the Canton region dwell on charges of molestation of women by soldiers, and especially by Indians, whose colour was another irritant.[97] The French, who have prided themselves on realism, sometimes rewarded their Senegalese soldiers with captured women, styled *épouses libres*.[98]

Orderly collection of prize-money was liable to break down, each man grabbing what he could for himself: at Delhi the prize agents themselves, as well as very senior officers, were accused of joining in, and the official haul, 13½ lakhs of rupees, must have been far less than the private takings. There was an equally unedifying scramble at Peking in 1900 by officers and men of all the allied forces. Enough money stuck to a few ordinary soldiers' fingers to enable them to buy their discharge and return home in comfort. But it must have been a nagging suspicion that officers, besides being entitled to far bigger shares, used their position to smuggle away far more loot. This was said for instance of the treasure seized in the palace at Lucknow in 1858. Alcohol was responsible for some unlicensed self-help, as on Chusan island in 1841 when British soldiers swallowed, *faute de mieux*, quantities of 'the fiery abomination' *shamshu*, and looted a town in a drunken frolic.[99] Petty pilfering was the weakness of camp-followers, among whom there were always bad characters. A good many ended on the gallows. On top of all this there was sheer vandalism, the 'wanton mischief' Pennycuick was angered by in the first Burma war: 'some of the most beautiful buildings I have seen in the country were destroyed without any reason whatever.'[100]

The record is a chequered one, but it shows clearly enough that Western civilization, brittle enough in its own clime, was a fragile thing to transport across the world. All European armies had a great deal to reproach themselves with, even if their grand crimes were exceptional. Such a one, the worst in the conquest of Algeria, occurred in 1845 and made a great stir at the time. A force led by Pélissier trapped some five hundred men, women and children in the Dahra caves, and kept fires burning at the entrance until they were all suffocated. A European outcry did not prevent Pélissier from rising to be French commander-in-chief in the Crimea, Marshal, Duke, Senator, Ambassador to the Court of St James; he died in 1864 governor-general of Algeria. Not from amorous dalliance alone, the first Afghan war left the British name, Sleeman wrote in 1848, 'intolerably odious to the mass of the people'.[101] There is evidence of attempts by Macnaghten, the political representative, and others to arrange the murder of Afghan chiefs;[102] the machinations of the CIA and similar secret services of our day have precedents of respectable age. Destruction at Kabul and elsewhere before the final withdrawal in 1842 was 'cruel, wanton, and unnecessary', as ministers at London could not but perceive.[103]

In the British case a crop of later mischief can be traced to the blight of 1857 on army mentality, especially on impressionable tiros, among whom were several field-marshals of the future. Wolseley arrived during the outbreak to listen to stories of horrors at Cawnpore and vow revenge. A letter from him at Lucknow gleefully described the sport of peppering 'niggers' trying to escape by swimming the river.[104] Young Roberts 'never enjoyed a gallop more' than when he took part in a ten-mile chase of fugitives begging in vain for mercy; six or seven hundred were given their quietus.[105] Twenty years later the rising at Kabul, starting with a mutiny of Afghan soldiers and British deaths, was just the thing to bring memories of 1857 back to life. Roberts was sent with instructions from the viceroy, Lytton, which gave him all the latitude he could desire. 'It is not *justice* in the ordinary sense, but retribution that you have to administer. . . . '[106] Forty-nine men were hanged; they must have been picked out more or less at random.

As officers, or settlers, in other parts of the empire many lesser actors of 1857 carried with them minds warped by that dark year. In 1866 one of them, General Chute, was directing punitive operations against Maoris. Sir J.G. Wilson settled in New Zealand, with a retinue of Indian servants, 'after presiding at mass executions following the Indian Mutiny'. Major M. Noake, another Maori-hunter, had been in the repression in Ireland after the famine, and in action against Chartist demonstrators in Yorkshire, as well as in the Mutiny; in New Zealand he was a trusted assistant of Sir George Whitmore, a veteran of the Kaffir wars.[107] A retired Maj.-Gen. T.B. Strange, settled in Canada on a huge ranch, who was given military charge of Alberta during the 1885 rising, was another man of 1857, and both an envenomed hater of Red Indians and a scourge of striking workers in the streets of Quebec.

A turn from easy optimism about the civilizing and liberating mission to a harsher realism was very apparent on the China scene. In 1900 there was no more thought of uplifting, as there had been in the previous wars, only of punishing, and Europe acting in concert did not behave better than its nations on their own. As always it justified its conduct by accusing opponents of worse things. 'The Chinese are perpetrating terrible atrocities upon the wounded', *The Times* reported.[108] But all the way along the invasion route from Tientsin to Peking outrages by the allied forces were heard of; returning along it to his post a little later the Dutch minister was oppressed by 'a feeling of inexpressible shame that men of the white race were after all so little removed from medieval barbarity.'[109]

In the later decades Western arms were penetrating regions, black Africa most ominously, whose inhabitants could be portrayed more plausibly than Chinese or Persians as benighted primitives. Here many features of the first age of European expansion were recapitulated. Boers and Portuguese in Africa were links between old and new, and later comers were not slow in emulating them. Thomas Campbell thought British conduct in south Africa worse than French in Algeria, which some Britons were so critical of. England had 'no right to call herself sinless in Africa – as the hapless Caffres can bear witness'.[110] As conquest quickened, a book on it could introduce Africa as a continent delivered from native barbarism by breech-loaders, Maxims, etc., 'with still more deadly cheap alcohol', and go on to hail any mass slaughter by the latest weapon as 'a deadly blow dealt at barbarism; a triumph gained for humanity and civilization.'[111] Growingly fashionable 'Darwinian' talk about survival of the fittest races supplied a further sanction. 'Civilization drove forward in a mortuary cart', one high-flyer wrote when famine cleared the ground by removing large numbers of Kaffirs, 'but it was civilization. The spirit of Kaffraria had been quenched.'[112]

Racialism, most virulent among settlers, had a long incubation in the West Indies. Only a handful of whites were killed in the revolt in Jamaica just before slavery came to an end, but retaliation was unsparing. In 1865 there was a much smaller disturbance, no more in fact than a noisy demonstration by a few hundred blacks hard hit by economic depression. When a Royal Commission was sent to investigate the sequel it found that 22 individuals, not all white, had lost their lives in the rioting; none of the atrocities alleged by Governor Eyre had taken place; 354 were executed by court martial, 85 without any form of trial; others were flogged; a thousand houses were burned down. 'The soldiers enjoy it', an officer on the scene is said to have remarked.[113] There was heated controversy in Britain, and passion stirred up against the blacks 'was to be of incalculable importance for the whole world',[114] by further poisoning racial attitudes in the era of accelerated conquest about to begin, in Africa above all.

Colonists in Britain's West Indian islands had always been permitted far too much control of government, and now this was being repeated in other parts of the empire. When ministers were questioned in 1881 about the plundering and wholesale destruction of crops and property that was a feature of the Basuto war, the reply was that all that was the affair of the colonial authorities,[115] that is of men elected by settlers who may have been fit to govern themselves but were certainly not fit to govern other races. Shuffling off of responsibility on to chartered companies had still worse conse-quences. At the time of the Matabeleland expedition the High Commissioner at Cape Town called the attention of officers and men to 'the requirements of humanity'; but he had to admit that they were not under military law.[116]

Europe's newer colonialists, in haste to catch up, could not be expected to be any more finical about their methods. Settler violence was sometimes shortsighted enough to overreach itself. As young Ironside found in south-west Africa, German planters were short of labour, but in their rage at the killing of some families at the outset of the Herrero rebellion 'they would be satisfied with nothing less than the annihilation of all coloured men.'[117] 'The Italian methods have been simply brutal', the British ambassador at Berlin wrote about Libya in his diary in September 1911 ' – and more those of Brigands than of a respectable people.'[118] As to the new colonial powers outside Europe, in China in 1900 General Stewart admired Japan's soldiers, but he saw no respect among them for enemy dead or wounded; 'some of the sights were very horrible!'[119] To America, self-liberated from George III, the ideology of liberation always made a strong appeal; but Negro servitude and Amerindian wars combined to produce there too the peculiar imperial squint. Several commanders in the Philippines had cut their teeth in Indian warfare. Guerrillas were treated not as patriots but as bandits, as some American books still call them. News which got into the American press included horrific details of torture. To a British observer the conquest appeared 'one of the blackest records which has ever stained the pages of history.'[120]

11

EUROPE AND ITS CONQUESTS

i. Publicity and the public

War reporting began with despatches from commanders. In colonial campaigns these came to be supplemented by narratives of more informal cast, composed for local newspapers by officers taking part; in the case of minor commotions this went on quite long. In 1894 Richard Ewart was both supply and transport officer to a batch of 'Piffers', or men of the Punjab Frontier Force Regiments, setting out from Bannu, and correspondent for the *Civil and Military Gazette* of Lahore.[1] His copy was transmitted by heliograph, and a signaller's mistake brought a stern rebuke from Simla about supposed ill-treatment of some of the enemy; agreeable evidence of a vigilant eye in high places. All reports from the army may have been prone to exalt small doings into grander ones. So Pennycuick, grumbling his way through the first Burma campaign, believed. 'Such are the trifles', he wrote, coming on the scene of a recent scuffle, 'magnified into great battles against these unfortunate savages.'[2]

Professional war-correspondents got their real start in the Crimea, with the celebrated W.H.Russell leading the way. This Anglo-Irishman and the Scotsman Archibald Forbes were the two who achieved most eminence; among other celebrities were H.M.Stanley and G.A.Henty, while a writer as distinguished as Winwood Reade covered an Ashanti war for *The Times*. Generals did not much care for these interlopers. From the later stages in the Crimea they were subjected to a form of army censorship, which could be used to gag them. Roberts got rid of an irksome reporter in Afghanistan by accusing him of breaking the rules. Chirol of *The Times* considered General Macdonald very unfit for the command in Tibet, and suspected him of descending to mean subterfuges to silence the pressmen.[3] Kitchener disliked the whole breed. So did Wolseley, who in a work called *The Soldier's Pocket-Book* referred to them as 'the curse of modern armies', useless drones eating rations and doing nothing to earn them.[4]

There was a brisk market for books by officers about exciting recent campaigns, and some of them brought latent literary talent to light and showed the officer corps to be not altogether so un-idea'd as it looked. They were likely to be based on diaries; few privates kept these, but a good many were fond of writing letters home, especially after primary education and cheap postage came in, and their epistles might be surprisingly graphic and well-expressed. Zululand produced a spate of them, not censored as soldiers' letters came to be later, a change that may have been partly due to the glimpses these gave of sagging morale, and regret for having taken the Queen's shilling. 'I am now indeed sorry for it', one penitent wrote from Zululand. 'I was under the influence of drink when I did so.'[5] Too many sighs like this found their way into the press. More suitable for the public ear was an expertly edited volume of extracts from Boer War letters.[6] In this officers and men were a band of brothers; horrors of war were not concealed, but it was portrayed as a nurse of many virtues, a trial stirring and ennobling as well as arduous, a school of citizenship transforming ordinary men into heroes.

Sketching was an accomplishment of the earlier 19th century among gentlemen as well as ladies; some who ventured into print adorned their pages with illustrations of their own, like W.R.King in Kaffraria. Other impressions dashed off on the spot were touched up by artists. An aquatint based on a sketch from south Africa shows a surprise attack on troops descending a steep forest track, Kaffirs springing out on them from the bush. Barker's painting of the generals meeting after the relief of Lucknow was done from sketches by eye-witnesses.[7] One of the most successful practitioners in this line was R.Caton Woodville, who had worn uniform in his time. He did Abu Klea, a fashionable subject, and the charge of the 21st Lancers at Omdurman, colliding with a dervish array lying in wait in a hollow: the lingering heroics of war instead of the machine-guns. In other countries too the brush was at work preserving or embroidering history. Horscheldt painted the surrender of Shamyl to Bariatinski, the victor seated on a rock under a tree, the defeated chief, seen from behind, modestly standing before him.

'Special artists' began accompanying armies in the 1850s. They had competitors from the first in photographers, beginning with amateurs like the John MacCosh who had a camera with him in the second Sikh and second Burma wars. Official army photography got its full start in Napier's Abyssinian campaign. In 1898 Kitchener's army had a film cameraman with it. By the time of the Libyan war the cinema was growing up, but it was alleged that its displays of Italian soldiers covering themselves with glory were completely bogus.[8] Another invention that could play a part was the gramophone. A very early and wheezy record was a dramatic reconstruction of the scene on the deck of the troopship *Birkenhead*, wrecked off the African coast in 1852 with reinforcements for the Kaffir war – the men standing in their ranks, drums rolling, billows crashing, and the commander declaiming: 'Soon the ship will sink beneath the waves, and we, officers and men of the 74th Highlanders! will be no more. . . .' Why they did not swim ashore instead (as a quarter of them did in the end) is a question that only later, smaller minds would think of. This was the parade-ground spirit at its sublimest.

Monuments provided another kind of record, imposingly permanent and eye-catching. St Patrick's Cathedral at Dublin has a memorial to the fallen of the 18th Royal Irish in the second Burma war, on which are carved troops advancing in exact formation towards the entrance of the Shwe Dagon Pagoda at Rangoon; on its steps lies a prostrate soldier. On the parapet of the North Bridge at Edinburgh a knot of Scottish soldiers in dire peril still face an unseen Boer enemy. The Royal Marines' monument in London is surmounted by two bronze bayonet-wielding figures, one recumbent as if wounded; reliefs on two sides exhibit the scaling of a rocky height in south Africa, and Chinese soldiers in ignominious flight.

From 1880 an annual Naval and Military Tournament in London re-enacted thrilling episodes, in 1892 from the Zulu war, in 1894 from the Sudan. On the stage imagination could be given a freer rein, as in the *Siege of Delhi* which G.O.Trevelyan saw at Astley's, with an Irish sergeant dancing a jig and falling in love, and the curtain falling on sepoys about to be blown from the guns.[9] At a more vulgarizing level still, someone home from India saw in a fairground in 1860 'a large canvas daub' depicting that Mutiny villain, the insignificant-looking Nana Sahib, as 'a terrific embodiment of matted hair, rolling eyes, and cruel teeth'.[10]

Despite all this fuel, empire enthusiasm in Britain was fitful, only burning brightly among ordinary folk when fighting was going on somewhere, and not always then. At best it was a complex, unstable compound. Public moods were volatile, and easily damped by the thought of taxes to be paid for war-gambols. In thrifty Scotland the press reflected a distaste for the second Sikh war, following so hard on the first; it ensured a hearing for Cobden's advocacy of military economies, and fed 'the growing conviction that the Empire was not worth its cost and trouble.'[11] Men in the seats of power were obliged to take account of the man in the street's coolnesses as well as fevers. No one in Britain cared about triumphs in Sind or Afghanistan, Peel told the incoming governor-general Hardinge, recommending peaceful constructive policies instead.[12] Peel may of course not have read the public mind correctly, and the Crimean War was soon to show Cobdenite gospel routed by Palmerstonian. Even so, it did not do to loiter on the stage; quick, conclusive success was always preferred to anything long drawn out. Baron Gros in China reported his British confrère Lord Elgin as telling him in 1860 that the war had come to be so much detested in England that it must be wound up somehow or other before long.[13] By 1888 some of the responsible men in Burma were conscious of newspaper-readers at home growing 'very weary' of their doings. Even at the end of the century Milner and Chamberlain had to tune up public opinion very carefully for the war they were preparing in south Africa.

While the majority might sometimes be apathetic, a small minority was usually ready with positive criticism, audible enough at least to be resented by men in the firing-line. At the end of the second Afghan war when Hartington as Secretary for India moved the customary vote of thanks to the officers, a stormy debate broke out. An Irish member, Healy, wanted to know why they should be thanked for 'slaying a number of people with whom we had no righteous quarrel', and compared the invasion with the conquest of Ireland. Sir Wilfrid Lawson condemned soldiers as mercenaries, pledged to any work however vile; Illingworth maintained that nobody approved of the war except the gentry and their army relatives, eager 'to glorify the war system'.[14] Aggressive frontier policies regularly enjoyed more favour at Calcutta than in London, partly because at home public opinion was some deterrent. Anglo-India itself might be sharply divided at times, as it was over the Tirah campaign in 1897–8, when civilians were scathing about so mammoth an armament being set in motion in a barren waste. Army men felt on the contrary that they were fighting 'perhaps the most difficult campaign in history', and getting niggardly thanks.[15]

Abd el Kader received French newspapers, followed debates in the Chamber, and knew that many liberals favoured evacuation. At Paris in 1846 Cobden was told by a minister that Algeria was a very heavy burden, and that once when the Chamber voted unanimously against any reduction of troops and costs 'he knew that four-fifths of the members were in their hearts opposed to the retention of the Colony altogether – but the state of public opinion (I should call it public madness) deterred them from acting upon their convictions.'[16] Prudence or better motives were always at odds with the appetite for glory bequeathed to the *Grande Nation* by Louis XIV and Napoleon. On holiday in the south of France in 1861 Tennyson witnessed 'a grand puppet show, a sham fight between the French and Chinese' in the recent war. 'The English were conspicuous by their absence.'[17] Marx's daughter Laura Lafargue in Paris was struck by reactions to a reverse in Indochina, the emotional shock of any bad military news for Frenchmen, workmen as much as any others. 'The fact', she wrote to Engels, 'that a few hundred Frenchmen have fallen on foreign battlefields will, at any time, sting them into madness.'[18]

Talk of the sacredness of life, one writer cried, when Tonking was under discussion, or of no race being superior to any other, was nonsense. As to the expenses that some economists were jibbing at, a great country like France must be great in the world; they might prove that expenditure would outstrip profits, but that was a base *calcul d'épicier*.[19] Viewpoints clashed anew over the western Sudan, for instance when right-wing efforts to hush up atrocities committed by an expeditionary force failed. But in 1890 a *Comité de l'Afrique française* came into being, and by the end of the century the right wing, long distrustful of distant adventures because of its revanchism against Germany, came round to the doctrine that the bigger the empire the better.

Among bodies of organized opinion, most Churches everywhere and their flocks could be counted on to underwrite it. From 1905 the Bank of Rome, with close clericalist connections, was taking part in Italy's programme of economic penetration of Libya, and when war came it was endorsed by many Catholic journals, while some bishops had the prayer *Tempore belli* read from their pulpits.[20] They were following in the footsteps of the Spanish prelates who gave their blessing to the attack on Morocco in 1859, when the Patriarch Iglesias praised the army in a pastoral letter as a worthy heir of the heroes of old who 'carried civilization and the faith, along with conquest, to America and Asia', and spoke of Europe watching with admiration.[21] At Potsdam William II was wont to don the surplice and preach sermons to himself and his courtiers in his royal chapel; he took God seriously, and had no doubt that God took him equally so. When his men were on their way to China he held forth on an invigorating text about smiting the Amalekites. In the Church of England the same triumphalist note was swelling, and fury with Boers found vent in sanguinary sermons at Windsor in which the Amalekites were again roughly handled.

Some fellow-feeling for peoples under the imperialist hammer touched nationalists in unfree countries of Europe. A Polish exile of the 1840s recommended his countrymen to study the Afghan repulse of British aggression, as a useful lesson for their own struggle against Russia.[22] There were Irishmen who could view Afghans or Boers as exemplary patriots, and in the Boer War the Dublin Fusiliers were faced by an Irish Brigade of nationalist volunteers. Socialism might have been expected to take a firm stand against colonial wars, but it had a divided mind on the whole question, and on the whole did not prove more of an obstacle to them than liberalism in Britain or France. In the Libyan war a majority of Italian socialists were ready to support it: this wing was largely southern, and it was the poverty-stricken south that dreamed seductive dreams of a better life for colonists in Africa.

Like suppressed nationalities, or the working class, women were another section of humanity beginning to seek a better place; but the more articulate of them were to be found among the upper classes, and often shared their strenuous imperialism. In India women were always 'the fiercest advocates of Strong Measures on all political occasions'.[23] One of the most remarkable women of her time, Florence Nightingale, had one of the most unfavourable estimates of her sex. 'Let the peace-people croak as they please', the heroine – a general's daughter – in Hall Caine's very progressive novel about Egypt writes to her army lover, 'it is war that brings out the truly heroic virtues.'[24] Wives of army men in the wilds were often their inspiration. Napier on the road to Magdala, Roberts to Kabul, were always writing to their helpmeets. Many of these women came of military families and could appreciate shades and gradations of success or failure in the profession imperceptible to the uninitiated. When Younghusband was insulted, as he felt, after his return from Lhasa with a pinchbeck KCIE, his wife as well as his father, he told a friend, were 'thrown into a profound melancholy. My wife burst into tears and had a severe heart attack.'[25]

Numerous English writers had family or other connections with the empire, but they seldom turned to it and its battles as a leading theme. Still the imperial ozone was pervasive, and must be part of the cause of the 'general shift to the right in the literary world in the 1880s'[26] which has been noticed. The few who had any direct acquaintance with the empire were usually minor figures like Haggard. One of higher rate, R.L.Stevenson, was living in Samoa at the time of the 1893 rising, and saw 'Manono all destroyed, one house standing in Apolima, the women stripped, the prisoners beaten with whips ... all under white auspices.' 'Barbarous war is an ugly business', he wrote during the fighting, 'but I believe the civilised is fully uglier. ...'[27]

In other countries too literary reflections were of every hue, the McGonagalls the most uncritical and exuberant, subtler writers' feelings often mixed. 'Pierre Loti' was a naval officer second to none in patriotic anglophobia, but he earned official disfavour in 1883 with over-candid articles about the conduct of French soldiers at Hue in Vietnam. His novel *Le roman d'un Spahi* (1881) is about a simple youth from the Cevennes serving in west Africa, demoralized by monoton-ous exile in an incomprehensible land, where he loses his life in the end in an obscure expedition whose dead will soon be forgotten. In 1911 the Futurist writer Marinetti hurried to Tripoli and poured out praises of the army, down to its horses with their lustrous Sicilian eyes, whose neighing seemed an endeavour to pronounce the word *Italia*.[28] Empire rhetoric was uniformly inimical to any sense of the ridiculous.

Borodin's tone-poem 'In the Steppes of Central Asia' evoked a peaceful caravan rescued from marauders by Russian troops appearing on the scene. Russian writers had a more intimate acquaintance with wars of conquest than any other country's; no seas flowed between them and their empire. The Caucasus was the romantic land that stirred imagination most, though Lermontov took the road to it involuntarily, transferred from his Hussar regiment at St Petersburg as punishment for his verses on the death of Pushkin in 1837. Tolstoy was stationed for nearly three years, in the early 1850s, in the wooded hill country south of the Terek river, and took part in hazardous rides against Shamyl and the Chechens. He was all eagerness, as he wrote to a brother, to help in 'destroying the predatory and turbulent Asiatics';[29] it is no wonder if more ordinary young men on imperial frontiers felt the same. In his novel *The Cossacks* his hero or alter ego Olenin is proud at being 'accepted into the comradeship of the gallant Caucasian army'. All the same, Tolstoy does not shut his eyes to the cruelty of soldiers breaking into Tartar villages and killing children, or his ears to the death-song of a party of outlaws, cornered and making their last stand, strapped knee to knee so that none of them can try to run away.[30]

ii. Political consequences

Modern Spain has been affected more profoundly than a stronger country would have been by empire, loss of empire, ghosts of empire;

the darkest consequences came to fruition only in the 20th century. In the early 19th century there could be some beneficial effects of lost dominion. The Liberal revolution of 1820 was made possible by the unwillingness of the army gathered at Cadiz, by special conscription, to be shipped across the Atlantic. One means by which conspirators worked on its feelings was reading out to the soldiers lurid descriptions of what the rebels did to prisoners. A flock of officers came back to Spain after the defeat and helped to militarize Spanish politics, though there were some, like Espartero, Regent in 1840–3, who adopted a mildly liberal posture. General Prim gained a title and acclaim in Morocco, took the lead in the revolution of 1868, and was virtual dictator when assassinated at the end of 1870. From then on the army was more single-mindedly reactionary. Ten years' fighting in Cuba bred a new generation of commanders accustomed to be a law to themselves. One of them, Martínez Campos, fought the rebels there both before and after initiating the counter-revolutionary coup which restored the monarchy in 1875, and crushing risings of workers in Barcelona and other towns. 1898 left the army smarting under its humiliating failure, and biding its time to take a vicarious revenge on opponents at home and new colonial opponents in Morocco.

Army rule in Cuba had resemblances to army rule in Turkestan. In a book on the region in 1876 the American diplomat Schuyler at St Petersburg, quoting a Russian officer, said that the worst men in the army were sent out there, and intrigued for lucrative berths, with the result that military and administrative functions were hopelessly confounded; in addition officers were allowed to dabble in commercial enterprises.[31] In Algeria an early institution was the *Bureau Arabe* of officers versed in Arabic, set up to control the population, with the Zouave captain and later war minister Lamoricière as its first head. It was accused of arbitrary and despotic proceedings, which could scarcely indeed have been otherwise. In fact the army was completely in power, inevitably again when the French were fighting for so many years against the people, not as the British in India usually were against princes. In Castellane's time a general was 'a second Providence', an 'absolute master', in his area.[32] Down to 1870 the army could turn a blind eye to any instructions from Paris. During Bugeaud's tenure 'military insubordination was raised to the level of an art'.[33] With extra pay, and service counting double (this came to be the practice in several armies) posts were competed for by men who wanted to get on.

Louis Philippe was content to squeeze all the political advantage he could from Algeria for himself and his family; to them it was a means of catching the public eye. In 1837 one of his sons, the Duc de Nemours, held a command. The Duc d'Orléans led a division in 1839, and next year both he and another prince, Aumale, saw action; in 1847 the latter succeeded Bugeaud as governor-general. After Louis Philippe's fall Algeria had an important bearing on the rise of Bonapartism, that precursor of fascism. Cavaignac made his way up in the Algerian fighting, becoming governor-general just before the revolution of 1848; the new liberal government brought him back as war minister, in time to crush the Paris workers in the bloody fighting of June. His right-hand man was Lamoricière. A republican, Cavaignac was soon overtaken by Louis Napoleon, who was surrounded with 'Africans', commanders hardened in the Algerian wars, like St Arnaud, or Magnan who was appointed to the Paris garrison. With their backing the coup d'état of December 1851 could be carried out, and the Second Empire installed. A host of its opponents were deported to Algeria, where many perished. After the 1870 war MacMahon, who had long served there and been governor-general, was put in charge of the Versailles army and the suppression of the Paris Commune. His right-hand man, the ferocious Marquis de Gallifet, had served the Second Empire in both Algeria and Mexico.

Zouaves and Legionaries helped to destroy the Commune. They were not the only troops called in for such purposes who had been toughened by colonial fighting. An early case is that of 'Kirke's lambs', the regiment from Tangier led by Colonel Kirke which fought at Sedgemoor in 1685 and butchered defeated rebels. With tsarist generals, the great Suvorov among them, stamping on rebels at home and other peoples in Asia were always twin employments. Paskievich's two titles epitomized this: victory over the Persians in 1828 made him Count of Erevan, over the Poles in 1831 Prince of Warsaw. Skobelev won his spurs against the Polish rebels of 1863 before turning his attention to Turcomans and Turks. Native troops could be made use of within Russia at times. After the 1905 upheaval, Liebknecht wrote, Circassian and other irregulars were 'loosed over the land like a pack of wolves in the Baltic counter-revolution.'[34] For them it must have been a chance to retaliate against the Europeans who conquered their fathers.

British territories, India notably, were under civil rule. Army men frequently chafed under it, and looked on the civilians they had to take orders from with a disrespect bordering on contempt. Young Roberts in India in 1857 made no question that the Mutiny was really the fault of the Indian government, 'men who have never been out of Calcutta in their lives'. 'Our civilians have ruined India by not punishing natives sufficiently. . . . Poor Nicholson was the man. His was an iron rule.'[35] Governorships however quite often went to men from the army. This was likeliest to happen in raw settlements where there might still be fighting to be done. Sir Harry Smith came to govern the Cape in 1847 fresh from his defeat of the Sikhs at Aliwal, and a new town was given the name of the battle. Individuals in the higher flights could soar to the highest altitudes. A great-grandson of the first Earl of Minto, governor-general of India, spent some time in the Guards, rode in several Grand Nationals, was a volunteer with the Turks against the Russians in 1877, in Afghanistan in 1879, Egypt in 1882, western Canada in 1895 for the Red River rebellion: in 1898 he became governor-general of Canada, and finally in 1905 viceroy of India. He was a not too illiberal ruler; but Kitchener was put in charge of Egypt in 1911 specifically as a man to stand no nonsense from the nationalists.

Englishmen were fond of saying that other countries did not know how to keep their colonial agents and soldiers on the leash. In 1894 when Siam was in trouble with France the British chargé d'affaires at Bangkok was sure that, while his French colleague was decent enough, 'the military and naval people at Chantabun [in the disputed borderland with Indochina] and in the French colonies and protectorates snap their fingers at him and the French Foreign Office, and act only to please the Colonial party.'[36] The mad Admiral Pierre's conduct in Madagascar in 1883, Lord Granville the Foreign Secretary's biographer wrote, 'was only an extreme instance of the aggressive conduct in every corner of the world of French agents' who often had links with the press and believed that ministers dared not disavow them.[37] But some Englishmen were disturbed by symptoms of their own representatives going the same way. An MP made a strong case against individuals up and down the empire being licensed to make treaties and wars off their own bats. His seconder quoted a suggestion by someone in Russia that any officer sent out should be given in advance all the medals he could hope to win by wars or annexations, and forfeit one for every quarrel he got into.[38] Gladstone wound up the debate, sweeping the dust under the carpet with a practised hand.

Colonial wars brought army chiefs into the limelight, but they never felt that they were getting enough of it, or of the rewards that ought to come with it. They learned to further their objectives or their careers by taking advantage of the new channels of publicity, playing to the press gallery. Wolseley might abominate war-correspondents, but he fully understood how helpful the more amenable of them could be to an ambitious soldier. Kitchener received hints from Colonel Repington, military correspondent of *The Times*, on how to 'manufacture a public opinion'.[39] Royalty was happy to share the limelight. There was a lengthy spell when Victoria was as much in need of it as Louis Philippe to rescue the throne from unpopularity, and she was whole-heartedly an imperialist. On a single day in the course of the occupation of Egypt she plied the War Office with eighteen letters, meddling indeed in a fashion that Gladstone considered gravely unconstitutional.[40] There was talk of the graceless Prince of Wales going to Egypt to do his bit; the Queen vetoed this, but let her favourite son the Duke of Connaught go. Some princes trod the quarterdeck, two accompanied the final expedition into Ashantiland, one died there.

Empire soldiers as a race were highly sensitive to attitudes in Britain. At the beginning of the century Sir John Malcolm's grievance was that nothing in British India was esteemed great except British crimes.[41] At the end of the century Churchill on the north-west frontier was outraged by censures in England on the actions of Englishmen facing 'the most ferocious savages in Asia'.[42] 'It was no ignoble little raid, as ignoble Little Englanders were saying', Younghusband protested of his climb up to Lhasa.[43] Nearly all imperial functionaries, the soldiers and those close to them most of all, belonged to the far right in politics and were convinced that the Liberal party's dearest wish was to sabotage the empire. In 1885 Wolseley fumed in a letter to the Queen about 'the foolish public' which would rather trust tradesmen turned politicians than 'the gentleman who wears your Majesty's uniform.'[44]

Privately he hoped to see 'frothing talkers' like Gladstone ousted by army rule under a new Cromwell.[45] One of the men who went to Lhasa remarked in his narrative that the exploit had been authorized because HMG was 'not yet undermined by hostile demagogues;'[46] he clearly feared that it soon would be. Imperial policies could only be 'slow, clumsy, and hesitating', wrote Younghusband, so long as 'an officer in the heart of Asia' was to be trammelled by 'the "will" of "men in the street" of grimy manufacturing towns in the heart of England.'[47] General Sir Ian Hamilton thought of the army, very much as a Prussian Junker might, as custodian of the national character, threatened with corruption both by labour unruliness and by upper-class luxury and materialism.

Britain had the biggest empire; nevertheless it also had the stablest political life. It was a favourable circumstance that all its possessions except Ireland were at a safe distance. Still, it could not be altogether unaffected by currents which were influencing other imperial nations so powerfully. Men so ready to believe that they knew best what ought to be done on the frontiers might come to think that they ought to have a say in decisions nearer home. All the generals in the public gaze had won their reputations in imperial wars; and both Lords and Commons were thronged with army men, often with colonial experience or connections, and former governors or their relatives. Clode's book on the armed forces in 1869 contained a warning of the possibility of civil supremacy being compromised.[48] Some military writings of the 1890s, it had been pointed out, paid only lip service to the principle. In 1903 Shaw Lefevre, writing to Campbell-Bannerman, expressed a fear that the new Committee of Imperial Defence might turn into an inner cabinet, rigged by the generals – 'another link in the chain of militarism which is being forged'.[49]

Ireland, rather than Britain, bore the convergent weight of imperialism and reaction. Anglo-Irishmen ruling dependencies were not much less numerous than the Anglo-Irish officers who helped to conquer them; one, Lord Dufferin, while viceroy of India was worried about the land-war in Ireland, and his rents, and viewed it in the same light as the Burmese resistance he was trying to suppress. Both, he was certain, were being stirred up by a few self-seeking agitators.[50] If W.S. Blunt was correctly informed, coercion in Ireland and intervention in Egypt were decided on at the same cabinet meeting in 1882.[51] 'Undoubtedly,' an English heretic in India was to write, 'the Black and Tans in Ireland were the lineal descendants – politically speaking – of the punitive police we had been employing for so many years in India.'[52]

For Europe at large expansion afforded an outlet to impulses of violence, and could relieve internal tensions, but there was always a chance that it might recoil and intensify them instead. If conquest was doing something to civilize the outer world, it was also doing something to barbarize Europe. In 1900, during the Boer War, Bryce in a letter to Goldwin Smith lamented 'the England of today, intoxicated with militarism, blinded by arrogance, indifferent to truth and justice'.[53] One sinister omen was a recrudescence in Europe of police torture, whose taproots in colonial warfare and repression can scarcely be missed. The first salient case, which shocked a Europe still innocent enough to be shocked, came to light in a trial of labour agitators in the Montjuich fortress at Barcelona. It happened in 1897, near the close of the long years of vicious warfare in Cuba.

178

12

THE GREAT WAR

i. The colonial background of 1914

Every European nation, wrote an English officer in China in 1860, 'is closely watching us, and marking how we are likely to come out of the great fight hereafter to be fought. . . .'[1] Beyond all local colonial wars lay always this prospect of an ultimate trial of strength among European rivals. It would be a conflict ramifying over the continents, as the old Anglo-French wars did. Lanessan recommended Indochina in 1886 partly by stressing its utility to France in case of war; Saigon could be made a strong naval base, British trade routes cut, India menaced. Bülow quoted, seemingly with approval, a *Times* dictum that the rapid growth of the German navy dated from the acquisition of Kiaochow on the Shantung coast in 1898.[2] During most of the 19th century, despite all jealousies and tiffs, colonial expansion had been a safety-valve for European tensions, as well as for internal pressures within the countries concerned. But towards the end a series of international crises in the colonial world itself – Tunis, Siam, Fashoda, Manchuria, soon followed by Morocco – threatened to ignite European war, as formerly nothing outside Europe except the Anglo-Russian feud in Central Asia seemed capable of doing.

When war finally broke out in 1914 it had very many and complex causes; among them the colonial perspective can offer a useful view from one angle. By the close of the 19th century the British empire was over-extended and vulnerable, and in 1891 its two old rivals, France and Russia, had come together in the Dual Alliance. In 1899 a warning voice told Britons that they would soon have to choose between conscription for service in India, or losing India to Russia.[3] The Anglo-Japanese alliance of 1902, a throw of the dice by Britain with some air of desperation, emboldened Japan to challenge and defeat Russia in Manchuria in 1904–5. Defeat brought on the 1905 revolution, and then, because of tsarism's need to regain prestige after both these hurricanes, renewal of Russian activity in the Middle East, and in the Balkans where it led directly towards 1914: Italy's attack on Turkey had a further disruptive effect on the precarious balance there. In this light the 'civil war' which did so much to weaken Europe in the world was largely due to its ascendancy in the world having already begun to crumble.

After the Boer War the War Office divided Intelligence into three departments, one of them for imperial concerns: it set about pondering a plan for defence of India. In 1908 London was still debating how to reinforce India against a Russian attack, when preparations to send an army to prop France against a German attack were already taking shape.[4] It was the moment of change when one vision of coming war was melting into another. To escape from the prospect of a collision with France and Russia combined, Britain entered a Triple Entente with them, which was primarily or ostensibly a settlement of colonial differences, but which secret diplomacy speedily transformed into an unavowed alliance. The three old imperialists were not burying the hatchet, but turning its edge against Germany. In other words Britain was risking war inside Europe, with allies, for fear of having to fight outside Europe, without an ally except a problematical Japan, and with India in acute danger, both from Russian invasion which war technology would now make easier than in the past, and from deepening internal unrest.

The very small ring of politicians and officials who were making this calculation were supported by the generals, men who having gathered all their laurels far away looked forward now, it may be supposed, to the grand climax of an appearance on the European stage. 'In regard to any questions which are not purely technical', the Secretary for War wrote in 1904 of the men he was getting to know in the newly-formed Army Council, 'many of these Officers are like children.'[5] In so far as the hidden pressures fashioning Britain's policy before 1914, and drawing the country towards participation in a European war, can be traced to imperial and military sources, it may be said that it had to pay a very high price in the end for colonial conquest.

Imperial success lent the Entente nations the confidence which Germany owed to triumphs inside Europe. In one sphere the colonialists, Britain in the lead, were far better equipped for the propaganda struggle which has been so essential a part of twentieth-century warfare. They were well versed in the art of denigrating opponents, in order to justify their own less laudable acts, and obviate fault-finding at home or abroad. In 1899, and then on a larger canvas in 1914–18, passions and prejudices long worked up against other races were diverted against a new target, with Germans in the role of 'Huns'. The alleged war-aim of liberating Germany and Europe from 'Prussian militarism', 'a heroic effort in sanitary engineering' as H.G.Wells called it,[6] was of a piece with the redeeming of Afro-Asia from its past. Once again civilization confronted barbarism. To be sure, for Germany it was not difficult to pose as saviour of Europe from barbaric Russia.

By this time the British army fought in costume of the sober khaki ('dusty') colour it owed to India. How much else colonial experience had to offer in the way of practical guidance might be another question. It was certain to exert a strong influence, when so many Allied generals owed their positions to it. Algerian warfare brought undeniable benefits to the French army, by encouraging initiative, simplifying uniforms, and so on. To argue from this that Algeria was 'an excellent training school for the French army' was proved fallacious in 1870, in many ways a rehearsal for the disasters of 1914. Various of the senior commanders were products of the colonial school and its exhilarating simplicities, like Bazaine and Canrobert, who surrendered at Metz, and MacMahon, captured at Sedan.

A gap remained and widened between the two spheres, what was happening in Afro-Asia and what might be expected to happen in Europe. Few British officers overseas could see any relation between the two. Frenchmen overseas continued to practise tactics of rapid, daring movement, and with them to imbibe firm self-reliance and 'a profound suspicion of anything that smacked of military science',[7] the same obtuseness that Shakespeare's Ulysses met with under the walls of Troy. Stay-at-homes in Europe, for their part, were sometimes inclined to dismiss colonial campaigning, on the Indian frontier for instance, as meaningless; and after 1870 there was more warrant for arguing, as an American did, that it was undesirable for officers to get most of their training in colonial warfare, which might mould them on inappropriate lines.[8]

About 1800 European methods were benefiting from lessons learned in North America. A hundred years later there was still something to be gleaned from the colonial environment, but only with careful consideration of what elements in it were valid in an era of vastly intensified fire-power. Neglect of this showed most glaringly in the notion that machine-guns and the like could only be decisive against barbarians. 'Sepoy generals', as Napoleon called them, could not grasp that the time was at hand when the machine would supersede the man; their faith in human superiority was too deeply rooted in certitude of the superiority of white man over native, compounded by that of officer over private and aristocracy over masses. Robert Graves discovered in the Great War that senior officers of his regiment thought the proper way to handle French civilians was to treat them 'just like "niggers" – kick them about'.[9]

Where colonial routine fitted in with conservative preconceptions, it could count on a ready, sometimes regrettable, welcome. 'A passive defence is forbidden', Upton learned in India, 'as being fatal to the *morale* of the troops'.[10] The maxim was drummed into every second-lieutenant in India, Colonel Henderson the military theorist wrote: '"Never refuse battle", "never show a sign of hesitation".'[11] Germany reached a similar philosophy by a different route; the Prussian élite instinctively adopted whatever tactics seemed best calculated to preserve its ascendancy over a nation in arms. 'The General Staff breathes "Attack, attack!" – attack everywhere,' wrote the lecturer on military studies at Edinburgh university, a retired engineer officer. 'These are virile ideas', he went on, well suited to produce 'the spirit that leads to victory. But the bullet of the magazine rifle does not spare high spirit', and German soldiers might have to 'suffer beyond endurance'.[12] Offensive doctrine found its purest and most atavistic expression in the cavalry charge. Its exponents, Henderson pointed out, were still hypnotized by their fantasy of horsemen 'thundering forward' to 'the supreme satisfaction of riding down a mob of panic-stricken fugitives'.[13] On the Western front this felicity eluded enthusiasts like Haig, but they went on throughout 1914–18 repeating the same folly with infantry in place of horsemen.

Colonial practice was not all of a piece. Mechanically drilled evolutions, controlled volley-firing, have been regarded as hallmarks of 'the small war mentality'.[14] It was after all by virtue of disciplined steadiness and obedience that the European soldier made his tremendous impact on Asia and Africa, moral as well as physical. But there were some more novel features, whose reception by the British army was hidden by the distance within it between the more gentlemanly element at home and the workaday officer types in India or elsewhere. Troops in India were trained for the offensive, but, as Upton also discovered, taught to attack economically, taking whatever cover offered, advancing in open skirmishing order. Common sense of this sort was drawn on to some extent in the Boer War, but inadequately because organization was too rigid. There was moreover a professional prejudice against it in all armies. Ideas on use of cover such as Roberts stood for 'were widely decried by

Continental theorists and above all by the Germans', who thought them cowardly.[15] Spanish officers in Morocco in 1859, Italian officers in Abyssinia, suffered unnecessary losses because they thought it necessary to their dignity and authority to stay on their feet when their men were lying down. Wolseley reprobated any recourse to entrenchments, as poor-spirited and demoralizing, and preparation for it was scamped by the British army.

Once the Great War got into its stride trenches became a necessity, and once they became continuous lines there was no room for the open-order tactics mastered on terrain like the north-west frontier. Of the teachings of colonial warfare only the most elementary, worse than useless in Flanders, could still be clung to, determination to get the upper hand by being continually on the attack. In 1893 a reporter wrote of Matabeles throwing themselves over and over again at a machine-gun battery.[16] It was as if they were fast in the spell of their old invincibility, unable to comprehend that their world had altered. Mass charges like theirs, or those of the dervishes, were the final spasms of a dying order. In the Great War both sides went on and on charging like dervishes. Archaic social systems and faiths were fighting against history, thrust on by the dead hand of the past.

ii. Colonial forces and campaigns

Hobson predicted in 1902 that a parasitic Europe would come to depend on huge native armies, as well as on colonial industries. With the Triple Entente arraying the three chief imperialist powers against it, clearly it was Germany that had most to fear from any such prospect. Use of native troops in European wars might not be strictly illicit, in the view of the *German War Book*, but the bringing of 'Turcos' from Africa into the Italian war in 1859 was universally disapproved, and their use in 1870 was 'a retrogression from civilized to barbarous warfare'.[17] As 1914 approached the French were looking more and more to colonial manpower to make up for the German lead in numbers. Colonel Mangin, who devoted most of his life to colonial 'pacification', was a leading proponent of the idea, and in 1910 was touring west Africa and submitting proposals; plans for increased recruitment, partly by conscription, were adopted. Bernhardi warned his countrymen that France's newest territory, Morocco, offered 'excellent raw material for soldiers', and that a large African army might enable it to turn the tables against Germany.[18] A Turkish alliance must have seemed all the more desirable to Germans, as furnishing an analogous supply of cannon-fodder.

Most British recruiting of native troops during the war continued to be voluntary, though in India it had to be extended to fresh areas and communities, in the later stages conscription was being considered, and enough pressure was exerted on villagers to provoke riots and disturbances in the Punjab and elsewhere. In all 1,300,000 Indian soldiers were employed, and more than 100,000 casualties incurred. In Egypt labour conscription, mostly of villagers and their draught animals, stirred resentment. With no sophisticated national movement like the Indian to worry about, France was eager to persuade Japan and even China, both nominal allies, to contribute manpower; but the Indian government had very strong objections to Japanese troops being brought into any theatre near India.[19] It would not do to let Indians guess that the Sahib was no longer capable of doing his own fighting. There were other imperial obstacles. In 1916 a War Office panjandrum assured J.C.Wedgwood that he was not at all opposed to enrolment of black troops: 'I am only too anxious to get all I can and have been scouring the world to find out where they can be raised.' But South Africa was the most promising recruiting-ground, and unhappily its government was offering 'strenuous opposition'[20] – thus, it might be added, for bad reasons giving its black subjects some real protection.

In the Russian army Colonel Oraz Sirdar was a son of the defender of Geok Tepe against Skobelev, and a cavalry corps which took part in the invasion of East Prussia in 1914 was commanded by General Khan Nakhichevansky. Caucasians and some Central Asians were, like Finns, exempt from conscription, but a mass of Asian labour was collected. Of all men serving with the French colours in 1914 about 9 per cent were non-French; during the war more than half a million were recruited in the colonies, and nearly a quarter of a million labourers. From west Africa more than 160,000 men were obtained, 'after strong resistance and severe repression'.[21] Discontent enabled the leader of a small tribal rising at Bussa in Nigeria in 1915 to swell his following with men from across the border. British sources confirm that revolts broke out that year in Dahomey and other areas, under pressure of 'intensive recruitment for the army, forced labour, heavy taxation'; considerable French forces were needed to put them down.[22] In Senegal chiefs were paid a premium for each man they brought in, much as in former days African chiefs sold slaves to the white men. Most of the hundred thousand labourers got from Indochina were rounded up by force. They left their homes

184

embittered, and many came back full of new-found anti-French ideas. Such non-combatants may have been more open than soldiers to political infection, being less cut off from civil life.

A letter supposedly written by a Senegalese sub-lieutenant to be read to a battalion decorated during the war congratulated his countrymen – 'You are the first among the Blacks, for the French, first among the Whites, have conferred distinction on you.'[23] After so many wild African onrushes during the European conquests had been halted by bullets, the army was persuaded by men like Mangin that a mass assault by Senegalese, a human battering-ram, could perform what no one else seemed able to, and break through the enemy lines. The result, on the Somme in 1916, was catastrophic.[24] News must have trickled back into the soldiers' homelands, and intensified dread of conscription. Use of African troops in 1914–18, and then in the French occupation of the Rhineland, must have fostered the racialism which Hitler exploited, and spread the Nazi doctrine that the true Europe, hemmed in by barbarism, was Germany. Frenchmen might have done well to recall the painful memories which haunted them for years after 1814, when the tsar's Cossack and Bashkir irregulars rode to Paris.

Despatch of Indian forces to Europe was decided on at once, a marked change from not long since when the Boer War was kept a white man's preserve. The Lahore and Meerut divisions, comprising 24,000 British and Indian troops, of whom nearly 10,000 were casualties before the end of 1914, had an ecstatic reception at Marseilles,[25] and also in some British newspapers. An officer not connected with them thought the press talk 'An awful lot of nonsense', disgusting to British soldiers who knew their own pre-eminence over any native troops. He admitted that the Indian Corps 'put up quite a good show at first, but they could not stick it for long', and without their British officers would be helpless.[26]

One of these, H.V.Lewis, attached to the 129th Baluchis, was relieved to find them behaving wonderfully well. 'Our men are very cool under fire, don't seem to mind a bit, I think', and they were splendid at night patrolling.[27] Another, second in command of a Garhwali regiment, strongly disagreed with an impression he felt had got about 'that in some way the Indian soldier was found wanting'. But he thought harm had been done by the sensational press raising impossible expectations about 'the marvels of night scouting, surprise attacks and kukri work which would be performed by Indians', Gurkhas especially. His own estimate of relative merits wavered. Officers thought highly, perhaps too highly, he wrote, of their Indian soldiers, but 'never for one instant imagined them the equals of the British soldier. If they were, India would not be a British dependency.'[28] Here was the real rub. Of old, when sepoys were intended for use against other Indians, second-rate soldiers could be reckoned adequate. Now they were not. Britain wanted to think its native troops good enough to help win the war, but not good enough to be able to break away from the empire. On the voyage to Europe, the Baluchi officer noted, 'The general opinion was that an Indian victory over white troops would have a bad effect on India.'[29]

Germany built many hopes before the war on plans for fomenting colonial rebellions. Formerly the West was liberating Afro-Asia from its own bad governments, now Westerners were ready to liberate it from one another. There were rosy illusions at Berlin, but shortage of experience made Germans far less familiar than Britons with the arts of manipulating native peoples, inciting tribesmen, tickling sheikhs. Their most ambitious scheme, to promote the 'Ghadr conspiracy' of Indian nationalists, mainly Sikh emigrants in North America, in the end came to very little. Where some real successes were scored was through the Turkish and Islamic channel, though even here they were modest. Turkey's entry in October 1914 set up some ripples at once in the Indian army, in the form of desertions from border regiments; a jehad was being preached by what Army HQ called 'the ignorant and fanatical priesthood'.[30] A company of the 10th Baluchis, embarking for Mesopotamia, shot its officer; the whole regiment was sent to Burma instead. On the Western front a plane dropped leaflets in Hindi calling on Indian troops most of whom were Hindus to join the holy war proclaimed by the Sultan. Less maladroitly, but not it seems much more effectively, similar appeals were addressed to Senegalese Muslims at Gallipoli. Central Asia was another field.

In February 1915 religion helped to provoke a startling mutiny at Singapore, of the 5th Native Light Infantry. This was a 'one-class' unit, composed of men from the same community, Punjabi Muslims. It was on its way to Hong Kong, but the men thought their destination was Europe and evidently did not like the prospect. This must have made them more receptive to the preachings of a holy man in a mosque, calculated, the court of enquiry held, to have a dangerous effect on men 'whose gullibility and credulity are almost beyond belief'.[31] Singapore was a lurking-place of Indian nationalists, who may have had a finger in the pie. British officers with the regiment were divided into hostile cliques, it came out.

Early on the 15th about half the men, in the Alexandra barracks, mutinied all of a sudden, killed some officers, seized the ammunition, and then, with little sign of planning or leadership, set out in groups through the town. Their sole purposeful action was to release some hundreds of interned Germans. Panic reigned; there were no British troops, only armed police, many of them Sikhs, and volunteers, some of them Chinese. A valuable addition came from the crew of a small gunboat in the harbour, the *Cadmus*, and later on French sailors joined in, and some Japanese were enrolled as special constables. The authorities were weak and hesitant, in the court's view: 'The time honoured maxim of "l'audace toujours l'audace" when dealing with Orientals was apparently lost sight of.' A Colonel Brownlow, an old NWF fighter, took the lead, and with a scratch force, including a naval squad with a Gatling mounted on a lorry, attacked the mutineers in their barracks at dawn on the 16th. They showed little cohesion, and were quickly routed.[32] A trial was held, in due form; 47 were sentenced to death, the rest to penalties ranging from transportation for life. Large crowds gathered to watch the executions, European women among them. The condemned men showed more fortitude in suffering than boldness in action. The first two set the example. 'Facing the firing party at eight paces their bearing never faltered.... Whatever their crime, their calm and dignity at the end was impressive.'[33] What was left of the regiment was reorganized and sent to the Cameroons.

In 1916 at Darfur on the edge of the Sudan, where Turkish arms were finding their way, once again tribesmen rushed out of the past at a British square, and were mown down. Far away in South-West Africa a campaign of a different sort was fought by the South Africa of Botha and Smuts, now reconciled to the empire, against the Germans in South-West Africa, who were joined by some dissident Afrikaners. German strength was little above 8000; the broad belt of desert was expected to keep Smuts's forces out, but he managed to get them across it, utilizing 'the new-fangled motor-car' to carry supplies.[34] In such a region motor transport could work a more immediate transformation than in western Europe with its short distances and many railways, and Smuts's son and biographer called the campaign, one of swiftly co-ordinated movements over a vast area, 'a revelation to students of military history'.[35] Still greater novelty, one or two aeroplanes were on the wing. Men of a Rhodesian regiment taking part were pestered while pursuing the enemy by a German biplane; its bombs always missed them, but 'Skinny Lizzy', their anti-aircraft gun, failed to hit it. British airmen brought in useful plans of the defences of Kalkfeld.[36]

In the joint Franco-British occupation of the Cameroons the log of HMS *Dwarf* shows the Germans arming tribesmen as snipers, Commandant Mathieu in return giving captured rifles to some friendly natives, 'who go out and occasionally return with a head or two!'[37] In East Africa the Germans were able to keep up a tenacious resistance to the very end of the war, and the decisive factor – a very unpalatable one to white men in southern Africa – was that here they had a splendid force of native fighting-men to rely on. Unlike the ill-starred Senegalese on the western front, these Africans were fighting on their own soil, in familiar conditions, even though with immense odds against them. It was a miniature epic, resembling the Boer War in the way that multitudes of soldiers had to be called in from everywhere to crush a small, mobile opponent. In February 1916 when Smuts took over the Allied command things had been going badly. It may be hard, as some found it at the time, to see why the Germans were not simply left alone. 'From what I saw of the country', one junior officer wrote at the end of a brief narrative, 'it was hard to imagine what we were fighting for, and I felt that the best thing to do was to give the country to the Germans and make them live there.'[38]

Allied heterogeneity was one stumbling-block. Besides Britain and South Africa there was Belgium, and after its entry into the War in 1916 Portugal. A Rhodesian regular army had its beginnings here; 10,000 white men and 14,000 blacks joined. Far the least useful were the Portuguese of Mozambique, 'bad commanders and ill-trained troops', in the view of Brigadier Northey, and officials and police who ran away from their posts on the enemy's approach, leaving a state of anarchy.[39] Imperial wars made strange bed-fellows, or grave-fellows. One column was composed of Nigerians and Kashmiris.

German strength was limited, but unified. If ability to train native troops was a test of fitness for empire, no Europeans were fitter than the Germans, to judge by the askaris who made up the bulk of Lettow-Vorbeck's little army. In the summer of 1915 there were estimated to be about 2200 Germans, about 11,000 African regulars, and some 3000 irregulars. Lettow had formed most of them into companies of 160 men, each with 16 Europeans. Many askaris were Muslims, and a proclamation by the governor, Schnee, summoned all the faithful to take up arms against the Sultan's foes.[40] In a clumsy attempt to counter this, British propaganda produced a document purporting to be a pre-war circular from Schnee asking his officials what could be done to check the spread of Islam, and saying that experts recommended pig-breeding.[41]

At the outset Lettow feared native risings, and he felt renewed apprehensions as the enemy pushed deeper into the country. 'The native has a fine sense of the transfer of real power from one hand to the other', he wrote in his war memoirs, and firmness was required to ensure compliance with the army's growing demands for food and porters.[42] His 'firmness' was a euphemism, if Allied versions were even a quarter correct. One spoke of women as well as men being roped together as carriers, and hundreds perishing; of 'sights of grim horror' along the route, as if the slave trade had come back. Northey too wrote of 'terrible' treatment of impressed carriers, worked to death or 'shot indiscriminately if they attempt to escape'.[43] On the Allied side too, large numbers of carriers were needed, if they did not have to be obtained by methods quite so draconic; the country was deadly to draught animals.

To avoid encirclement Lettow had to keep dodging about, and it turned into a sort of guerrilla war, half buried in thick bush. The climate was fatal to men as to animals; a very high proportion of the troops were always down with malaria, and sickness inflicted thirty times as many casualties as battle. But patrolling in the bush was nerve-racking work, because of constant danger of ambushes, and being fired at from close at hand – worse than the western front, Lewis thought.[44] Here too he found his Pathans excellent, really 'having the time of their lives'. One of them, Ayub Khan, wounded in a night attack, he called 'the bravest man I ever knew'. All the Indians were doing well. 'But', he wrote home, 'you won't hear much about it as the "gallant South Africans" are very jealous and I think politically they want every ounce of credit in this country and can afford to part with none.'[45]

Smuts would have liked to arrange a capitulation, had Lettow been willing. The continuing demonstration of the black man's ability to fight the white on equal terms must have perturbed him and his countrymen. Shortage of numbers was compelling conservative Germany to play a revolutionary part, as it did in Europe when it sent Lenin back to Russia. 'The white man cannot teach the blacks of Africa how to kill his brother white man', a war-correspondent wrote, 'without breaking down many of the ethical principles upon which European rule in Africa is based.'[46] General Molitor, the Belgian commander, denouncing German treatment of European prisoners, dwelt heavily on the 'vile, the unspeakable regulations ... that destroyed the prestige of the white man in the native's eyes.'[47]

In terms of the philosophy of race the antagonists were not really far apart. The governor of the Cameroons taxed the Allies with being the first to use black troops in the contest there; it must have been obvious, he declared, what would happen when 'the blood-thirsty beast has been aroused in the black and set upon the white opponent.'[48] After the war Lettow and Smuts became fast friends. But the mischief, for white supremacy, had been done. The spectacle of the askaris was part of what made the Great War 'a significant turning-point' for black Africa.[49] A ferment of ideas was churned up out of which much African nationalism would emerge. Millenarian preaching was in the air, the War was talked of as Armageddon. A portent for the future was the brief episode in 1915 of John Chilembwe's rising in Nyasaland.

13

CHALLENGE AND
RESPONSE: 1919–45

i. New empire problems

At the end of 1918 Europe was crippled, and the victorious Western allies, whose empires were now expanding afresh, did not escape its enfeeblement. Morally as well as physically its ascendancy was fatally undermined. In Britain itself Lord Milner deplored the vista of 'conquest, of domination, of the oppression of the weak by the strong', that the word 'empire' now widely conjured up.[1] Old hands in the outposts were jarred by an altered mood at home which they could not comprehend, and in early post-war days especially were inclined to mark their rejection of it by behaviour hardened by four years of mass killing in Europe. This affected the rank and file as well as their superiors. As a police officer in Burma in the 1920s George Orwell 'was constantly struck by the fact that the common soldiers were the best-hated section of the white community', and very deservedly.[2] It was against this bleak background that General Gwynn was trying to formulate procedures that would put colonial policing on a more civilized basis. One of his observations was that women were playing a growing part in subversive movements, and that this must raise delicate problems. There was fuel here for much anti-imperial propaganda. 'In your country', the new Communist International proclaimed to the peasantry of Iraq, 'there are 80,000 English soldiers who plunder and rob, who kill you and violate your wives!'

To the ferment of Asia the revolution of 1917 was a great contributor, as colony-owners were resentfully aware. But while it could blow sparks of revolt far and wide, Leninist doctrine and organization could as yet reach very few. For the colonial world the interwar years were a time of confusion, of groping towards new leadership and methods, which it would take another world war to bring, here and there, to maturity. Meanwhile there was only too much likelihood of relapse into atavistic forms of struggle, especially where religion was still predominant; of ancestral voices prophesying war, ghosts of old warrior bands returning from the grave. Russia was plagued with them like the rest: tsarist empire could only by painful degrees be transformed into Soviet Union. In Central Asia there were by Soviet admission 'Basmachis' at large at least as late as 1922–3, who like their congeners in other territories could be classed either as Muslim irreconcilables or as brigands. In 1926 there was revolt in Outer Mongolia against the Soviet-protected local government which had emerged. It was incited by two of the wealthy lamaseries, and led to separation of Church from state.

In India, Nehru wrote, nationalism was spreading, while 'the great prop of British rule in India – prestige – was visibly wilting'.[3] In the Punjab, the vital military province, among the British there was something like a revival of the panic of 1857. The worst consequence, which did them irreparable harm, was the massacre at Jallianwala Bagh in Amritsar, the holy city of the Sikhs, on 13 April 1919, when General Dyer with a detachment of Gurkhas and Frontier soldiers opened fire on a crowded meeting in a walled enclosure, and killed at least four hundred. He was censured by the Hunter Commission of enquiry, and removed from his command. In England he was lionized by conservatives, as the saviour of the Raj. To Gwynn his violent action was anachronistic and senseless, and his contention that he had to kill people in Amritsar in order to strike fear into the whole Punjab, or India, was clearly unacceptable.[4] Still, Gwynn had misgivings about the effect his dismissal might have on other British officers. One of these, who was with Dyer in the shooting, bitterly declared that the government had merely 'sat on at High Olympus, i.e., Simla', giving no lead – 'They let those sweltering down in the plains do the dirty work', and then found fault with them.[5] Army Headquarters in India held that 'the rioters were cowed by heavy casualties, especially at Amritsar', and that Dyer's 'knowledge of the Oriental was profound';[6] an example of how Europeans talked themselves into thinking Asiatic psychology so recondite as only to be penetrated by an occasional expert.

Later that year there broke out the rebellion of the Moplahs, a poor peasant people of the interior of Malabar in India's far south-west. Providence had created them, or so that second providence the British Raj assumed, to be exploited by landlords and traders. Since these were Hindus, while the Moplahs were Muslim, their chronic risings against their tormentors all through the 19th century took on a strongly communal colouring. They were always beaten down, and left more darkly and furiously religious. Now thousands of insurgents gathered, with some stiffening of demobilized soldiers: ordinarily Moplahs were not taken into the army, because of their fanaticism, but wartime needs compelled the admission of a number. On the other hand few of these were armed with anything better than swords or knives. Late in August their centre, Tirurangadi, and their leader Ali Musaliar, were captured, but they then broke up into bands, harder to come to grips with in broken hill country and jungle. More attacks on Hindus than on the army took place, and this enabled the government to pass the rising off as nothing but a communal disturbance. In the end the rebels were reported to have suffered four thousand casualties, besides a much greater number arrested; the army was accused of 'extraordinarily cruel' methods, and of shutting prisoners up in railway vans where they died of suffocation.[7] On their opponents the Moplahs succeeded in inflicting 137 casualties, a tally, as so often, pitifully small.

Up in the north-west the army had just been facing a sterner test, the third Afghan war. A chain of border incidents led to Britain declaring war early in 1919. On both sides it was a half-hearted affair. Memories of earlier happenings here could not embolden the British to plunge too deeply. The Indian army was below strength, and British troops on their way home from Mesopotamia had to be roped in, very much against the grain. At Peshawar 'it was a common sight to see senior officers being jeered at in the streets.'[8] As to the Afghan army, it was raised by conscription for long service of one man in eight, but did not get the best men because 'the more warlike and truculent tribes evaded their obligations', and other communities handed over the individuals they were most content to be without. Its role was to provide 'a stiffening to the hordes of armed tribesmen. . . .'[9] Its only success was won on the central sector, by General Nadir Khan; even that, according to the British, ended in defeat, but was claimed as a great victory: Nadir was promoted (he later promoted himself to the throne), and a column erected at Kabul with a British lion in chains at its foot. Europe was not alone in appreciating the arts of war publicity. After a few weeks of desultory manoeuvres King Amanullah was ready to ask for an armistice, and in August the treaty of Rawalpindi was signed. The campaign had witnessed the last charge of the King's Dragoon Guards, who captured from a mullah a green and orange flag now in the Clive museum at Shrewsbury. But HQ was left comfortably satisfied as to 'the soundness of our textbooks', the dogma of the 'vigorous offensive', and the paramount duty of infantry 'to cultivate dash, and a desire to close with the enemy with the bayonet.'[10]

For the Indian army a kind of St Martin's summer was setting in; a time when a British officer was conscious, as one has lately written, of an 'enormous respect' felt for him by his men, to bear the weight of which he had to be 'slightly larger than life'.[11] His pay bore no relation to the height of his pedestal. India was getting his services fairly cheap. Juniors were always in debt, because 'the Paymaster had calculated pay down to the last penny (anna) to permit bare existence'.[12] The supply of British privates showed signs of drying up; their lot in places like India was still unpleasant enough. Men of poor physique had to be accepted, inferior to the Indians with whom they shared the hurly-burly of the frontier. They might be equally below par in gumption. Out in the open, heedless of the sniper who might have been crouching behind any rock in his vicinity, a man was seen placidly reading the *Pink 'Un*. 'The British soldier simply would not take things seriously. . . .'[13]

Here was another reason for the Raj to want to be on good terms with its Indian soldiery. But the day had gone when the Indian army could be treated as an imperial maid of all work. In 1920 the viceroy gave London blunt notice of this: public feeling must now be taken into account.[14] Next year the Legislative Assembly at Delhi made a firm declaration. When troops were needed to guard oil-wells in Persia, a decision was reached that it would be imprudent to saddle India with the task. In 1935 Zetland as Secretary for India had to warn colleagues of 'increasing sensitiveness on the part of Indian opinion'.[15] This handicap was one aspect of an all-round shortage of manpower affecting all Western empires more or less. 'Our small army is far too scattered', F.M. Sir Henry Wilson confessed in 1920; 'in no single theatre are we strong enough'.[16] With its Moroccan war still on its hands, France was enlarging the Foreign Legion, drawing liberally on Austrians, White Russians, and the Germans it had so lately been denouncing as cut-throats and Huns.

ii. New technology

Above all, reliance was being placed on the new military technology to magnify manpower. It had been pushed forward rapidly by the Great War, which in this way fortified imperialism as much as in other ways it weakened it. During its course electrified as well as barbed wire was made use of on a turbulent sector of the north-west frontier. The armoured car showed its paces in the Afghan war, though only available in limited numbers. 'It possessed great fire power and mobility', the army reported, 'whilst offering a small and almost invulnerable target to the enemy.' 'Motor machine-gun batteries' were also now in service.[17] A grander chariot of wrath was the tank, an avatar of the elephant of older Indian warfare. But the true *deus ex machina* was the aviator, who had made his appearance in various colonial theatres during the Great War. A pregnant compliment from his commander to Flt-Lt Moore, carrying out low-level attacks in East Africa in 1917, was that 'The enemy's Askari have a holy dread of the Aeroplane. . . .'[18]

To empire men of Dunsterville's generation aviation promised, as his book makes clear, to be the trump card, the perfect means of keeping colonial peoples on the strait and narrow path. In the government this view had champions in Milner and Churchill. Before the War Churchill had founded the Naval Air Service, after it he was backing Trenchard, Chief of the Air Staff, against the claims of army and navy: the aim was to turn Iraq, whose defence was being entrusted to the RAF, into a showpiece of the new philosphy of air power. A quarter-century later Churchill would be beside himself with joy at the successful testing of the atom-bomb, as the perfect means of enabling the West to dictate to the Soviet Union.[19]

A dramatic vindication of the new gospel was forthcoming in 1920 when air power could claim to have finished off at one stroke the bothersome decades-old business of Somaliland. 'Operation Z' was planned to be carried out by air-force machines from Egypt and 'picked officers of experience, driving power, and initiative': speed, and 'economy in LSD', were laid down as essential principles. One machine was earmarked as 'hospital aeroplane'. Stores officer for this 'first independent air operation in history', as he proudly called it, was F.A.Skoulding, a Great War corporal who rose to Air Commodore. At the end of 1919 a species of challenge or declaration of war was issued by the governor, in the form of a proclamation couched in what must have been intended as very oriental language: it would be borne through the air, as if by birds, within an hour, and announced the Mullah's doom.[20]

On 21 January 1920, six planes took off for Medishe, now his chief stronghold. Only one was able to locate the target, but a bomb fell close enough to the Mullah to singe his clothes and killed his chief adviser, an uncle. On the next two days there was more bombing, and 'severe casualties' were inflicted on parties fleeing southward. On 4 February three planes bombed and machine-gunned the grand fortifications at Taleh; direct hits were scored, and hutments set on fire. 'Despite the terrible novelty of attack from the air, the Dervish garrison valiantly returned the fire.'[21] But resistance fizzled out, the Mullah died, the long war was over. As a new and far-reaching experiment, its denouement was watched by military and police experts all over Africa and Asia 'with the most profound interest'. Not all subscribed to the RAF's estimate of its achievement, and an expert on the country dismissed the idea that 'the savage peoples of Africa and Asia can be controlled from the air', as a dangerous illusion.[22] As usual, jealousies between Services came into the picture. It was the men on the ground who had the real work to do, a Camel Corps officer grumbled.[23] In Italian Somalia aeroplanes did not prevent hostilities from going on till 1927.

In the Punjab disturbances there was a first trial of aviation as a police weapon. A plane was sent to bomb and another to machine-gun objectives, a Sikh high school among them, in and near the town of Gujranwala. Both attacked from a low altitude, though only 12 people were killed and 24 wounded; in Governor O'Dwyer's opinion they saved the situation until troops could arrive. In the Afghan war planes were used to bomb enemy concentrations. They were obsolete machines, and one was shot down by marksmen concealed on a hillside, but it was judged that their 'moral' effect was great. A bomb on Kabul, which had thought itself safe among its mountains, was considered particularly efficacious. Work of this sort quickly became part of frontier routine. At the end of 1919 an officer in the Tochi valley was watching planes go over to bomb Waziri raiders, so as to help the light of reason to dawn on the tribal jirga or council – 'awful scallywags in dirty white rags for the most part'. Soon after, Mahsud tribesmen drew punishment on themselves, 'and in consequence their villages and lands are being destroyed daily.... I am afraid they will undergo most awful hardships this and next year.'[24] As a rule villages were supposed to be given warning in advance of a raid, so that only empty buildings would be demolished; but a rumour got afloat, and was believed by Nehru, of a new invention, of 'fiendish ingenuity', a delayed-action bomb which exploded after villagers had returned to their homes.[25]

In 1930 troops and airmen were coping with an unprecedented menace, tribal incursion in alliance with nationalists in Peshawar and its district. In the city a small squadron of armoured cars was made use of one day in April against riotous crowds, with disappointing results. They killed 30 individuals and wounded 33, but this only fanned public anger, and it was realized that these vehicles were vulnerable once brought to a halt, and unable to fire their machine-guns at close quarters. Bombing the attackers in the open proved ineffective: they soon learned to take cover, often in caves, and to move by night, in small parties. It was coming to be recognized that air action was not a complete solution. It was cheaper but more transient in its effects than ground operation. During the 1930s armoured carriers were being developed into light, turreted tanks, with machine-guns; on the frontier their thin armour was adequate, and they could scale rough slopes. Regular tanks were used for the first time in 1935, against the Mohmands. Still, the old drudgery and risks could not be done away with altogether. In 1938 an officer's letters described perspiringly a march through 'terrific country', infested with 'hostiles', between Razmak and Bannu.

It was in new territories where colonial rule had as yet no infrastructure that air forces could be looked on most of all as a short cut to control. In Iraq the British Mandate found few welcomers, and there were complications both in the north, where oil was expected, with Kurdish rebels, and in the south with Wahhabis, Muslim zealots raiding across the nebulous border from the new neighbouring kingdom of Saudi Arabia. A variety of operations were soon being undertaken by the RAF, on its own or in conjunction with ground forces under its direction. They were breeding a new type of soldier, a technician in uniform. A good specimen was the L.A.Simmons who joined the RAF as a 'skilled driver' in 1923, and spent 'two and a half quite unforgettable years' with armoured car units in Iraq, before moving on to Egypt. He rose to flight-lieutenant. The army was not concerned to notice that it had some enquiring minds now in the fold. No one told Simmons and his friends that they would be getting out of a train at Ur of the Chaldees. 'There was little or no "Briefing" in those days, everyone was kept in the dark about what was going on.' He arranged to have newspaper cuttings sent out from home, in order to get some clue to what he was doing.[26]

His No. 4 company of armoured cars had its base at Hinaidi, close to the capital Baghdad. Far-ranging patrols were carried out, by sections each of four cars, four Fords with Lewis guns, and a tender with radio and provisions. A car had a crew of five, all of whom had to be able to drive it and to handle any of its weapons. 'Our "armoureds" were greatly respected everywhere', he wrote. When men on the ground spotted the enemy in too much strength for them to tackle they radioed for planes to come and bomb him. Loose sand was a menace to both planes and cars. Thirst was the most persistent discomfort. Once a plane whose load included a crate of beer for Simmons and his comrades made a forced landing not far off, but they never saw their beer because 'the crew and guard sent to stand by the machine till it was made to fly again polished it off!!!! Were we wild about that or were we?!'

In Palestine Britain was busy making fresh trouble for itself; an empire running down always perhaps develops self-destructive impulses. London was committed to a Jewish National Home, as firmly as Washington to an expansionist Israel later on, and turned a deaf ear to anxious remonstrances from the Indian government, which, sorely in need of Muslim support against Hindu nationalism, kept pressing for concessions to the Arabs and a rein on Jewish immigration. Here too, despite misgivings felt by some, security was entrusted to the air force, but with little or no back-up on the ground. When in 1929 the 'Wailing Wall riots' spread from Jerusalem across the country, two platoons had to be flown from Egypt to Jerusalem to relieve the exhausted police; warships from Malta, one an aircraft carrier, landed men; motor transport multiplied scanty manpower by providing mobility; two armoured trains were improvised for the protection of Gaza. Technology was rising to the occasion, but from then on the RAF had ground troops at its disposal. In 1936 in spite of further warnings from India the cabinet resolved to put down Arab revolt by force, which meant bombing villages, shooting suspects without trial, and filling internment camps. Ten years later, on 22 July, British headquarters in Jerusalem were blown up, with ninety-one lives lost, by the ungrateful Zionists, who were showing themselves highly proficient in terrorist tactics and practised them against Arab and Briton alike. In May 1948 the miserable record of the Mandate came to an end, and its sequel, the first Arab-Israeli war, began.

In Egypt war burdens had inflamed national discontents, and in March 1919 deportation under martial law of Zaghlul and other leaders of the nationalist Wafd party provoked riotous demonstrations and sabotage. Students were in the van, as they were beginning to be everywhere in patriotic and left-wing movements. Lieutenant Mackie, Edinburgh graduate and wartime officer, returned from leave to find things in an uproar. A train from Bilbers with some officers on board was stopped by 'a howling mob armed with sticks', and Europeans were molested; they had to use their pistols, and, the track in front having been torn up, get the train back to its starting-point. 'As usual', he complained – the complaint was at least a very usual one from the army – 'the people on the spot had their hands tied from Whitehall' in the first days.[27] But there were still plenty of troops on hand from the War, Indians among them, so that General Bulfin was able to act at once over the whole country, and with energetic help from bombers and armoured cars order was restored within a month.

From what Gwynn learned, the army went about its work in the enlightened spirit he advocated, the troops showing 'admirable restraint'.[28] But history as written and history as scribbled may differ widely. 'It must be admitted', another officer wrote home about the British troops, 'that the behaviour of a minority had done little to improve the British image'.[29] Mackie recalled later how 'Each agitator that we got hold of gave away another after a little gentle persuasion.' This was the function of Serg.-Maj. Robson and a rhinoceros-hide whip. He extracted money from his patients as well as information, it was surmised, and pocketed most of it. Yells were heard, but our phlegmatic young Scot 'did not enquire too deeply into his methods'. Mackie was reticent too about a shipload of Australians, homeward bound, who were stopped and called in as reinforcements. 'What the Australians said, and what they did to the Egyptians is not for me to write about!' Gurkhas at Bilbers were 'a trigger happy crowd'; one of them raked a throng of demonstrators with a machine-gun before he could be pulled up.[30] In the eccentric British style, a concession followed: early in 1922 Egyptian independence was recognized, but subject to British control of defence and the Canal.

In the Sudan most junior officers were Egyptians from the Cairo military school, who brought with them too many newfangled political ideas. In 1924 the murder in Cairo of Sir Lee Stack, governor-general of the Sudan, allowed the British to demand removal of all Egyptian troops. Egypt acquiesced, but there were mutinies of Sudanese in Khartoum and elsewhere. In the capital an army building where some diehards held out had to be reduced by howitzer fire. 'None of the desperate garrison was found alive.'[31] Among such men the old Mahdist passion could still flare up, while the small new educated class was turning to different ideas. After this episode the Sudanese battalions were disbanded; again much trust was reposed in aeroplanes, which might get out of order but would never get out of hand. By the early 1930s there were a hundred landing-grounds distributed over the vast country.

In Burma too a discordant mixture of thinking old and new seems to show in the rising of 1930-2. Gwynn felt able to dismiss it as 'a widespread outbreak of banditry', displaying 'the natural instincts of the Burman when released from control.'[32] Saya San, the leader, appears to have been an extremist breaking away from the staid national movement, and going to the people, but by descending to their political level rather than trying to raise them to his. He had some disaffected monks as allies, and played on old superstitious trust in a tattooing rite to immunize against bullets. In the difficult terrain there was not much scope for the newer methods of warfare, and opposition had to be worn down by small columns slogging through the jungle, much as in the original pacification. Saya San was caught in July 1931 and hanged. But the experience must have contributed to Britain's disinclination to start once more on the uphill task, against much more sophisticated opponents now, after 1945.

Whatever inadequacies might come to light, air power was establishing itself as the grand new asset. It reflected and accentuated the widening estrangement between rulers and ruled brought about by nationalism and repression. In 1932 at the Disarmament Conference the British government joined in the cry against bombardment of towns from the air, but it could not bring itself to renounce its new-found celestial empire. It would not give up 'the use of such machines as are necessary for police purposes in outlying places'. Its representative congratulated himself on having saved the bombing aeroplane. As Lloyd George put it in homely phrase, other countries would have agreed to a ban, 'but we insisted on reserving the right to bomb niggers!'[33] Imperial chickens would soon be coming home to roost in places like Coventry. After Guernica what had seemed a godsent means for Europe to maintain its sway over other peoples wore the look of a way to self-immolation instead.

Other empires too were having their distempers, and needing all the aid that technology could offer them. In the Dutch East Indies economic conditions provoked labour struggles and attempted risings, culminating in 1926 in a communist-led revolt in western Java and Sumatra. Javanese troops seem to have wavered in their allegiance, and it was with the help of others from the ever reliable Christian island of Amboina that the rebels were crushed. Very harsh reprisals followed, the alarmed Dutch trying to put down not only the Left but all nationalist activity however moderate. In Indochina the French were doing the same. Vietnam however differed from Indonesia in being a nation, and it was close enough to its past to remember independence and the struggle to defend it, but far enough from it now to be capable of a new orientation; and like all the Far East it was free from the religious obsessions of India and the Islamic world.

Armed resistance on the old lines was petering out by 1900; the Great War hastened the transition from one era to another. As in French Africa, conscription of soldiers and labourers caused risings;

and many of those who returned from Europe brought back with them what in Japan were called by the police 'dangerous thoughts'. In 1925 a communist party was founded. At the end of the 1920s nationalists were concentrating propaganda on soldiers, who were receptive because many were serving unwillingly, and most of these were taken from among the poorest countryfolk. A rising was planned for early 1930, with the Yen Bay army base in the north as its central point. On February 10 the garrison rose, and a red flag was hoisted from the citadel. But co-ordination was poor, and the response elsewhere inadequate. Rebel villages were bombed, with heavy loss of life. Much of the leadership was caught and summarily executed. Ho Chi Minh escaped to Hong Kong; and in effect the French, by trying to destroy liberal nationalism, were opening the door wider to communism. Labour unrest went on in the 1930s, under the spur of the world depression which worsened the misery of the whole colonial world. The iron-fisted governor-general Robin made free use of the Legion, whose malign shadow had lain on the country ever since the conquest.

Repression and torture aroused protest in France, though as in every such case not nearly enough. Meanwhile in its Syrian mandate France was meeting with the same unfriendliness as the British in Iraq, and was less willing to retire after a while to the back of the stage. In October 1925 Damascus was subjected to two days of shelling, and machine-gun fire from tanks, which had an opportunity to demonstrate their versatility, taking the place of infantrymen in the street fighting which they always detested. In Morocco there were outbreaks in 1933-4. When George Orwell was convalescing at Marrakech in 1938, Frenchmen watching Senegalese soldiers march by seemed to him to be saying to themselves: 'How long before they turn their guns in the other direction?'[34]

iii. Imperialism and fascism

While the colonial world was stumbling towards more progressive modes of thinking, Europe was being dragged backward by fascism. In its witch's cauldron imperialism was a chief ingredient. Göring was the son of a colonial governor. Aimé Césaire wrote of the brutalizing influence at home of brutalism in the colonies – 'l'*ensauvagement* du continent', a grotesque reversal of the civilizing mission. In France fascism gained considerable ground. Portugal was under its clericalist version of dictatorship, closely geared to control

201

and exploitation of the African territories. After 1931, under the 'National' government, Britain shifted a long way to the right. Nehru felt that British rule in India was getting worse, and verging on fascism. An English dissident there noted the spread of police espionage in Britain, with a general in charge of Scotland Yard. 'Have our Indian police methods crept homeward . . . ?'[35]

Mussolini's Italy is a glaring case of this interplay. Libya helped to lead it into the Great War, the War into fascism, fascism back into Africa. His credit shaken by the Slump, at the close of 1934 Mussolini issued a directive to his commanders for the conquest of Abyssinia. It threw some of them into alarm, and there was 'almost total confusion' in the preparations.[36] But invasion was launched in October 1935, the main thrust from Eritrea in the north. A quarter of a million Italian soldiers were soon in the field; the bloated armies of Europe's own battlefields were going to be needed now for colonial wars. Five-sixths of them were conscripts, often jealous of the better conditions and more liberal praise enjoyed by the Blackshirts, who by some accounts performed less well when it came to fighting. They volunteered partly in the hope of 'cheap and exotic pleasure with the native girls', and the army's favourite song was '*Faccetta nera, bella abissina*'.[37] There were also some 60,000 native troops from Eritrea and Somalia, a certain number of whom deserted to the other side. These huge forces were accompanied by 150 planes, a figure increased as the campaign proceeded, 700 cannon, 6000 machine-guns, and 150 tanks. In addition there were 200 machine-gun carriers, copied from a Vickers model, lightly armoured and manoeuvrable.

De Bono, the first commander, very soon had to be replaced by Badoglio, with orders to push on more energetically. Planes went in advance, native troops, to whom was reserved the honour of most of the rough work, came next. Progress was still not rapid, and not only because of forest and ravine. Abyssinia was fighting for its life. Its forces still as in Menelik's day consisted of a small regular army, and ill-armed feudal or local levies. Four bodies of these auxiliaries barred the way to Addis Ababa, too often exhausting themselves in hopeless stand-up fights. As so often, there was nothing else that an array so out of date could do. At Enderta in February 1936 Badoglio's artillery fired 23,000 shells, his airmen dropped 396 tons of explosives. Next month at Shire the Italians suffered nearly a thousand casualties, and Ras Imru's men only four instead of ten times as many. Resistance was stiff enough to sting the invaders into indiscriminate bombing of villages and lavish use of mustard gas, which had horrific effects. There was also it seems deliberate razing of foreign Red Cross stations, practically the only medical aid the defenders had. Fascism had to win quickly, because a long-drawn war would be embarrassing both at home and internationally. It was a relief to Badoglio when Haile Selassie at length decided to risk his own trained corps, the only one left intact, in a pitched battle. It took place at Mai Chew, on ground more favourable to the invaders, and was their decisive victory, bravely though the Abyssinians fought. Most of the Italian losses fell on Eritrean troops.

Both the Duce's sons, and his son-in-law Ciano, as well as sundry royal dukes – following the Orleanist example in Algeria – were in the war, gathering glory for themselves and the regime; Vittorio Mussolini wrote a book about his exploits as an airman, with an account of the pleasure of watching a band of horsemen turn into a blossoming red rose as a bomb fell among them. As Lord Wavell, turned historian, puts it, this war 'showed how greatly the application of science to war had widened the gulf between the forces of civilized and uncivilized nations.'[38] Two hundred correspondents flocked to Abyssinia at the outset, but few went far or stayed long. Foreign opinion followed mostly predictable lines. It ranged from condemnation of Italian aggression to the flippant indifference of a British journalistic allusion to 'that vivid show in Abyssinia'. Pious Italians had the comfort of knowing that the Catholic world was on their side. Their own Catholic journals played on the theme of the true faith following the flag. Haile Selassie was painted as a bloodthirsty tyrant, just as Theebaw and so many others had been. Hungry Italians were being promised land for settlement, but development was sluggish and costly` because guerrillas kept the countryside in turmoil. Immigrants were shut up in towns, their soldiers in forts. Mussolini's orders for all 'rebels' to be shot were scarcely needed by the viceroy, Marshal Graziani, already 'a by-word for brutality' in Libya.[39]

Fascism had carried fire and sword into Africa, and Africa was soon to assist in imposing fascism on another European country. Spain's Moroccan colony had all along been a peculiarly meaningless one, where any army could safely be expected to appear at its worst. 'Fraud and favouritism reigned in most sectors of the military hierarchy'; in the garrison stations life 'seems to have been about as dissolute as a depraved imagination might conceive.'[40] A force of Moorish *regulares* was enrolled in 1911; all its NCOs as well as officers were Spanish. In 1920 a sort of foreign legion, the *Tercios de Extranjeros*, was set up, with Franco as its first commander. Most of the men were in fact Spaniards, of the most disreputable sort, or soldiers willing to stay on in Morocco. They were needed to help in coping with a rebellion, caused in part by stories of molestation of women, in the Riff mountains of the coastal area opposite Gibraltar, rising steeply not far inland. It found a gifted leader in Abd el Krim, educated son of a headman. His people were tribesmen of Berber stock, often at odds among themselves as the Kabyles of Algeria had been, but like them ingenious at learning to use captured equipment. Many of Spain's native recruits had come from these mountains.

In 1921 a heavy defeat was inflicted at Annual on a Spanish army trying to penetrate the region. Losses in the retreat, or rather panic flight, and then at other posts, may have totalled over 8000 dead, with hundreds more taken prisoner. It was one of the worst disasters ever suffered by European arms. Spain was staggered, and the government fell. Like the Kurds, the Riffians were a race divided by alien frontier lines: many lived on the French side, and the struggle spread there. France's war hero Pétain was sent to direct the French share in the largest joint colonial undertaking since the second China war. His offensive got under way in September 1925; bombing from the air was an important adjunct. A Spanish landing in the Bay of Alhucemas, not far from Abd el Krim's makeshift capital at Axdir, led to its surprise and capture.

Alfonso XIII had been compromised by the catastrophe of Annual, and was glad to safeguard himself by welcoming General Primo de Rivera as dictator in 1923. He was the son of a governor-general of the Philippines, and had served both there and in Morocco. The 1925 success shed some lustre on him, which was reflected on to the throne. When he was compelled to retire in 1930 it was only a year more before the monarchy fell. Morocco remained as a nursery of reaction. It attracted ambitious career officers, who could win promotion quicker there than at home, and enjoy more power. In its atmosphere of repression and brute force were being reared the *africanistas*, men of the same breed as Napoleon III's *Africains*, who were to overthrow the Republic. Franco was one; Mola, who came of an old Cuban military family, another; Queipo de Llano a third.

Moorish regulars and legionaries were brought into Spain in 1934 to take part in crushing the miners' rising in Asturias. Without the Moroccan base the rising of 1936 could scarcely have got going. Spanish and Moorish troops were ferried over by air, with Mussolini's help. Moors were promptly despatched to all the most critical areas, and further supplies, largely hired through feudal chiefs, were collected. Altogether during the war, by official figures, about 80,000 of them were employed. They made excellent cannon-fodder, displaying 'blind obedience' to their Spanish officers.[41] Very likely however they were happy to take a vicarious revenge on any white men. Outside Madrid they 'as usual bayoneted the wounded'.[42] A prisoner from the International Brigade found that Moorish guards were allowed to enter cells and beat their occupants daily, and that it was a good idea to scream as loudly as possible; they were then sooner satisfied, and went off on their rounds.[43]

Franco in power kept a Moorish bodyguard, and Spain's place in Africa was made the most of to impress the public. In 1940 when Italy joined in Hitler's attack on France there was an eruption of imperial ardour in the Spanish press, as if, wrote Lord Templewood, in Madrid as special envoy, all Morocco was about to be conquered and the African empire of Charles V's dreams carved out. Templewood (Sir Samuel Hoare), for years Secretary for India, had a 'sympathetic and attractive friend' in the foreign minister, Colonel Beigdeber, who had made his name in Morocco. 'To Franco and Beigdeber', he cautioned the Foreign Office, 'Morocco is as much as ever India was to Lord Lawrence, or, in our own times, to Michael O'Dwyer....'[44]

iv. The Second World War

Delvers into the causes of the second World War in recent years have been finding one of them in Britain's insecure position in Asia, which became an argument for appeasement in Europe. In February 1932 for instance, at the time of the Japanese onslaught on Shanghai, the chiefs of staff warned the Committee of Imperial Defence of how perilously exposed was Britain's whole stake in the east. Whether or not there was some wilful overstatement, the effect was the same, and the empire can be said to have helped to push Britain into the second World War as into the first, even if it also helped the country to fight its way through both. Churchill's 'finest hour' oration in 1940 wound up with a call to defend not Britain but the British empire, and keep it intact for the next thousand years.

By contrast with 1914-18 there was now no united front of empire-owners, and propaganda and counter-propaganda to colonial peoples played a far bigger part. Japan found many willing listeners. But in addition it had been fighting for years in China, and although that most gigantic of all colonial wars was only half won a great deal was learned from it militarily. The fruit could be seen in the use of air power, and of specially designed types of planes, or in the artfully constructed bunkers and fox-holes or machine-gun pits that made the Japanese so tenacious in defence, as in Burma or New Guinea. During the war Britain had painful lessons to learn, both military and political; they taught it both skill and prudence in confronting colonial nationalism after the war. Holland and Portugal had no such chastening experience, France not much; America, coming up on the sidelines as the next claimant to hegemony, had too little, because its war in Asia was mostly on the sea or in the air: it took over far too uncritically the European mirage of government from the skies.

Japan like its predecessors made considerable use of colonial troops; Britain was still, if for the last time, supreme in this department, with its Indian army as always in the forefront. It grew from 189,000 men in 1939 to two and a half million in 1945, the largest volunteer army ever to serve under any flag as a panegyrist said.[45] Although Indian national consciousness was far stronger now than a generation earlier, far more soldiers were raised than in 1914–18, and more easily. There was more pressure now of need for jobs, and opportunity for more diversified talent. Recruiting was extended to provinces and communities previously classed as non-martial, and the army thus became more representative of the nation. Anxious care was taken to keep morale high, through radio programmes from stations like Cairo, army publications, a corps of popular entertainers visiting the fronts; it was a far cry from the old days of the Company and its ill-used sepoys. 'Indianization' of the army was being transformed from fiction to fact: from a thousand the number of Indian officers rose to nearly sixteen thousand. This by itself was enough to make long-continued British rule impossible, but for the time being it did much to ensure loyalty. A British officer in the Indian army thought that 'for reasons of prestige and home interest' British press reports were more open-handed with praise to British than to Indian exploits, and that Indian press accounts were more reliable.[46] There was a far bigger Indian press than at the time of the Great War, and All India Radio was fairly well developed, and run almost entirely by Indians.

On a minor scale a second Indian Mutiny occurred, among troops overseas who fell into enemy hands, chiefly at Singapore, that eastern Dunkirk without a rescue. In April 1941 the extremist Congressman Subhas Bose made his way to Germany, seeking co-operation. All he got was a long monologue from the Führer in his Wolf's Lair: India he was told would not be fit for self-government for another century and a half.[47] At Tokyo in June 1943 he was better received; he could fit into Japan's ostensible purpose of liberating Asia from its Western rulers. An Indian National Army was formed, chiefly from war prisoners, some though not all of whom joined under intimidation.

Taking part in the drive through Burma to the Indian frontier, they lost heart at finding no welcome from fellow-Indians on guard there. Inside India feelings were of the mixed kind likely to flourish in a country deprived of political responsibility. People found an emotional satisfaction in listening to Bose's rhetorical broadcasts, but went on working with or for the British. Still, the INA's existence was part of the writing on the wall for the Raj. Another was the naval mutiny at Bombay in February 1946.

Africa was a rich recruiting-ground, as in 1914-18, with the salient difference that, luckily for its African soldiers, France dropped out so quickly. In British Africa the King's African Rifles were prominent. In peacetime, one of their officers felt that although duty with them might demand more than average competence, 'good service with the KAR is rarely appreciated in Whitehall'.[48] Now the force was enlarged, and for the first time saw service outside the continent, in Burma. African soldiers were evolving more quickly than white attitudes towards them. What they all shared, a British officer of Christian convictions wrote, was 'the perpetual subconscious irritation that they are regarded as an inferior race'; he saw some army doctors treat them 'as though they were like rather loathsome animals'.[49] Settler mentality showed most superciliously among former cavalry officers in Kenya, who not only looked down on 'nigger troops' but found it hard to be civil to officers of the KAR, mostly drawn from less stylish regiments than those they had adorned.[50] Some of the men came from American mission schools, and sang marching songs about black Americans landing from the air to deliver them from white rule.[51]

In Abyssinia by 1938 Italy had increased its native troops to about 200,000, many of them Muslims; but when war came a good proportion of them abandoned their employers. A resolute stand was made at some points, especially at the mountain fortress of Keren. None the less, Italy's power crumbled quickly. The brutality of the conquest, so fresh in its subjects' memory, helped to ensure its collapse, once challenged from outside. In the fighting here the 4th and 5th Indian divisions were conspicuous, and men of the KAR also took part. So did South Africans, whom Smuts after a visit to them described euphorically in a radio talk as 'the happy warriors' of a new dispensation, upholding 'the spiritual order of the universe'[52] – no doubt including apartheid.

14

THE DISMANTLING OF THE EMPIRES

i. A new era

On the old order in Africa the second World War had a deeply unsettling impact. Over most of Asia western domination was now broken, or fatally compromised by its easy collapse in face of the Japanese. In 1942 the little attachment of the Burmese to the retreating British could not be blinked; desertions from the 1st Burma Division were numerous. Even in the Soviet Union old bitternesses might return to the surface. Germany was able to tamper with some of the Caucasian peoples; conservative Muslim dislike of Soviet rule, or modernity, feeding on memories of the resistance to the tsars, had gone on smouldering. Four of the seven nationalities of the northern Caucasus were deported *en bloc*. Britain was prudent enough to avoid the post-1918 folly of hanging on to the whole of an empire now beyond its strength. India, Burma, Ceylon were all abandoned before the end of 1947, and resources thus freed for other areas. That the delirium of dying empires was to be so convulsive and prolonged was the responsibility, more than of anyone else, of the French.

To combat the new mass awakening of the third world, the West could again, as after 1918, pin many hopes to new strides in military technology, improvements on what Dunsterville had called 'the various ingenuities of frightfulness that accompany modern war'.[1] In 1942 experts working at Harvard University invented napalm, to supersede the petrol used by old flame-throwers. Large quantities of it were also used in the incendiary raids on Japan, and in the Korean war 165-gallon fire-bombs were 'dropped with devastating effect on enemy troops'; in Vietnam too it was 'used with telling effect'. Helicopters were only in an experimental stage before 1945, but came on the scene in the Korean war. They were soon evolving into gunboats of the air and becoming an indispensable requisite of colonial administration. On the ground there were now tanks for every purpose. It was chiefly with colonial disturbances in view that the Saracen armoured car, still in service today, was being developed in the early 1950s, with a speed of 45 mph and sterling cross-country performance.

In addition the War had hatched corps of paratroopers and others trained to special toughness and ruthlessness, who could be trusted to make good use of any new means of killing people. They were élite formations, romanticized by themselves and their advertisers, but often in practice very much like such forerunners as the death-squads of Hitler's SS. The empires would have to fight far harder to keep their hold than they had in the past to gain it, and would go to any and every length. Too often ingenious technology was accompanied by equally sophisticated methods of terror, including the scarcely concealed use of torture. Partly to distract public attention from this side of things, partly as a last chapter of the old naïve faith in the blessings of empire, repression sometimes alternated with benevolent policies, or promises, intended to disarm hostility by kindness, to 'win hearts and minds' as the British learned to say in their 'confrontation' in Borneo.

1945 saw a prompt patching up of differences among empire proprietors, a return to the readiness to collaborate against native mischief-makers shown intermittently in the past. British generals in Asia at the end of the War – by whom Mountbatten is said to have been overborne – took the lead; soon a network of regional pacts and pledges of mutual support was being spun, a kind of new Holy Alliance. It was directed against nationalism, but ostensibly against communism, because this gave it a better look, and with a good measure of realism because the most energetic and resourceful colonial leadership was communist. Callwell was aware before 1914 that the true guerrilla fighter was 'on an altogether higher plane than the savage or the normal irregular';[2] now there was the further asset of modern-minded political leadership. Where communism took root it was the best guarantee of a movement acquiring the virtues of organization by which in earlier days Europe triumphed over Afro-Asia. Recognition of social problems, and of the need of social programmes to give nationalism a broader base, was bringing into action the mostly peasant masses. At the other end of the scale was the increasing prominence of intelligentsias, drawn from student movements more and more radical in outlook.

Old colonial movements defended the past, the new ones were creating a future. Similarities of outlook could facilitate co-operation between movements in neighbouring countries, countering the mutual aid of the imperialists, or help from countries which regained their independence to those still struggling. During the epoch of conquest outside help had been virtually unknown, each people waging its fight and going down by itself. Together these novel sources of strength could be a combination impossible for any technology to overcome. 'The Communists have displayed almost unbelievable staying power', a journalist writing on south-east Asia in 1969 admitted; communist movements there had shown 'tremendous capacity' for undergoing huge losses without breaking.[3]

In Indonesia, immediately on the Japanese surrender, Soekarno proclaimed a free republic. A British force arrived, to take custody of the Japanese but also to restore Dutch rule. In November 1945 there was hard fighting at the naval base of Surabaya between it and the patriots, and air bombardments and harsh repression followed.[4] A protest was lodged by Nehru against the use of Indian troops in this and similar operations, last and least creditable of all the countless actions fought by the Indian army under British direction. Early in 1946 an American woman war-correspondent visited the nationalist-held area of Java, and found it a scene of confusion; she saw Soekarno, with insight, as an eloquent windbag.[5] Poor rebel organization enabled the Dutch, now reinforced, to launch in July 1947 what they called a 'police action'. Blockaded and short of ammunition, the nationalists were penned into a part of southern Java, while elsewhere the Dutch, profiting by regional discords, set up puppet governments.

At the end of 1948 they broke off a truce and resumed the offensive, seizing Jogjakarta and most of the insurgent leadership. In face of their 100,000 soldiers the nationalists were reduced to guerrilla tactics, but in these they proved quite skilful. Further than this their leaders' compound of populist demagogy and religious appeals could not carry them. But the puppet regimes crumbled, and international opinion was hardening against the Dutch. In 1949 they were obliged to negotiate, and the next year Indonesia became fully sovereign. Only West Irian, or western New Guinea, useless except as a face-saver, remained Dutch. In 1956 American missionaries, when a mission station was raided by Kapauku tribesmen, saw Dutch soldiers land from a squadron of planes and at once proceed to lob mortar shells into thickets where the marauders were hiding, before tracking them down one by one; nearly two hundred were killed.[6]

After 1945 'there were few periods when part of the British Army was not engaged in active operations somewhere.'[7] Old habits and hankerings kept Britain meddling in the Middle East. In Egypt 1954 brought Colonel Nasser to power, and in July 1956 the Suez Canal was nationalized. It has been alleged, not too improbably, that a plan for Nasser's murder was submitted by MI6.[8] Instead the Tory government entered into a clumsy conspiracy with France and Israel. Israel invaded Egypt, providing its partners with an excuse to intervene under pretence of safeguarding the canal. There was a chorus of denunciation of this brigandage by the UNO, USA, and USSR, and in Britain itself. Inglorious failure and the unseating of the prime minister Eden made the rash adventure a milestone in Britain's imperial decline.

In 1962 Aden with its military base was tied into the Federation of South Arabia, a bundle of reliably medieval sheikhdoms, in order to suffocate urban opposition. Unexpectedly revolt broke out against the feudal rulers, and in the spring of 1964 bombing raids were made on the tribesmen, while 'food control' measures that winter meant burning of crops and driving thousands out of their villages in the hills – a *modus operandi* derived from north-west frontier policing, and by remoter ancestry from the conquest of Ireland. Resistance was firm enough, with some protest in Britain over what was learned of the repression, to make the government decide on closing the Aden base and surrendering power in 1967 to a republic of South Yemen. Oman, the protected sultanate at the other tip of southern Arabia, was the one British success hereabouts. Occasionally a glimpse of protracted repression there, again including destruction of food supplies, got into the British press, but a conspiracy of silence was kept up by the front benches. British officers went on being lent to the sultan, as a species of official mercenaries, and found Oman a useful training-ground for experiments in counter-insurgency. Sporadic fighting went on until 1975, with Iran and Pakistan and half a dozen other despotic regimes joining in against the rebels.[9] The colonialist united front was by now much broader than the West alone.

Another territory where Britain was prepared to fight and go on fighting, on a much bigger scale, was Malaya, with its tin and rubber. Capitalist interests had brought in large minorities of Chinese and Indians, inevitably obnoxious to the Malay population. Jungle resistance by some Chinese to the Japanese occupation forces left behind a core of perhaps five thousand devoted communists, past masters in such fighting, and with able leaders in men like Chin Peng. When trouble broke out in 1948 and a state of emergency was declared, government and left wing each accused the other of being the aggressor; the government did at least jump at an opportunity to strike hard at the trade unions. Very little active support for the rising was forthcoming except from sections of the Chinese community; militants never numbered more than eight or ten thousand, and their exploits could not go far beyond surprise descents on police-posts or plantations.

Sir Henry Gurney and his assistant General Briggs resorted, like so many other colonial governments, to a wholesale uprooting of people, in this case the Chinese squatter population, which was rounded up and removed to 'new villages'. Here, surrounded by barbed wire fences, they were under watch and ward of searchlights and machine-guns. Thereby the officially designated 'Communist Terrorists', or 'CTs', were cut off from a source of recruits and supplies; an extra gain was a pool of cheap labour available for employers. Gurney was ambushed and killed in October 1951, the insurgents' most successful year. General Templer then became High Commissioner, civil and military authority were more completely fused, and before he retired in 1954 the back of the rebellion had been broken.

Quite large forces had to be deployed. British troops included 'national service' men: imperial exigencies kept conscription going for several years after the World War. Besides a large force of Malay armed police, there were Gurkhas, Africans, and at one stage a band of Dyak head-hunters from Borneo, esteemed as trackers. Thousands of arrests were made, many were deported, some executed. Most of the CTs killed, a regimental history tells us, 'were caught in skilfully laid ambushes, which usually were based on Special Branch information.'[10] In 1950, when helicopters were brought into play, it was announced that new bombing techniques were being worked out: bombers would be used as artillery, seeking their own targets instead of being only appendages to ground operations.

In 1953 a total of 4500 air strikes in the past five years was reported,[11] and in 1956 an Australian squadron of 'Hell-bombers' could boast of 40 sorties in four days and 480,000 pounds of explosives dropped.[12] Little by little resistance was worn down, but it was not without political consequences. In 1957 Malaya was granted independence, under conservative Malay rule, and in 1958 the 'Emergency' was declared at an end. Ten thousand rebels had been killed, nine thousand, most civilians, on the other side. Lessons learned by the army were codified at a Jungle Warfare School in Malaya, and British methods were widely admired and came to be regarded as 'a model of counter-insurgency': Americans and others bound for Vietnam received training at the school.

ii. Wars of liberation against France

1945 found France's Afro-Asian subjects rising up against it very much as its subject peoples in Europe did in 1813–14. Among the varied motives and passions which impelled the French to react so pugnaciously, those of the army stand out. Most of its officers belonged to a force which had suffered humiliating defeat in 1940 and inglorious inaction thereafter, at home or in Africa, and they were now in an ugly and cantankerous mood. Their ranks underwent very little of a purge at the end of the War; they far outnumbered the Free French contingent which gained a place in the officer corps. Both sorts agreed on keeping out men from the Resistance, which was largely communist. All this meant that the colonial wing of the army was more powerful than ever. In one sense the officer corps was growing more democratic, with fewer entrants coming from St Cyr and the École Polytechnique, more being promoted NCOs or rankers. But this was far from making it any more progressive; it may in some ways have had an opposite result.

To pull it together at the end of the World War, action was imperative, a washing of the spears as a Zulu might have called it. In May 1945 a stormy demonstration at Sétif was fired on, from the air as well as by ground troops, and some 15,000 Algerians may have been killed. During 1947–8 an unknown but very large number of rebels or suspects were killed in an abortive rising in Madagascar. Bleeding was still the imperial cure for all political distempers, just as it was once the universal nostrum of the medical faculty. An attempt to regain control of Syria by force in 1945 had fizzled out, partly because Britain disliked it as a further unsettlement of the Middle East. It was apparently decided in London that the French must clear out, and in return would be helped to reassert themselves in Indochina, where they could do no harm except to the Indochinese.[13]

With the World War the Vietnam nationalist movement crushed so remorselessly in 1930 raised its head, and there was again harsh repression after a revolt in the south in December 1940, with thousands killed and many other thousands arrested. In May 1941 a gathering of exiles in south China, initiated by Ho Chi Minh but including a variety of parties, set up the united front which came to be known as the Vietminh. The French rulers were soon losing face by their tame submission to the Japanese. In September 1945, with the Japanese collapse, a republic headed by Ho Chi Minh was proclaimed. British forces arriving to take charge of the surrendering

Japanese were under the command of General Gracey, an officer of aboriginal type whom the thought of treating with upstart natives, who might actually be communists, filled with horror. He re-armed the French, and went on to give them energetic backing. Many of his troops were Indian; the British lion was using its false teeth to the end. Soon the nationalists were driven out of Saigon, where their strength and unity were less than in the north.

With the provisional government at Hanoi in the north Paris negotiated, or prevaricated, until late in 1946, when the army felt strong enough for another move. On 23 November it issued a declaration of intent by bombarding the northern port of Haiphong from the sea; at least six thousand people seem to have been killed. All the bigger towns fell to the invaders; Hanoi in February 1947 after an obstinate defence chiefly by its workers. Throughout that year the French were striving to complete their reoccupation of the north, making use of armoured river vessels and dropping parachutists in surprise attacks. But the Vietminh remained unbroken. Under desperate stress the whole coalition was pushed further to the left, just as happened in the Spanish civil war. Communist party discipline, and useful foreign links, helped to ensure it the guiding role.

In the armed struggle another communist, Vo-Nguyen Giap, was taking the lead as decisively as Ho on the political front. Born in 1909, in a peasant family in the north, he studied at the university of Hanoi, where he was impressed by the history of the French Revolution and its lessons in mass mobilization. France may not have planted any tree of liberty in its colonies, but it did plant a tree of knowledge, which bore unpredictable fruit. At first guerrilla activity was the limit of what was possible, but it was always carefully directed. Small arms such as bazookas and grenades could be made in jungle workshops; presently heavier equipment too was produced in rear bases, while growing quantities were captured from the French, often of American origin. It was an immense advantage when, with Chiang Kai-shek finally dislodged, China became a friend and supplier to the Vietminh. Meanwhile the nucleus of a regular army was being put together, each unit retaining the ability to manoeuvre on its own; this was essential particularly in the south.

Complain as the French army might of the politicians at home, conscripts could not be sent to Indochina. As an élite striking force a sort of imperial gendarmerie was being formed, with Vietnam as its starting-point, the *Parachutistes Coloniaux* or *Berets rouges*, with a central reserve at their base at Bayonne. Now with a parachute battalion of its own, the Foreign Legion was flocking back to

Indochina from early in 1946, about half of it Germans indoctrinated by Nazism. Troops from Africa included Moroccans, Algerians, and Senegalese. In the name of a puppet emperor, Bao Dai, recalled from his haunts on the Riviera, some 200,000 men were recruited to a 'National army', by compulsion or by the bait of food and pay held out to the classes suffering most acutely from poverty and wartime dislocation. As soldiers they were of dubious value, and desertions were many. This inordinate number of non-French troops put a heavy strain on the cadres of the regular army, the officers and NCOs who had to command them; a high proportion of the 20,000 Frenchmen killed belonged to these ranks. Financially too the war was a heavy drain, but this was relieved by subsidies from America, outraged by the loss of China and in 1950 plunging into the Korean war in order to bolster its position in the Far East.

Like most imperial wars of the final phase this one reproduced appallingly the worst features of nineteenth-century conquest. Besides outbursts of savagery among men unhinged by the strain of danger close at hand, there was now the more cold-blooded diabolism of the new military technology, to which enemies of alien race were no more than animal pests, or germs to be 'flushed out'. As in Malaya, multitudes were being herded into settlements which were also prisons. Crops were destroyed in the fields. It is not hard to believe the allegation that to keep up the sagging morale of the puppet troops they were given *carte blanche* 'to destroy, rape and pillage'.[14] 'Pacification' was coming to mean air-bombing, massacre, systematic use of torture. A French participant describes a captured saboteur being taken up in a plane and thrown out.[15] In a speech to the 12th Congress of the French Communist Party in April 1950 André Marty declared that it would not do to ascribe all the atrocities to SS men in the Legion: most of them were committed by Frenchmen whom the war was turning into criminals. When a sensational trial took place of those indicted for the shooting and burning of civilians in the village of Oradour during the occupation of France, a West German newspaper could retort: 'In Indochina there is an Oradour every week.'

In France there was deepening dislike of the 'dirty war'. Too flagrantly this 'defence of the West' against communism was only defending the profiteers who were making fortunes out of it. Every long war breeds its own vested interests; there was for instance a ramifying racket in currency exchange. To the army it seemed that it was being neglected, forgotten, its sacrifices ignored, and this showed in its hatred of press reporters. Late in 1950 France's best-known soldier, De Lattre de Tassigny, was sent out with full powers both military and civil. He converted much of the army into flexible *groupes mobiles*, intensified air operations, dropped more napalm; but he was soon compelled by illness to retire. His successors lost ground to the tenacious Giap, who warily avoided pitched battles but struck relentlessly at exposed points. By 1953 he was getting a firm foothold inside the Red River delta, where the French in the north were being cooped up, opposing to their chairs of blockhouses a network of fortified villages with tunnelled bolt-holes, very much as the communist-led Chinese peasantry had defended themselves against the Japanese. It was only in the daytime that the countryside still belonged to the French.

In May 1953 the world saw a new commander-in-chief, Navarre, paying his respects at Washington before taking up his duties. There was a buzz of talk about a 'Navarre Plan', which would roll the enemy up in a sequence of phases plotted with true French logic, starting with a drive to demolish the Vietminh in the south once for all. Giap's book on the war shows that he did not underrate his antagonist, but he soon found comfort in a conviction that Navarre was dissipating his strength – given as 230,000 men from Europe and Africa, 160,000 local levies – too widely. They were drawn into a further diversion by a Vietminh offensive in an area still French of the mountainous north-west. To block this, on 20 November a French force was dropped from the air to occupy Dien Bien Phu, a valley a dozen miles long close to the frontier with Laos. Giap's reply was to begin an encirclement. Prestige rather than utility forbade the French to withdraw; it was resolved to hold on, come what might.

The garrison was brought up to about 16,000, mostly Europeans and Africans; a large proportion were Legionaries. A fortified camp was formed partially sheltered by trenches, barbed wire, minefield. Though materials were lacking to complete these works, the position was a hard enough nut to crack, considering that heavy guns and supplies had to be hauled long distances, from the Vietminh rear bases, over forested hills, by the soldiers and thousands of labourers. On 13 March 1954, when the formal attack opened, Giap could claim a threefold superiority in numbers, and heavier fire-power. It was an artillery duel, with the assailants pushing their trenches closer and closer, and overrunning outlying posts one by one. Planes brought supplies from Hanoi; in all these colonial wars it was a vital factor that the westerners had total command of the air. But anti-aircraft guns took toll of the transport planes, and the two airfields were coming under fire. Both sides suffered heavy losses, and severe strain.

Giap hints at a crisis of nerve among his men, who had never before had work like this to do, in spite of the political teaching steadily carried on.[16] But morale in the polyglot French camp was sinking much lower. When the final assault came on 7 May there were still ten thousand defenders, but surrender was not long delayed.

It was the first victory over the West, except by Japan, in a battle fought by the two sides with equal weapons and on the same highly professional lines. Its repercussions were far greater than its significance simply in terms of French losses. France was tired of the contest. At Geneva a conference had met in April to wind up the Korean war, and it provided a convenient forum for ending the Vietnam war too. France dropped out; unhappily the USA took its place, and stopped fighting in Korea only to start fighting in Vietnam.

Meanwhile the French were jumping still more hastily out of the Vietnam frying-pan into the Algerian fire. Technically Indochina had been for the army 'an incomparable experience', imparting valuable lessons and suggesting novel experiments; but it did not teach French generals to open their eyes to the new reality of Afro-Asian nationalism. And the army was 'sentimentally and passionately attached to French North Africa',[17] as the scene of its most brilliant colonial successes, much as the British army had been attached to India. This meant principally Algeria, and there the intransigence of army and settler population reinforced each other. There could be no thought of belated concessions when sporadic outbreaks began in 1954, at first chiefly in the eastern uplands. Discontent must have been fanned by news from Vietnam; empires no longer consisted of scattered territories ignorant of one another's existence, and some of the cannon-fodder in Vietnam was Algerian; men who had served there came indeed to form 'the hard core of the rebel army'.[18]

When disorder spread into Morocco, with another Riff rising, Paris acted fairly promptly, conferring independence on Morocco and Tunisia in 1956 in the teeth of strong army disapproval. But Algerian revolt was spreading and taking on a more organized character. It benefited from the first by the sympathy of fellow-Muslims. It was at Cairo, late in 1958, that the FLN or National Liberation Front set up its provisional government, recognized by all Arab states. Arms came from Egypt; Morocco, and still more Tunisia, provided a sanctuary for rebel forces. Elaborate barriers with electrified wire had to be constructed by the French to seal the frontiers, and adjacent zones cleared of inhabitants.

Resistance did not develop the same heroic proportions as in Vietnam. Population was smaller, and there was less here than in the Far East either of national tradition or of genius for collective organization. Politically the FLN stood on a lower level than Ho Chi Minh's party, and produced no equivalent leadership; there were frustrating jealousies among the heads of the *wilaya* or military districts into which the country was divided. The main force was normally in reserve, much of it outside the country. It incurred heavy losses when it ventured on a series of regular engagements near the Tunisian border early in 1958. Mostly the struggle was waged by guerrilla action, and by terrorist methods, often of the kind that Fanon deplored, though he could comprehend them, in one of the most illuminating books inspired by any war of liberation.[19] It could seem at times that bombs were being thrown in order to coerce ordinary people into supporting the rebels; as with similar IRA doings, the psychology moulded by an intolerant religion demanded political unanimity. But French repression did far more to drive the Muslim population into approval of the rebellion.

To deal with something like 40,000 active opponents alive at any one time, given their high death-rate, the army of occupation was built up to about ten times that number. As was first shown by the Boer War, to wear down a determined enemy defending his homeland with modern weapons an immense numerical superiority is required. A proportion of the troops brought in were from black Africa. Algeria being in legal fiction part of metropolitan France, there could be no bar to employment of French conscripts. There was some draft-dodging, and some officers felt it incumbent on them to give their men simple lectures justifying the war. In many cases these officers must have been a good deal less intelligent or well-informed than some of their audience. There were conscripts who within the twenty-eight months to which the term of service had to be extended could be conditioned by the army into 'glorying in military exploits, brutality and medals.'[20] On the other hand there were impressive cases of Europeans in Algeria risking death and worse to help the rebels.[21]

Most of the ordinary troops were tied up in routine occupation duties and patrolling, systematized in the *quadrillage* or grid pattern of garrisons and outposts covering the entire country. This left only a limited reserve, and for a striking-force there was more and more reliance on the 45,000 or 50,000 paratroopers and Legionaries, with helicopters to add to mobility. Paratroopers prided themselves on being the élite of the army, and gazed self-consciously into the mirror of history, or historical fantasy; in the age of novelette, 'comic', cinema, radio-play, this kind of false consciousness, or deliberate acting of an artificial role, has entered increasingly into mass mentality. It was to General Massu's 10th Paratroop Division that police control of the city of Algiers was handed over, and it was by its ruthless efficiency that terrorism there was curbed.

'Counter-terrorism' was the order of the day, and torture in regular use. Once again the now familiar device of population removal was employed, and by 1959 two million villagers, a fifth of the population, had been transferred to new locations under military watch. There was enough tincture of French intellectuality in the army to set it spinning theories about a 'revolutionary war' against revolution, a blending of persuasion with coercion; a bureau was set up to direct 'psychological warfare'. Since blandishments were not and could not be accompanied by any tangible concessions, to appease land-hunger especially, not much came of it.

Psychological warfare may have had most effect by introducing officers to politics: 'a large number of them found it to be a fascinating game'.[22] If the FLN could not defeat the French army, it could bring down not merely a French government but the short-lived Fourth Republic. In 1958 suspicion of weakening determination at home started a ferment, chiefly among junior officers and paratroopers, and led to a seizure of power in Algeria and, on the demand of Massu and the commander-in-chief Salan, the return to office on 13 May of General De Gaulle. Diehards were soon disillusioned by his ambiguous tactics. At the end of March 1961, unable to sit on his uncomfortable fence any longer, he agreed to talks with the FLN, and there was a cease-fire. Next month revolt exploded among the French in Algeria, with a group of commanders seizing control: parachutists of the Legion were their heaviest battering-ram. Between 22 and 26 April there was a furore in France, with the prospect again as in May 1958 of parachutists descending on Paris and being welcomed by the right wing. But the revolt quickly lost momentum. Probably the army as a whole shrank from a Spanish-type civil war. Muslim demonstrations in Algeria finally deflated the myth cherished all through the fighting by French conservatives, of the mass of the people being at heart pro-French. It seems that conscripts may have had a share in paralysing the army coup, by showing their unwillingness to follow its leaders.

There was a tailpiece to the war in July at the French naval base of Bizerta, which was being enlarged while Tunisia was pressing as often before for its evacuation. A parachute force was sent, and took revenge for the failure in Algeria by bombing and machine-gunning the Arab town indiscriminately. A reporter's photograph showed a dead Tunisian with a circle and cross carved on his chest with a knife, the emblem of a French neo-fascist movement *Jeune Nation*.[23] The civilizing mission in north Africa was having an appropriate finish. Algerian independence, confirmed at last in March 1962, found the country wrecked and ruinous, with enormous numbers of dead and war-cripples, but also shaken free by the hurricane from much lumber of ideas and customs, the dead weight of a dead past. Women had been brought into the struggle by an early decision of the FLN, and responded courageously; prejudices against modern medicine as foreign were jettisoned.[24]

iii. Black Africa

In 1960 De Gaulle took a long step towards an Algerian settlement by conferring independence on France's possessions in black Africa. Freedom so granted might be little more than an extension of long-practised methods of indirect rule through dependable local managers. French governments have shown themselves very ready since then to intervene forcibly in these territories; colonial war has been transposed as it were into a fourth dimension. All the same, the second World War had given black Africa a more vigorous shaking up than the first. In the British sphere it was in Kenya that the consequences were earliest felt. In October 1952 attacks on white farms led to a state of emergency lasting nearly eight years. Kenya had never been a nation, and was indeed very much a jumble of squabbling tribal groups. Among these the Kikuyu people was the most important, but though most of the outlaws came from it and tribal brotherhood provided a loose framework, the embitterment that goaded them was primarily agrarian. In Kenya with its 'White Highlands' the evil of land-robbery by settlers – a repetition of the embezzling of village commons by landlords in nineteenth-century western Europe, especially England – was exceptionally gross. In the two World Wars, an old man said to an enquirer, Britain asked Africans for their young men to go and fight Germans and Italians, and now there were German and Italian planters occupying land from which they were shut out.[25] Resentment among poor Kikuyu peasants, and some town-dwellers, was turned against more prosperous fellow-Africans and Kikuyus as well as against whites, and the better-off Kikuyus were loyal to a government under which they were faring well enough.

Because the fighters came mostly from the poorest, most illiterate strata, with scarcely any leadership of more modern outlook, the rising took on the aspect, like many earlier ones in Afro-Asia, of a religious or magical cult. 'Mau-Mau' had some grotesque features which made it easy to denigrate the whole movement as a relapse into an abysmal past. Rebel weapons were at first not much more up to date, a few home-made guns the best of them. Nothing like a regular force emerged from the guerrilla bands; the army was making wide sweeps across the country to round them up and prevent them from combining. 'National service' men were again involved; like conscripts of other nations they were much less useful at this kind of work than professionals. As a rule the army seems to have behaved with restraint, the more easily preserved because it suffered scarcely any casualties; the police were much worse.[26] The special prisons where those considered incorrigible were incarcerated, or made away with, were probably as bad as any similar Nazi or Japanese establishments. As often in colonial wars, some of the worst crimes might be committed by native auxiliaries. The number killed in the fighting, or executed, was at least ten thousand, perhaps far more.

In earlier times this would have been the end of the matter. But the world was a different one now, and British statesmen could not be oblivious of the winds of change. To the fury of the settlers and their friends, there was concern in Britain at reports of what was happening, churchmen and many others were protesting, MPs visiting the country. Non-white members of the Commonwealth had to be taken into account, and Nehru, now Indian premier, was critical of the repression from the outset. By 1960 London was ready to think about independence, and at the end of 1963 this was granted. The new government headed by Jomo Kenyatta was conservative, its policies designed to benefit the propertied more than the poor who had done the fighting. Withdrawal could not stop with Kenya. The notion of an indefinite series of other such conflicts was uninviting. Just as Algeria compelled French withdrawal, real or nominal, from black Africa, Kenya compelled British.

It was the oldest empire in Africa, the Portuguese, that hung on longest, and, like its Spanish coeval in America and Asia, behaved worst as it neared its last gasp. Transition elsewhere in Africa helped to kindle aspirations in the Portuguese colonies. Angola rebelled in 1960, Guinea in 1963, Mozambique in 1964. By its obdurate rejection of any change Portugal was condemning itself to an ordeal shared by no other imperial nation, of having for a whole decade to fight three distinct colonial wars at once. Military preparedness for it was very scanty. Troops in Africa at the start were astonishingly few; African patience or inertia was regarded as inexhaustible. In quality they are not likely to have been much better than those described by a British officer in East Africa in the Great War as 'badly commanded, untrained, undisciplined and disorganized', along with African soldiers mostly 'just raw natives, impressed and given uniforms.'[27]

In the 1960s when large forces had to be put into the field Portugal would have been incapable of arming them had it not been for the benevolence of its allies, who tacitly allowed it to make use of munitions of all sorts, napalm among them, given it by NATO supposedly as part of Western defence against communism. Arms-manufacturers were happy to coin an extra penny out of the war, and by now their trade was one of the principal motors of the 'free world' economy. Bombing from the air could therefore be carried on *ad lib*; the navy too was in action, patrolling coasts and making dashes up rivers. Methods as well as weapons were being borrowed. Training in counter-insurgency drew on British experience in Malaya, defoliants were dropped on forest hide-outs as in Vietnam. Man-power Portugal had to find for itself. For a long time after the initial outbreaks the army hesitated to use black troops, until necessity obliged it to take the risk. In 1967 service for Portuguese conscripts was extended to four years, two of which had to be spent in Africa. Before the end of 1968 between 120,000 and 150,000 men, out of a total army strength of 180,000, were in Africa, vastly more than Britain ever required to garrison India. There was massive emigration from Portugal, largely of draft-evaders or deserters.[28]

Rebellion began in 1960 in the northern part of Angola, in a premature, chaotic fashion, closer akin to Mau-Mau than to the well-led movements in other parts of the third world. Barbaric attacks on white settlements and their African dependents, fearful reprisals by the settlers, left the insurgents by the close of the year quelled or in flight; the death-roll was estimated at 2000 whites and 50,000 Africans. Tribal frictions and rival leaders further weakened the cause. Of the three organized movements which took shape the one that posed in course of time a serious challenge to white rule was the MPLA. It was led by Agostinho Neto, one of the many intellectual men of action now being thrown up by colonial movements. He and his lieutenants were careful to disclaim any racial animosity against white men, and to insist that they were fighting only against imperialism. But after failure in the north in 1966 they had to shift to new, safer, but less promising terrain, in the dense eastern forests. A friendly neighbour, in this case Zambia, was a crucial factor as in the Algerian war. Tanzania was another well-wisher, and some equipment, most of it from communist countries, came in trucks, and then on men's heads, from the east coast two thousand miles away. Still, in 1970 only half the five thousand or so fighters had proper weapons, and they were cut off from the rest of the territory.[29]

In Portuguese Guinea, smallest and poorest of the three colonies, whose population of less than a million was an ethnic and linguistic mosaic, another outstanding intellectual came to the front, Amilcar Cabral, in 1956 one of six founder-members of the PAIGC party. This was revolutionary and Marxist in outlook, but distrustful of ideas like Che Guevara's that the first thing to do was to start an insurrection, somewhere or anywhere, and count on its attracting spontaneous support.[30] Several years were devoted to political preparation before armed action was initiated in 1963. As in Angola, there was much faith at first among volunteers in the protection of *mezinhas*, or fetishes; the leaders did not try to ban these, but left their men to learn by trial and error that 'the best *mezinha* is the trench'.[31] In 1966 their numbers were estimated at 6000, and by 1968 a mobile force, the nucleus of a small standing army, was getting into its stride. Arms and medical supplies were sought from other African countries and from outside the continent. Cabral was assassinated in mysterious circumstances in January 1973, but the struggle went on. By then airmen were no longer safe; low-flying planes and helicopters were being hit by ground-to-air missiles.

FRELIMO, the liberation movement of Mozambique, was formed by a meeting of several groups of exiles in Dar es Salaam in 1962. It was plagued by dissension, and like many others had to go through a process of shedding older, more conservative and tribalist leaders, who were supplanted by more modern-minded figures. It was from Tanganyika that the first raids came in 1964, across the northern border. Little by little the rebels were able to win control of a northern zone, and to push southward through the eastern uplands fringing Lake Nyasa (Malawi). They were trying to break out into other areas, while the Portuguese endeavoured to hem them in. Exploiting tribal grudges in a familiar imperial style, they were recruiting auxiliaries from among the Makua, who had old scores to pay off against the Makonde, backbone of the FRELIMO forces. Forcible resettlement under military supervision was being carried on urgently, on a massive scale.

By 1969 the insurgents were forcing their way down into the Tete region south of the lake, and threatening the huge Cabora Bassa dam being built on the Zambezi. Their armoury was steadily improving:

223

in 1973 powerful Soviet rocket-missiles were in use. Portuguese reactions became more and more brutal, a symptom of desperation. On 16 December 1972, the inhabitants of three villages were massacred at Wiriyamu. This was brought to light by Father Adrian Hastings, and other missionaries were making known abroad other atrocities, including the burning alive of the people of one whole village.[32] News was leaking out too, partly through disgusted Portuguese officers, about the sinister DGS, or security police, among whose methods torture ranked first. In spite of all such efforts, late in 1973 and early in 1974 determined guerrilla offensives were opened. It may have been pressure here, much more than in the other colonies, that brought the breaking-point of the imperial will.

On 24 April 1974, Caetano, who had succeeded the old dictator Salazar in 1968, was overthrown by a 'Movement of the Armed Forces', and General Spinola put in power. It was one of the very exceptional cases of an army bred by colonial warfare making an irruption into the politics of the metropolis in a progressive instead of reactionary direction. Spinola himself was no liberal, and had been heavy-handed enough while in Africa, but he was realistic enough to see the hopelessness of going on. Attempts were made to reach a compromise with the rebels, but it was too late, and at the end of July unconditional withdrawal was announced. It was received by the public with mixed feelings, but on balance with relief; within a very few years the empire was no more than a fading memory.

In November 1965, rather than tolerate any possible interference from Britain on behalf of the native majority, Rhodesia made its unilateral declaration of independence. Settler loyalty is always conditional on the assurance of a free hand with the natives. Africans everywhere contrasted Britain's readiness to use force against them, or against Asians, with its refusal to act now. All along, indeed, and very notably in the history of Kenya, the British lion showed a craven fear of asserting itself against recalcitrant settlers.[33] Ministers could not be sure of backing from public opinion at home, or rather could be sure of conservative opposition; since 1914 in Ulster, they could not count on the obedience of the officer corps.

A first spluttering of revolt came in 1966–7. Two African bodies, ZAPU and ZANU, were already in being; they kept at arm's length from each other, or at most joined in a very loose Patriotic Front, in spite of both moving towards acceptance more or less of Marxism – as all colonial movements that meant anything were by now virtually bound to do. From 1972 rebellion was taking on broader proportions, and securing advanced weaponry from outside. Zambia and after

1974 Mozambique both offered supply routes, and sanctuaries. Tactics resembled Algeria's. Considerable forces were mobilized, but they were kept for the most part in reserve, in the bush or across the borders, instead of risking battle on a bigger scale than harassing raids and skirmishes. Joshua Nkomo, leader of ZAPU, though not a Matabele had his main strength in the old Matabele region round Bulawayo. Robert Mugabe's ZANU was drawn mainly from the Shona majority, and seems in general to have done, as it claimed, more of the fighting. Of the two the Matabele had been far more a warrior people, and 'martial races' have sometimes, but not always, been in the vanguard of liberation movements. Defeat and loss of their arms may rob them of their old spirit, while previously more pacific peoples may be readier for new forms of struggle, which in modern conditions may have to be military but must be also political.

'The fascist terror and the striking power of the Rhodesian police cannot be overemphasized', an Indian observer wrote; it had been trained for years in counter-insurgency, on South African or European lines.[34] In September 1977 a 'Catholic Commission for Justice and Peace in Rhodesia' reported wholesale killing of suspects by the security forces. Religious and missionary feeling about colonial bloodshed was coming to be strikingly different from what it had been not long since, and it was not without weight. Increasing help had to be sought by the Smith regime from South Africa. White manpower was very limited, and there was draft-dodging, or emigration to avoid conscription, especially by the large non-British element. Some black auxiliaries had always been made use of, and now it was necessary, though risky, to add to their number by the conscription announced in January 1979.

But if the guerrillas were not winning the war, they were proving that their rulers could not win, and they were transforming the external situation. Liberal opinion abroad was hostile to the white regime; conservative opinion in Britain, though always very well disposed towards it, was perturbed by the danger of prolonged conflict bringing a further spread of communist influence in southern Africa. The upshot was that at the end of 1979 a very right-wing government in Britain had to compel Smith to abdicate and make way for free elections, which brought to office next year a coalition led by Robert Mugabe. It was left to South Africa to take over the torch and keep the flag of 'civilization' flying, and to go on fighting a similar war in Namibia. It too has perforce had to go in for training native troops to augment its manpower; whether this can be a success in today's altered Africa must be doubtful. In January 1979 the centenary of Isandhlwana was celebrated by Africans in London; doubtless it was remembered by many at home.

15

EPILOGUE

Even with the aid of machine-guns and high explosives, the total of deaths inflicted on Afro-Asia by Europe must have been trifling compared with the number inflicted on it by its own rulers, in Africa chiefly through wars, in Asia chiefly in crushing revolts. Nowhere was the brutality of power and possession more extreme than in bland Confucian China, or the destruction of life remotely so huge; the Taiping rebellion alone and its suppression in the mid-nineteenth century may have cost twenty to thirty million lives. Against the price of Western conquest has to be set the cessation it brought of old endemic bloodshed. Nevertheless, the loss of life in the ranks of the conquered must in sum have been very great, though impossible to compute. To it must be added the mass of native troops who perished in European service, from long before the time when, in Macaulay's mordant words, to enable Frederick the Great to rob a neighbour of a province in Europe 'black men fought on the coast of Coromandel, and red men scalped each other by the Great Lakes of North America.'[1]

Afro-Asia was helping to forge its own chains; on a more sanguine interpretation it was preparing, in a very roundabout way, for its eventual liberation, which had to begin with liberation from a great part of its own past. But when countries emerging from imperial rule resumed, or began for the first time, an independent existence, among their many predicaments might be a soldiery trained by the foreigner, dragons' teeth with a harvest of wars and army coups. In a minority of cases successful armed struggle for freedom had swept it away. Even then the outcome might be unfortunate. Dutch obduracy and Indonesia's political backwardness left a country encumbered with too many men in uniform, and a plethora of ambitious generals who in 1965 were responsible, along with religious venom, for a colossal massacre and inauguration of rule by military terror under foreign patronage. Too often armed forces have continued to be, in effect, what they were before, 'native troops', servants of a camouflaged Western ascendancy in return for armaments and other means of maintaining their power.

There have been uncomfortable legacies for the West too. If the Papacy was the ghost of the Roman empire, the British empire's is an apparatus of espionage and counter-insurgency techique for expertness in which, and willingness to sell tuition and arms to others, this country has a certain reputation.[2] Besides malign consequences for the third world, repercussions on political life at home may still have to be feared; imperial fevers have not yet had time to work their way out of Europe's system. The men now at the head of the armed forces in Britain came up by way of Kenya, Malaya, Oman, Cyprus and Ulster. In other shrinking empires too their practitioners have been coming back from the frontiers to positions of authority in the metropolis. One of the last acts of Giscard d'Estaing's right-wing presidency, in early 1981, was the appointment as head of the defence staff of a youngish general, Lacaze, born in Vietnam, wounded there, a specialist in military business combined with espionage. France's overseas intelligence organization has been credited with dozens of open or clandestine intrusions in former colonies and elsewhere in Africa. In January 1980 when there was an outbreak at Mecca, of all places, a team of French undercover advisers with 'anti-terrorist equipment' was on the spot as promptly as a jack-in-the-box. Empire armies were always polyglot, they are now in a new sense multi-national.

Nostalgia for glorious days gone by, among those who shared the glory, is very natural. One memoirist, who draws a very unattractive picture of army life in India, looks back all the same on the old British regiments as 'small but steadfast flames' lighting up the island's history.[3] In Evelyn Waugh's novel tall candlesticks lighting up a mess table 'commemorated the military history of the last century in silver palm trees and bowed silver savages.'[4] Sir John Fortescue closed his long line of volumes on the history of the British army with words of commiseration for a disconsolate Indian peasant of days to come, sadly remembering the British soldier who once gave him peace and protection. Such images, not entirely false but only very imperfectly focused on reality, could not easily drop out of Western conscious-ness, of ordinary folk as well as men at arms. When the drums beat again at Suez there was instant acclaim from a large section of the middle classes, jubilant at the lion still being able to roar when its tail was twisted; also from a good many workers, mostly of the older generation which grew up with the lion's roar in its ears. Vietnam and Algeria stirred similar French feeling, for much longer.

Division of British opinion over the crime of Suez was to a considerable extent between younger and older. A writer referred with some disapproval to 'the sense of guilt over Britain's imperial past which many young people seem to feel rather unthinkingly.'[5] It could take many forms; one was the 'sick humour' of a motto seen on the front of a young fellow's shirt in 1978, inviting the passer-by to join the army, visit exotic lands, get to know their fascinating people – 'and kill them'. In the main, what empire memories hold today is an attraction akin to that of story-books read in childhood. While the British empire stood immovably upright, its majestic posture could invite ridicule. A woman novelist, E. Arnot Robertson, wrote about a family accustomed to dying 'on all the best frontiers'. Now that those frontiers have disappeared, or are paced by other sentinels, dissolving shapes of the past take on a new life. Tales of the north-west frontier have the same appeal as the Wild West for Americans; an appeal for Americans as well, it would seem, as Sahara and Foreign Legion have had for English schoolboys. On this plane too the empires are merging into a common stock.

When the USA was occupying the Philippines its loudest imperialist, Senator Beveridge, visited the islands, and went on to China to consult British officers who were dealing with the Boxers on how native races could best be handled. 'I think', Colonel The O'Gorman replied, 'you must do nothing but fight them. When we are in a row with Orientals, that is what we do. They do not understand anything else.'[6] Since then it has often seemed as if America had taken The O'Gorman's advice very literally, and could not understand anything else. But it is far easier in our day than in the past, for any who wish, to enter into the feelings and thoughts of third-world rebels; so many of them now share Western knowledge as well as weapons, and have ideas to offer to the West. In April 1977 a Red Cross proposal to add to the Geneva Convention of 1949 the same protection for 'combatants' in colonial liberation struggles as for regular soldiers, was approved by a Diplomatic Conference on Humanitarian Law at Geneva, with a vote of 66 governments out of 86 (Britain abstaining). Aid has been given to these combatants by the World Council of Churches. Certainly most Churches have much leeway to make up, and much room for repentance and reparation.

Somewhere in the Scottish hills young Robert Louis Stevenson fell in with an old tramp who had been a soldier and lived through the frenzies of the Mutiny, and yet could tell him scarcely anything about it; everything had faded in his mind into a blur.[7] Men's collective memory of their past is not much better, and at times one must feel that this is as it should be. War of any sort is not much more than 'a series of errors and accidents', wrote the historian of the Peninsular War, who took part in it.[8] Its annals have more to tell us of man's nature than of anything else. Those of colonial war, in particular, leave us to wonder whether the conqueror's violence has been an authentic expression of human nature, or a derangement of it. They display frequent gallantry among the builders of empires, heroic devotion to duty, as well as much else, the same mixture of qualities we admire and are repelled by in the Romans. Victoria Crosses were never won easily. Far more still has been added to the record of human endurance by those who resisted or rebelled. As a symbol, such as mankind will always need, of indestructible courage, for our century Vietnam has become what Troy was for the ancient world, the Troy of Virgil that neither Diomed, nor Achilles lord of Larissa, nor ten years conquered, nor a thousand ships.

There are, after all, good reasons for prying into the past with the historian's telescope, and trying to see more clearly what happened, instead of being content with legend or fantasy. Of all reasons for an interest in the colonial wars of modern times the best is that they are still going on, openly or disguised. They have been besides a momentous part of a transformation of the earth, traumatic but epoch-making and irreversible; landmarks along the road mankind has been treading, as tortuous and perilous as any march of vanished regiments to Magdala or Mandalay, Samarkand or Timbuctoo.

NOTES

CHAPTER 1

1. W.Watts, *Memoirs of the Revolution in Bengal, Anno Dom.* 1757, p.161 (London, 1764).
2. Marx, *Eastern Question*, p.413.
3. Hibbert, *Wolfe*, pp.25-6.
4. Wintringham, pp.126-7.
5. Moyse-Bartlett, *Nolan*, p. 78.
6. Kaye, vol.1, pp.327-8.
7. Letter to Hobhouse, 3.10.1819.
8. Malcolm, vol.2, p.110.
9. Marx and Engels, *India*, pp.60,64 (Aug.1857).
10. Alfred de Vigny, *Servitude et Grandeur Militaires* (1835), Part 3, ch.1.

CHAPTER 2

1. Walmsley, pp.39-40.
2. MacBeth, p.153.
3. G.F.R.Henderson, pp.126, 130.
4. J.G.Lockhart, *Life of Sir Walter Scott* (1838), ch.42.
5. *The Book of Snobs* (1848), ch.10.
6. Dalhousie, p.350.
7. 'Naval and Military Promotion and Retirement' (1840), p.xxix.
8. W.Fleming, letter 15.4.1849.
9. G.R.Pearson, in *New Left Review*, no.9 (1961), p.63.
10. Welch Regiment Museum, Cardiff Castle.
11. Ryder, p.11.
12. L.Robertson, in *The Scotsman*, 4.6.1966.
13. James, p.464.
14. Hanham, p.161.
15. Pollock, p.26.
16. Stuart, vol.1, pp.69,73.
17. Waterfield, p.103.

18. Emery, p.143.
19. Foster, p.4.
20. Nicholson, pp.3, 4, 6-7.
21. Fleming, p.110.
22. Ryder, p.50.
23. Dunsterville, p.38.
24. Trotter, *Outram*, pp.154, 207-9.
25. Wetherall.
26. Auber, pp.582-3.
27. Pearson, Diary of 1824-25, pp.42, 71.
28. Stuart, vol.2, p.277.
29. Buckle, p.402.
30. Doveton, pp.1-2.
31. Duthie, p.47.
32. Trotter, *Outram*, p.89.
33. Backhouse, p.68 (8.5.1839).
34. Doveton, p.65.
35. Barat, pp.181-3.
36. Waterfield, p.107.
37. Dillon, pp.44-5.
38. Ségur, *Aide-de-Camp*, pp.358-60, 402.
39. Baddeley, p.129.
40. Walmsley, p.164.
41. Ségur, *Aide-de-Camp*, p.274.
42. Walmsley, pp.31, 51.
43. F.Garrido, *L'Espagne contemporaine* (Brussels, 1862), p.364.
44. *Anuario Estadístico de Espana* (Madrid, 1859), p.700.
45. Alatas, pp.101-2.
46. Alatas, p.26.
47. Roy, pp.319-21.
48. Cubitt, p.123.
49. Vagts, p.329.
50. Pennycuick, 7.12.1825.
51. Pughe, p.64.
52. M.Lewis, p.571.
53. Dalhousie, pp.224-6.
54. Ferrier, p.466.
55. Trotter, *Outram*, pp.47-8.
56. Ewart Papers: notes on Waziristan expedition,1894.
57. Fenwick, pp.45, 83.
58. Waterfield, App.E.(J.Ryder), pp.174-5.
59. D.H.Caldwell, *The Scottish Armoury* (Edinburgh, 1979), p.52.

60. Callwell, p.399; cf. p.376.
61. Buckle, pp.456, 459; Pearson, Letterbook, pp.29 ff.;Lehmann, *Smith*, pp.220-1.
62. Pasley, p.337.

CHAPTER 3

1. Anon., Notebook of 1817.
2. Pearson, Diary of 1824–25, pp.13–14.
3. *Ibid.*, pp.44, 50.
4. Foster, p.10.
5. Pearson, Diary of 1824–25, p.59.
6. Foster, p.10.
7. Sita Ram, p.71.
8. Lyall, p.320.
9. Waddington.
10. Stuart, vol.2, pp.124-5.
11. Lambrick, p.45.
12. Yapp, pp.527, 538.
13. Pughe, p.124.
14. Lyall, pp.323-4; cf. Trotter, *Hodson*, pp.21-3.
15. Pearson, Letterbook, pp.110-11.
16. Pughe, p.127.
17. Pearson, Letterbook, pp.125-6,132.
18. *Ibid.*, p.138; cf. Sita Ram, pp.141-2, and Lehmann, *Smith*, pp.214-15.
19. Pearson, Letterbook, pp.119, 132.
20. Ryder, pp.41-2; cf. Pearman, p.36.
21. Ryder, p.69.
22. Waterfield, p.78.
23. Pollard Papers, item 21; cf. Daly, pp.49-50.
24. Daly, p.26.
25. Buckle, pp.555-7.
26. Ryder, pp.127-30.
27. 'Subaltern', p.150.
28. Ryder, p.173.
29. 'Subaltern', p.154.
30. Ryder, p.176.
31. Dalhousie, p.57.

32. 24.3.1849; *Letters of Queen Victoria 1837–1861* (London, 1908), vol.2, pp.216-18.
33. Doveton, p.70; cf. p.305.
34. Capper, p.201.
35. Doveton, p.292.
36. Doveton, p.22.
37. Blackwood Papers, item 9.
38. Doveton, p.22.
39. Pennycuick, 16.2.1825.
40. Dalhousie, p.233.
41. Laurie, *Narrative*, pp.64, 82.
42. Dalhousie, pp.198, 226.
43. Laurie, *Narrative*, pp.91ff.
44. Dalhousie, p.203.
45. Dalhousie, p.283.
46. Trotter, *Hodson*, p.80.
47. Dalhousie, pp.101-2.
48. Pollard Papers, item 71: narrative of Adjutant C.Browne.
49. Trotter, *Outram*, p.147; cf. Malcolm, vol.2, pp.228ff.
50. Malleson, p.397.
51. Sherer, p.189.
52. Spiers, *Army*, p.135.
53. Roberts, p.145.
54. Trotter, Hodson, p.191.
55. Hibbert, *Mutiny*, p.310.
56. James, p.40.
57. Hibbert, *Mutiny*, p.372.
58. Cooper, p.111; cf. p.142.
59. Daly, p.157.
60. Callwell, p.80.
61. Stuart, vol.2, pp.172-3.
62. Trevelyan, p.242.
63. Mazumdar, p.153, 192ff.
64. N.Stewart, pp.49-50.
65. Marvin, p.32n.
66. Malleson, p.410.
67. Hira Lal, p.133.
68. Swindlehurst, 4.11.1919.
69. Swindlehurst, 22.10.1922.
70. Sita Ram, p.173.
71. Morris, p.82.
72. Steevens, p.356.

73. Count C.F.Vitzthum von Eckstaedt, *St Petersburg and London in the Years 1852–1864. Reminiscences* (English edn, London, 1887), vol.1, p.210.
74. A.T.Q. Stewart, p.107.
75. Burn, p.7.
76. Geary, pp.50ff.
77. Geary, pp.224, 237.
78. Crosthwaite, Preface; pp.13-14.
79. Pollard Papers, item 31 (late 1886).
80. Burn, p.6.
81. Burn, pp.12, 19.
82. Burn, pp.18-20.
83. Cole, p.378.
84. Crosthwaite, Preface.
85. Lambrick, p.61.
86. Prem Narain, p.232; cf. p.234.
87. Hira Lal, pp.192, 197.

CHAPTER 4

1. Baddeley, pp.297ff.,359.
2. Baddeley, p.340; cf. pp.271-3.
3. Baddeley, p.479.
4. Pennycuick, 9.4.1839.
5. Backhouse, p.56 (17.4.1839).
6. Pennycuick, 14.7.1839.
7. Pennycuick, 21.7.1839.
8. 'The Assault of Ghuznee', in *United Service Journal* (London), 1840, Part 1.
9. Trotter, *Outram*, pp.54-5.
10. Backhouse, p.133.
11. Dawes, 2.11.1840. Cf. Ferrier, p.131, ed.n.
12. Pughe, p.21.
13. Backhouse, pp.139-40. Cf. Sale, pp.221ff., 'The Retreat from Cabul'.
14. Backhouse, p.99.
15. Backhouse, p.232 (12.9.1842).
16. Pughe, pp.100-1.
17. Lambrick, p.317.
18. Hardy, 1.7.1857.

19. Mills, 8.2.1857, with account of the battle, and sketch.
20. Lambrick, pp.318-19.
21. Trotter, *Outram*, p.145.
22. See M.Cowling, 'War against Russia', in *Manchester Guardian*, 16.7.54.
23. Singhal, p.185.
24. A.Conan Doyle, *A Study in Scarlet* (1887), ch.1.
25. N.Stewart, pp.79-82.
26. Callwell, p.47.
27. Marvin, p.10.
28. Burnaby, p.96.
29. Durand, p.334.
30. Lyall, p.286.
31. Dalhousie, pp.222-3.
32. Pollard Papers, item 19.
33. Thorburn, p.68.
34. Andrew, p.54.
35. Martin, vol.2, p.94.
36. Callwell, pp.286, 321.
37. Spencer Papers, album of photographs with narrative.
38. O'Dwyer, pp.110ff., 132-4.
39. Spencer Papers, 'Some notes on Tibet Mission to Lhasa'.
40. Lamb, p.279.
41. Kawaguchi, pp.548, 551, 558.
42. Candler, pp.87, 90.
43. 'Pousse Cailloux', p.40.
44. Candler, pp.105ff. He was wounded in the fight.
45. Dilks, p.86. Younghusband admits that it was 'a terrible and ghastly business' (p.178). Cf.P.Fleming, p.151:'It was not a battle but a massacre.'
46. Spencer Papers, 'Tibet'.
47. *Ibid.*
48. Younghusband, p.228.
49. Gilbert, pp.17, 19.
50. Younghusband, p.419.
51. Rin-Chen Lha-Mo, *We Thibetans* (Madras, 1926), p.50.

CHAPTER 5

1. Campbell, vol.1, pp.269-70.

2. Cave, pp.93-4.
3. Campbell, vol.1, pp.316-17.
4. Cited by D.E.Sultana, *'The Siege of Malta' Rediscovered* (Edinburgh, 1977), p.33.
5. Castellane, vol.2, p.219; cf.Wolf, pp.217-18.
6. Castellane, vol.2, pp.143-4, 284-5.
7. Marshall, p.240.
8. B.H.Liddell Hart, 'Armies', in *New Cambridge Modern History* (1960), vol.10, pp.320-1.
9. D.F.Sarmiento, *Viajes ... 1845–1847* (1849), pp.218-19 (in Collected Works, vol.5).
10. Callwell, p.463.
11. Castellane, vol.2, p.13 (cf. pp.167-9).
12. Sarmiento, pp.206-7.
13. Walmsley, pp.246, 259ff.
14. Hardman, pp.4, 36, 61-2, 91.
15. Hardman, p.146; cf. p.175, and Engels, p.194.
16. Hardman, pp.274ff.
17. Atteridge, pp.308-9; Sir A.West, *Recollections 1832 to 1886* (London, 1899), p.384 (one-volume edn, London, n.d.).
18. N.Stewart, pp.112-13, 13?.
19. Smith, p.219.
20. Baird, p.151.
21. Strickland, 2.1.1899; 22.1.1899.
22. Malgeri, pp.292, 295.

CHAPTER 6

1. Marcus, p.22.
2. Atteridge, p.336.
3. Chirol, p.110.
4. I.Wilks, in Forde and Kaberry, pp.226-7. Cf. Turney-High, p.81.
5. Law, pp.124ff. Cf. Turney-High, p.250.
6. Burton, *Dahomey*, pp.160-1, 187, 260ff.; cf. pp.35, 50, 137.
7. J.Lombard, in Forde and Kaberry, pp.86-7.
8. Sibeko, p.23.
9. Kunene, pp.xxff.; cf. K.F.P.Otterbein, 'The Evolution of Zulu Warfare', in Bohannan. Cf. Turney-High, p.83.
10. Sibeko, pp.28-9.

11. Bailes, p.93.
12. Clammer, p.30.
13. Forbes, p.44.
14. Emery, pp.162, 198.
15. Emery, pp.127, 200.
16. W. Fleming, p.89.
17. W. Fleming, pp.93-4.
18. W. Fleming, pp.97-9; cf. Ransford, pp.192-4; Lehmann, *Smith*, pp.298ff.
19. Price, pp.182, 190.
20. Martin, p.158.
21. James, p.392.
22. Barclay, p.33.
23. James, p.354.
24. Ironside Papers: memoir by Col.R.Macleod, p.1.
25. *A Writer's Notebook* (1949; Harmondsworth edn, 1967), p.69.
26. Hardy Papers: Harold Hardy, 15.5.1901.
27. Spiers, *Haldane*, p.94.
28. Smuts, p.49; cf. Barclay, pp.27-8.
29. Smuts, p.72.
30. 'The Looker-on', in *Blackwood's Magazine*, Nov.1899, pp.716ff.
31. Kanya-Forstner, p.248.
32. Prem Narain, pp.250-1.
33. Gardner, pp.49, 144; cf. pp.128, 177; Plaatje, p.67.
34. Plaatje, pp.22, 34; cf. p.120.
35. Hardy Papers: Harold Hardy, 15.5.1901.
36. Bernhardi, p.44.
37. Charters, p.64.
38. W.S.Churchill, *My African Journey* (1908; London edn, 1972), p.118.
39. Livingstone, p.108.
40. Hibbert, *Wolfe*, pp.25, 28.
41. Emery, p.57.
42. King, p.208, cf. Lehmann, *Smith*, p.144.
43. King, p.138.
44. Livingstone, p.227n2 (29.9.1851).
45. Charters, pp.63-4.
46. King, p.171.
47. King, pp.255-6.
48. W. Fleming, p.15 (27.8.1846); pp.28-9 (13.11.1846).
49. W. Fleming, p.43 (2.2.1847).
50. W. Fleming, p.61 (16.9.1847); pp.65-6 (29.9.1847).

51. W. Fleming, pp.70-2 (20.11.1847).
52. W. Fleming, p.40 (24.1.1847).
53. W. Fleming, pp.80 (27.1.1848) and 87 (30.3.48).
54. Livingstone, pp.220, 236-7.
55. Connolly, vol.2, p.169.
56. W. Fleming, p.166 (5.7.1852).
57. King, p.145.
58. King, p.52.
59. King, pp.308, 311.
60. Emery, p.49.
61. Wills and Collingridge, p.26.
62. Galbraith, p.131.
63. F.C.Selous, in Wills and Collingridge, p.2.
64. Maj.P.W.Forbes, *ibid.*, pp.110-11.
65. Galbraith, p.307.
66. Loney, p.47.
67. Henderson Papers, pp.35, 234-5.
68. Ikime, pp.172-3.
69. Ikime, p.176.
70. Kanya-Forstner, p.87.
71. Kanya-Forstner, p.187.
72. Robinson, 'Partition', pp.600-1.
73. 'Judson and the Empire', in *Many Inventions* (1893).
74. Abshire and Samuels, p.64.
75. Summarized in Admiralty, *East Africa*, pp.211ff.; cf. p.86.
76. Rudin, pp.192-4.
77. Admiralty, *East Africa*, pp.200, 203.
78. German Colonial Office, Reply to England, p.176.
79. Ironside Papers: Macleod, pp.3, 45ff.

CHAPTER 7

1. A.P.Vayda, 'Maori Warfare', in Bohannan, p.359-61.
2. Pine, 30.4.1845.
3. Pine, 3. and 6.5.1845.
4. Pine, 8.5.1845. This shows Hulme was less foolhardy than Holt (p.86) thinks.
5. Milne, *Grey*, pp.126, 132-3. On Grey cf. Holt, pp.91ff.
6. D.Scott, pp.12, 27, 44.
7. Holt, p.228; cf. Turney-High, p.17.

8. See D.Scott.
9. Gordon, Preface.
10. Gordon, vol.1, pp.xvii-xviii.
11. Tarling, p.267.
12. Tarling, pp.137-8.
13. Roy, pp.198-221. On piracy cf. Tarling, pp.57ff., 63-4, 118-20, etc.
14. Roy, pp.327-34.
15. Hall, p.496.
16. Vlekke, pp.310-11.
17. Victoria, *Letters*, vol.3, p.427.
18. Hall, p.572; cf. Hodgkin, pp.158-9.
19. J.G.Scott.
20. Stead, p.10.

CHAPTER 8

1. D.Kincaid, p.204
2. See Clode, vol.2, pp.481ff.
3. Hunter, pp.245, 250-1.
4. For a fictional account, see Iltudus Prichard, *The Chronicles of Budgepore* (1870; reprint, Delhi, 1972), p.39.
5. Parry, p.358.
6. See Cunninghame-Graham.
7. Cubitt, pp.184,186; cf. Donghi, pp.87,97.
8. Foner, vol.2, pp.234-6, 252ff.
9. Callwell, p.132, citing Lt Barnes.
10. J.Costa Martínez, *Oligarquía y Caciquismo* (Madrid, 1903), pp.29-30.
11. Callwell, p.133 (Barnes); cf. p.143. On promotion from the ranks cf. Christiansen, p.37.
12. Denison, pp.261, 266.
13. Morton, p.133; cf. Denison, pp.19, 248, etc.
14. Dalhousie, p.351.
15. Hunter, pp.247-8.
16. Hunter, p.248.
17. Hunter, p.247.
18. Pomeroy, p.85.
19. J.D.Ross, ch.27.
20. Silva, p.31.

21. De Latre, reports of 14.3.1818, 27.3.1818.
22. Powell, pp.267-8.
23. Ludowyk, pp.45,47.
24. Harrison, p.185.
25. Vlekke, p.268.
26. See Wolfe, pp.211ff.
27. Mercer, p.99.
28. Binns, pp.218-21.
29. Gandhi, *An Autobiography* (English edn, London,1949), sections xxiv, xxv.
30. See Joshi, Part 3.
31. Goschen, pp.154, 294 ed.n.
32. See Steiger; Purcell.
33. Wu Yung, pp.25, 28, 36.
34. Kell, p.34.
35. Report of 29.6.1900, in *Parliamentary Papers*, Cmd 257; cf. *The Times*, 30.6.1900, p.11.
36. *The Times*, 28.7.1900, p.7.
37. N.Stewart, p.216.
38. N.Stewart, pp.231-2.
39. N.Stewart, pp.220, 342.

CHAPTER 9

1. Daly, p.40.
2. Bailes, pp.85, 87.
3. Downey, p.147; cf. p.155.
4. Upton, p.77.
5. Featherstone, p.154.
6. Wills and Collingridge, pp.247-9.
7. Callwell, pp.440-1.
8. Ellis, p.92.
9. Sanderson, pp.260-1.
10. M.Beer, *A History of British Socialism* (London, 1929), vol.2, p.264.
11. I.M.Lewis, p.52.
12. Callwell, p.438.
13. Prendergast, p.94.
14. Emery, p.142.
15. Durand, p.330.

16. Andrew, App.3: lecture by D.Ross, of the railway staff.
17. Theobald, *Mahdiya*, p.217.
18. Witte, p.74.
19. A.Marsden, 'Britain and the End of the Tunis Treaties 1894–1897' (*English Historical Review* Supplement, no.1, 1965).
20. Emery, pp.55, 58; cf. King, pp.37-8, on 'civilized cruelty' to draught animals.
21. Strickland, 2.2.1899.
22. Sir Evelyn Baring to Foreign Office, tel., 28.11.1883 (F.O.97. 493, P.R.O.)
23. Hansard, vol.288, May-June 1884, col.657.
24. Hibbert, *Mutiny*, p.172.
25. Hardman, p.188; cf. pp.194-6.
26. Pearman, p.77.
27. Sita Ram, pp.37-8.
28. Maude, vol.1, p.138.
29. Gibb, p.46.
30. Cunninghame-Graham, p.125.
31. Waterfield, p.111; cf. Cooper, pp.15-16; Fenwick, p.66.
32. Campbell, vol.1, pp.50-1; vol.2, p.176.
33. Ironside Papers: Macleod, p.16.
34. Marshall, pp.77-8.
35. *Peter Simple* (1834); cf. E.Howard, *Rattlin the Reefer* (1836), vol.2, chs. 9,10.
36. Pughe Papers, Introd., p.xviii.
37. Pennycuick, 2.12.1825.
38. McNeill, p.266.
39. 'Subaltern', p.100.
40. Burroughs, p.8.
41. Woodham-Smith, p.300.
42. Burn, pp.20, 32.
43. Pine, 11.8.1847.
44. Harries-Jenkins, p.103.
45. Bond, *Staff College*, p.130.
46. On prize-money regulations in the 1860s, see Clode, vol.2, pp.291-7.
47. Magnus, pp.306-7.
48. Gillard, p.23.
49. Pearson, Letterbook, 16.9.1845.
50. Mason, p.191. On officers' grievances cf.Stuart, p.266.
51. Wale, p.83.
52. Woodham-Smith, p.403.

53. 'Subaltern', p.32.
54. Backhouse, pp.159-60.
55. Roberts, p.128.
56. Spiers, *Army*, p.23.
57. N.Stewart, pp.85, 90-1; cf. p.378.
58. N.Stewart, pp.254-5.
59. Pearson, Letterbook, 19.12.1845, 29.1.1846.
60. Martin, vol.2, p.80.
61. Milne, *Epistles*, p.20.
62. Magnus, p.92.
63. Strickland, 7.3.1906.
64. Pughe Papers, Introd., p.xii.
65. Prendergast, p.76.
66. G.F.R.Henderson, p.270.
67. *Hired to Kill* (London, 1960).
68. Marshall, pp.94, 99.
69. Pughe, p.167.
70. 'Subaltern', p.68 (1848).
71. Riddell, pp.11, 21, 44.
72. Fenwick, p.xiii.
73. This passage owes much to the guidance of Professor Erickson, of Edinburgh University.
74. N.Stewart, pp.388-9.
75. Colvin, pp.171-2; cf. Magnus, p.58.
76. Sanderson, p.197.
77. W.O., *French Army*, pp.71-3, 114-15.
78. Ingold, pp.3,9.
79. Sanderson, p.223; I.M.Lewis, p.212n.
80. Burroughs, p.30.
81. Cobden, *Tour*, 3.1.1847.
82. Russell, p.50.
83. W.O., *Somaliland*, p.24.
84. Admiralty, *East Africa*, pp.28-113: 'Ethnography'.
85. Hansard, vol.253, June-July 1880, col.1424ff.; vol.256, Aug.-Sep. 1880, col.734.
86. Sardesai, p.275; cf. p.66. For an earlier Indian nationalist protest see Dadabhai Naoroji, *Poverty and Un-British Rule in India* (London, 1901), pp.360, 362, 522-6, etc.
87. Yapp, pp.341-3.
88. W.O., *Cost of wars*.
89. H.Thomas, *An Unfinished History of the World* (London, 1979), p.451.

90. Anon., *War Justified*, p.345n.
91. *Alan Quartermain* (1887), ch.6.
92. Bonner-Smith and Lumby, p.165; cf. p.168.
93. Geary, p.93.
94. Knight, p.438. On this campaign see also Keay.
95. Cave, pp.128-9.
96. W.O., *Somaliland*, p.23.
97. Barclay, p.30.
98. Jardine, pp.230-1.
99. Plaatje, p.127.
100. W.O., *Manual*, p.89.
101. Callwell, p.443.
102. Callwell, p.224.
103. Indian Army, *Afghan War*, p.7.
104. Jardine, p.104.

CHAPTER 10

1. Campbell, vol.1, pp.v-vii.
2. Anon., *War Justified*, p.200n.
3. Barooah, pp.83n, 85, 97.
4. Dalhousie, p.247.
5. Dalhousie, p.69.
6. Trotter, *Outram*, pp.90-1.
7. Alatas, pp.28-9.
8. In F.O.17.1059 (1885; P.R.O.).
9. Burn, p.54.
10. Strong, 15-16.9.1914.
11. 'Subaltern', p.93.
12. Dawes, 4.8.1839; 24.5.1840.
13. Mills, 15.2.1857.
14. Pearson, Letterbook, 25.2.1846.
15. W.Fleming, p.149.
16. Hibbert, *Mutiny*, p.187.
17. Castellane, vol.2, p.292.
18. Trooper F.G.Johnson, Imperial Yeomanry, in my mother's autograph-book, 16.2.1901.
19. D.Scott, p.96.
20. Doveton, p.155.
21. Swindlehurst, 14.12.1919.

22. Doveton, p.139.
23. Iglesias, p.6.
24. Dalhousie, p.255 (22.5.1853).
25. Pearman, pp.64-5.
26. Stuart, vol.1, pp.142, 307.
27. Lehmann, *Wolseley*, pp.106-7.
28. Hanham, p.159.
29. Sita Ram, p.24 and ed.n.14.
30. Stuart, vol.1, pp.141-2.
31. Hibbert, *Mutiny*, p.201.
32. Dilks, vol.2, p.85.
33. Gilbert, p.18.
34. Sanderson, p.307.
35. Jardine, pp.84-6.
36. German Colonial Office, Reply to England, p.262.
37. Wong, p.186.
38. *Blackwood's Magazine*, Dec.1834. See generally Best.
39. Calder, p.143; D.Scott, pp.34, 36.
40. Lehmann, *Smith*, pp.198-200, 274-5.
41. Underwood, p.89.
42. J.H.Morgan, p.62.
43. Bonner-Smith and Lumby, pp.50, 54-5.
44. Marx and Engels, *Colonialism*, p.115.
45. Callwell, p.40.
46. Cave, p.61.
47. Jardine, pp.56, 313.
48. *Natal Witness*, 30.1.1879. Lady Agnew kindly showed me a copy.
49. King, p.283.
50. Sanderson, p.187; Colvin, p.247.
51. Strickland, 23.2.1905.
52. King, p.149.
53. Underwood, p.91.
54. 'A Conference of the Powers', in *Many Inventions* (1893).
55. Malgeri, p.197.
56. Vagts, p.400; cf. Spiers, *Dum Dum*.
57. Major Broadfoot, 'British Bullets and the Peace Conference': *Blackwood's Magazine*, Sept.1899.
58. 'The Début of Bimbashi Joyce'.
59. Lecture of 1865, in *The Crown of Wild Olives*, section 84.
60. Magnus, p.143.
61. Sherer, p.125.

62. Yapp, p.549.
63. Sanderson, pp.152-3.
64. Sita Ram, p.73.
65. Yapp, p.302.
66. Dalhousie, p.414 (1858).
67. Callwell, p.82. Gwynn uses the word three times on pp.175-6.
68. Callwell, p.227.
69. Callwell, pp.229, 406.
70. Callwell, p.72.
71. Singhal, p.135.
72. Bonner-Smith and Lumby, p.182.
73. *Ibid.*, pp.244, 247.
74. *Ibid.*, p.103; cf. pp.202, 347.
75. Osborn, pp.9, 76.
76. Dalhousie, p.317.
77. Callwell, p.147.
78. Gordon, vol.1, p.410.
79. J. Finnemore, *Teddy Lester's Chums* (London, n.d.), p.187.
80. Callwell, pp.74,148.
81. P.Fleming, p.151.
82. Baddeley, pp.96-7.
83. German Colonial Office, Reply to England, p.12.
84. Baddeley, p.55.
85. Waddington, pp.8-9.
86. 'Subaltern', pp.110-11.
87. 'Subaltern', p.155; cf. p.152, and Pearman, p.103.
88. Magnus, p.151.
89. Hall, p.576.
90. King, p.266; cf. p.68.
91. 'The Exploitation of the Inferior Races', in F.W.Hirst *et al.*, *Liberalism and the Empire* (London, 1900), p.146.
92. 'Subaltern', pp.109, 119.
93. Pine, 28.5.1842, 31.7.1840.
94. Doveton, pp.86-7; Laurie, *Narrative*, pp.79, 122.
95. E.g., Ferrier, p.152, Ed.n.; cf Sita Ram, p.103.
96. Spencer Papers, 'Tibet'.
97. Wakeman, p.56.
98. Kanya-Forstner, p.272.
99. Lt J. Ouchterlony, *A Statistical Sketch of the Island of Chusan* (London, 1841).
100. Pennycuick, 8.2.1826.
101. Sleeman, p.xxxix.

102. Yapp, p.526.
103. Yapp, p.453.
104. Hibbert, *Mutiny*, pp.212, 344.
105. Roberts, p.81.
106. James, pp.108-9.
107. D.Scott, pp.23, 25-6, 32, 34.
108. *The Times*, 7.7.1900, p.7.
109. W.J.Oudendyk, *Ways and By-Ways in Diplomacy* (London, 1939), pp.103-4.
110. Campbell, vol.1, p.203; vol.2, p.84, etc.
111. Sanderson, pp.iii-iv, 205.
112. Milne, *Grey*, p.198.
113. Underhill, p.50.
114. C. Bolt, *Victorian Attitudes to Race* (London, 1971), p.83. On the use of martial law cf. Clode, vol.2, pp.492-7.
115. Hansard, vol.258, Feb.-Mar.1881, col.1652.
116. Maj. Sir J.Willoughby, in Wills and Collingridge, p.196.
117. Ironside Papers: Macleod, p.48.
118. Goschen, p.245.
119. N.Stewart, p.209.
120. J.D.Ross, ch.37.

CHAPTER 11

1. Ewart, pp.47-8.
2. Pennycuick, 16.2.1826.
3. Dilks, vol.2, pp.99-100.
4. Forbes, pp.353-4.
5. Emery, p.101.
6. Milne, *Epistles*.
7. Smailes, p.81.
8. Malgeri, p.277.
9. Trevelyan, pp.38ff.
10. Sherer, p.165.
11. Cowan, p.405.
12. Yapp, p.521.
13. Banno, p.252n.
14. Hansard, vol.260, Mar.-May 1881, col.1842ff.
15. Steevens, p.252.
16. Cobden, *Tour*, 11.8.1846.

17. Hallam Tennyson, *Alfred Lord Tennyson* (London, 1897), vol.1, p.474.
18. F.Engels and Paul and Laura Lafargue, *Correspondence*, vol.1 (Moscow, 1959), p.280.
19. A.Mangin, 'Aventures lointaines', in *Économiste Français*, 1885, vol.2, pp.166ff.
20. Malgeri, pp.17, 34-5; Jemolo, p.111.
21. Iglesias, pp.13-14; cf. Hardman, p.92.
22. Billington, p.508.
23. Kincaid, p.180.
24. Hall Caine, *The White Prophet* (London, 1909), vol.2, p.213.
25. Gilbert, p.21.
26. C.Harvie, in J.Calder, ed., *Stevenson and Victorian Scotland* (Edinburgh, 1981), p.112.
27. R.L.Stevenson, pp.226 (12.7.1893), 234-5 (Sep.1893).
28. Malgeri, pp.267-8.
29. Maude, vol.1, p.69.
30. Tolstoy, pp.210, 226, 327.
31. Schuyler, vol.2, pp.220, 226, 386.
32. Castellane, vol.2, p.109.
33. Kanya-Forstner, pp.8-9; cf. Hermassi, pp.126-7.
34. Karl Liebknecht, *Militarism and Anti-Militarism* (1907; English edn, Cambridge, 1973), p.29.
35. Roberts, pp.51, 75.
36. E.T.S.Dugdale, *Maurice de Bunsen* (London, 1934), p.118.
37. Fitzmaurice, vol.2, pp.315-16.
38. Hansard, vol.260, Mar.-May 1881, col. 1424ff.
39. Dilks, vol.2, pp.114-16, 125.
40. Hardie, pp.25-7, 47, 56.
41. Malcolm, vol.2, pp.31-2.
42. Singhal, p.164.
43. Younghusband, p.150.
44. Hamer, p.91.
45. Spiers, *Army*, p.227.
46. 'Pousse Cailloux', p.23.
47. Younghusband, p.133.
48. Clode, vol.2, pp.92-3.
49. Hamer, pp.157, 200.
50. A.T.Q.Stewart, p.174.
51. Blunt, *Secret History*, p.265.
52. Osburn, p.219.
53. C.Harvie, *The Lights of Liberalism* (London, 1976), p.237.

NOTES

CHAPTER 12

1. Osborn, p.87.
2. M.J.Bau, *Foreign Relations of China* (London, 1922), p.123.
3. Steevens, p.257.
4. Spiers, *Haldane*, pp.70, 72.
5. Hamer, p.25.
6. Wells, p.12.
7. Kanya-Forstner, p.9.
8. P.S.Reinsch, *Colonial Administration* (New York, 1905), p.394.
9. Cited by Osburn, pp.124-5.
10. Upton, p.302.
11. G.F.R.Henderson, p.102.
12. Johnstone, p.210.
13. G.F.R.Henderson, p.64; cf. p.54.
14. Harries-Jenkins, p.196.
15. James, pp.346-7; cf. Callwell, p.278.
16. Ellis, p.90.
17. J.H.Morgan, pp.66-7.
18. Bernhardi, pp.90, 146; cf. p.131, and Davis, ch.4.
19. Rothwell, pp.39-43.
20. Wedgwood Papers, letter of 27.9.1916.
21. J.D. Hargreaves, *The End of Colonial Rule in West Africa* (Hist. Ass., 1976), p.14.
22. Crowder, pp.114-15, 146-9.
23. Ingold, pp.97-8.
24. See Kiernan, pp.30-1.
25. Ewart, p.91.
26. Allen Papers: Great War diary, pp.29-30.
27. H.V.Lewis, 26.10.1914, 29.6.1915; cf. a tribute to the Indian troops by Mason, p.413.
28. Henderson Papers, pp.117-20.
29. H.V.Lewis, 1.9.1914.
30. Indian Army, *Afghan War*, p.11; cf. H.V.Lewis, article on the 129th Baluchis.
31. Dickinson Papers: Court of Enquiry report.
32. Brown, narrative by him and his wife, ch.5; cf. Dickinson's account (he was then a police cadet), pp.15-16.
33. Dickinson's account, pp.19-20, with police narrative and photographs.
34. Smuts, pp.155-7.
35. Smuts, p.158.

36. Maxwell-Smith, pp.4,7.
37. Strong, 19.12.1914.
38. Kellie, p.15; cf. memorandum by Gen.H.L.Smith-Dorrien, 1.12.1915, Secret, in Ewart Papers, vol. of miscellany.
39. Northey, pp.243, 279.
40. Northey, pp.68-9, with translation.
41. Ewart Papers, miscellany, Intelligence report of 1916 with alleged circular of 13.10.1913.
42. Lettow-Vorbeck, pp.33, 82.
43. H.V.Lewis, scrapbook, a press report; Northey, pp.96, 128.
44. H.V.Lewis, 18.8.1916; 10.5.1916.
45. H.V.Lewis, 2.4.1916; 26.12.1916; 10.5.1916.
46. H.V.Lewis, scrapbook, undated article.
47. Dolbey, pp.49-50.
48. German Colonial Office, Reply to France, pp.33-4.
49. S.E.Katzenellenbogen, 'Southern Africa and the War of 1914-18', in M.R.D.Foot, ed., *War and Society* (London,1973), p.117.

CHAPTER 13

1. Milner, p.112.
2. B.Crick, *George Orwell. A Life* (London, 1980), pp.81, 83-4.
3. *Autobiography*, p.70.
4. Gwynn, p.61. See generally Fein.
5. M.H.L.Morgan, pp.3,5,6.
6. Indian Army, *Afghan War*, pp.14, 51.
7. Nehru, p.87. See on the rising Gwynn, ch.5.
8. J.Morris, *Hired to Kill* (London, 1960), p.66.
9. Indian Army, *Afghan War*, pp.7, 22-3.
10. *Ibid.*, pp.133, 135.
11. Prendergast, p.61.
12. Prendergast, pp.42, 46.
13. Prendergast, p.89.
14. Chawla, p.3.
15. Zetland, p.202.
16. Chawla, p.60.
17. Indian Army, *Afghan War*, pp.17, 65-6, 134; cf. Dunsterville, pp.15, 313.
18. Northey, pp.144-5, 148.

19. A.Bryant, ed., *The Alanbrooke War Diaries 1943–1946* (1959; London edn, 1965), pp.373-4.
20. Skoulding Papers.
21. Jardine, p.272.
22. Jardine, pp.278-80.
23. Russell, p.57.
24. H.V.Lewis, 10.10.1919; 29.2.1920.
25. Nehru, *Glimpses of World History* (Allahabad 1934), p.379.
26. Simmons, notebook of 'RAF Memories' (no paging). On air-power in Iraq and elsewhere cf. Ivelaw-Chapman.
27. Mackie, pp.1-2.
28. Gwynn, p.70. On the events see Mansfield, pp.222-7.
29. Townson, p.8.
30. Mackie, pp.3-4.
31. Gwynn, p.169.
32. Gwynn, pp.299-300.
33. F.Stevenson, diary, 9.3.1934.
34. Crick, *op.cit.*, p.251.
35. Osburn, p.200.
36. Robertson, p.122; cf.168.
37. W.Guttmann,*Observer*, 22.10.1972, p.38.
38. *New Cambridge Modern History*, vol.12 (1960), pp.267-8.
39. Robertson, p.122.
40. Payne, pp.154-5.
41. R.de la Cierva y de Hoces, in R.Carr, ed., *The Republic and the Civil War in Spain* (London, 1971), pp.198-9.
42. H.Thomas, *The Spanish Civil War* (London, 1961), p.349.
43. A reminiscence of my friend the late Edinburgh city councillor Donald Renton.
44. Templewood, pp.37, 51-2.
45. Yeats-Brown, p.13.
46. Prendergast, pp.227-8.
47. C.Sykes, *Troubled Loyalty* (London, 1968), ch.14.
48. Lloyd-Jones, p.241.
49. D.H.Barber, p.48.
50. Lloyd-Jones, p.106.
51. G.A.Shepperson, in *Journal of American Studies*, Apr.1980, pp.52-3.
52. Smuts, p.406.

CHAPTER 14

1. Dunsterville, p.11.
2. Callwell, p.250.
3. R.Butwell, *Southeast Asia Today – and Tomorrow* (revised edn, London, 1969), pp.173-4.
4. Caldwell, *Ten Years*, p.37; cf. Shaplen, pp.50ff.
5. Gellhorn, pp.184ff.
6. R.T.Hitt, *Cannibal Valley* (1962; London edn, 1969), pp.158ff.
7. Margesson, p.75.
8. This has been alleged by a Conservative MP, J.Aitkin; see D.Leigh, *Guardian*, 23.2.1981.
9. See Halliday.
10. Margesson, p.67.
11. *United Services and Empire Review*, Oct.1953.
12. Reveille, vol.29, no.7 (1956).
13. Warbey, p.25.
14. Giap, p.43.
15. Riesen, p.43.
16. Giap, pp.107, 130.
17. Gorce, pp.394, 401-3, 412.
18. Thompson and Adloff, p.233; cf. Scholl-Latour, p.61.
19. Fanon, pp.24ff.
20. A.Werth, *Scotsman*, 31.7.1959.
21. Fanon, p.162.
22. O'Ballance, p.111.
23. C.Brasher, *Observer*, 30.7.1961.
24. Fanon, pp.51, 142.
25. Koinange, pp.62-3.
26. See Clayton; for some episodes from an African novelist's viewpoint, Ngugi wa Thiong'o, *Petals of Blood* (London, 1977).
27. Northey, pp.279, 292.
28. Da Ponte, p.26.
29. Davidson, *Angola*, p.270.
30. Davidson, *Guinée*, p.57.
31. Cabral, p.129; cf. p.116.
32. Father Hastings, *Observer*, 26.8.1973; cf. *Guardian* editorial, 8.8.1973.
33. See on this R.Robinson, 'The Moral Disarmament of African Empire 1919-1947', in N.Hillmer and P.Wigley, eds., *The First British Commonwealth* (London, 1980).
34. Gupta, pp.236-7.

CHAPTER 15

1. Essay on 'Frederick the Great' (1842).
2. See e.g., N.Davies, *Guardian*, 5.5.1980.
3. G.Foster, *Indian File* (1960; London edn, 1964), p.7.
4. E.Waugh, *Men at Arms* (1952; Harmondsworth edn, 1964), p.53.
5. T.R.Fyvel, *Intellectuals Today* (London, 1968), p.178.
6. C.G.Bowers, *Beveridge and the Progressive Era* (New York, 1932), p.109.
7. 'Beggars', in *Across the Plains* (London, 1892).
8 W.F.P.Napier, *History of the Peninsular War* (London, 1813), vol.3, p.519.

BIBLIOGRAPHY

This reading-list includes only materials drawn on, and makes no attempt at completeness. Asterisks indicate unpublished sources, chiefly in the National Army Museum (NAM) and Imperial War Museum (IWM). I am grateful to the staffs of all the libraries I have worked in, and in particular of these two and of Edinburgh University.

Abshire, D.M., and Samuels, M.A., *Portuguese Africa. A Handbook* (London, 1969).

Admiralty War Staff, Intelligence Division, *A Handbook of German East Africa* (Jan. 1916).

Alatas, Syed Hussein, *The Myth of the Lazy Native* (London, 1977).

*Allen, Wing-Commander D.L.: Papers (IWM).

Anderson, Olive, *A Liberal State at War. English Politics and Economics during the Crimean War* (London, 1967).

Andrew, W.P., *Our Scientific Frontier* (London, 1880).

*Anon.: Diaries and papers, including India and Burma, 1817–24 (NAM, 6807/337).

Anon., *Filipinas. Problema fundamental, Por un Espanol* (Madrid, 1891).

Anon., *War Justified: An Appeal to Scripture and Common Sense, by a Lover of Peace* (London, 1869).

*Arora, Abnash Chander, *British Policy towards the Punjab States 1858–1905* (Ph.D. Thesis, Panjabi Univ., Patiala, 1975).

Atanda, J.A., *The New Oyo Empire. Indirect Rule and Change in Western Nigeria 1894–1934* (London, 1973).

Atteridge, A.H., *Famous Modern Battles* (1911; London edn, 1913).

Auber, P., *An Analysis of the Constitution of the East-India Company* (London, 1826).

*Backhouse, Capt. J.E.: Journal, 1838–42 (NAM).

Baddeley, J.F., *The Russian Conquest of the Caucasus* (London, 1908).

Bailes, H., 'Technology and Imperialism: a Case Study of the Victorian Army in Africa' (*Victorian Studies*, autumn 1980).

Baker, V., *Clouds in the East* (London, 1876).

Banno, Masataka, *China and the West 1858–1861* (Harvard, 1964).

Barat, Amiya, *The Bengal Native Infantry. Its Organisation and Discipline 1796–1852* (Calcutta, 1962).

Barber, D.H., *Africans in Khaki* (London, 1948).

Barber, N., *The War of the Running Dogs. How Malaya Defeated the Communist Guerillas 1948–60* (1971; London edn, 1972).

Barclay, G.St.J., *The Empire is Marching* (London, 1976).

Barooah, N.K., *David Scott in North and East India 1802–1831* (Delhi, 1970).

Becker, P., *Path of Blood. The Rise and Conquests of Mzilikazi* (1962; Harmondsworth edn, 1979).

Bernhardi, F.von, *Germany and the Next War* (1911; English edn, London, 1918).

Best, G., *Humanity in Warfare. The Modern History of the International Law of Armed Conflicts* (London, 1980).

Best, G., and Wheatcroft, A., eds., *War, Economy and the Military Mind* (London, 1976).

Billington, J.H., *Fire in the Minds of Men. Origins of the Revolutionary Faith* (London, 1980).

Binns, C.T., *Dinuzulu. The Death of the House of Shaka* (London, 1968).

Bishop, E., *Better to Die. The Story of the Gurkhas* (1976; London edn, 1977).

*Blackwood Papers (Institute of South Asian Studies, Cambridge): G.F.Blackwood, Indian army, from 1857.

Blunt, Wilfrid Scawen, *The Secret History of the Occupation of Egypt* (London, 1907).

Blunt, Wilfrid Scawen, *My Diaries* (1919–20; London edn, 1932).

Boca, A.del, *The Ethiopian War 1935–1941* (1965; English edn, Univ. of Chicago, 1969).

Bohannan, P., ed., *Law and Warfare. Studies in the Anthropology of Conflict* (New York, 1967).

Bond, B., *The Victorian Army and the Staff College 1854–1914* (London, 1972).

Bonner-Smith, D., and Lumby, E.W.R., eds., *The Second China War 1856–1860* (Navy Records Society, vol.XCV, 1954).

*Brasted, H.V., *Irish Home Rule Politics and India 1873–1886* (Ph.D. Thesis, Edinburgh Univ., 1974).

*Brown, Maj. E.A. Narrative of the Singapore mutiny, 1915 (IWM).

*Bryant, G.J., *The East India Company and its Army 1600–1778* (Ph.D. Thesis, London Univ., 1975).

Buckle, Capt. E., *Memoir of the Services of the Bengal Artillery* (ed. J.W. Kaye, London, 1852).

*Burn, Lt-Gen. A.G.: Papers (IWM).

Burnaby, F., *A Ride to Khiva* (11th edn, London, 1877).

Burnes, Sir A., *Cabool: a Personal Narrative* (1841; Lahore edn, 1961).

Burroughs, P., 'The Human Cost of Imperial Defence in the Early Victorian Age' (*Victorian Studies*, autumn 1980).

Burton, Sir Richard F., *First Footsteps in East Africa* (1856; London edn, 1910).

Burton, Sir Richard F., A Mission to Gelele King of Dahome (1864; ed., C.W. Newbury, London, 1966).

Cabral, Amilcar, *Revolution in Guinea. An African People's Struggle* (London, 1969).

Caine, Hall, *The White Prophet* (London, 1909; illustrations by R. Caton Woodville).

Calder, A., *Revolutionary Empire. The Rise of the English-Speaking Empires from the Fifteenth Century to the 1780s* (London, 1981).

Caldwell, M., ed., *Ten Years' Military Terror in Indonesia* (Nottingham, 1975).

Caldwell, M., 'South East Asia from Depression to Re-Occupation' (*Sri Lanka Journal of the Humanities*, vol.2, no.2, 1976).

Callwell, Col. C.E., *Small Wars. Their Principles and Practice* (War Office, 3rd edn, 1906).

Campbell, Thomas, *Letters from the South* (London, 1837).

Candler, E., *The Unveiling of Lhasa* (London, 1905).

Castellane, Count P.de, *Military Life in Algeria* (London, 1853).

Cave, Capt. L.T., *The French in Africa* (London, 1859).

Chandler, D., 'The Abyssinian Adventure' (no.44 of BBC series, 'The British Empire', 1972).

Charters, Maj., 'Notices of the Cape and Southern Africa' (*United Service Journal*, 1840, Part 1).

*Chawla, Sandeep, *British Indian History and the Problem of Palestine 1917–40* (Ph.D. Thesis, Univ. of Delhi, 1981).

Chesneaux, J., *Contribution à l'histoire de la nation Vietnamienne* (Paris, 1955).

Chirol, Sir V., *India* (London, 1926).

Cholmondeley, R.H., ed., *The Heber Letters 1783–1832* (London, 1950).

Christiansen, E., *The Origins of Military Power in Spain 1800–1854* (London, 1967).

Clammer, D., *The Zulu War* (1973; London edn, 1975).

Clayton, A., *Counter-insurgency in Kenya; a study of military operations against Mau Mau* (Nairobi, 1976).

Clode, C.M., *The Military Forces of the Crown; their Administration and Government* (London, 1869).

*Cobden, Richard: Journal of a Tour of 1846–7 (BM).

Cole, Maj. D.H., *Imperial Military Geography* (1924; 9th edn, London, 1937).

Colquhoun, A.R., *The Truth about Tonquin* (London, 1884).

Colvin, Sir Auckland, *The Making of Modern Egypt* (1906; London edn, 1909).

Connolly, T.W.J., *The History of the Corps of Royal Sappers and Miners* (London, 1885).

Cooper, L., *Havelock* (London, 1957).

Cowan, R.M.W., *The Newspaper in Scotland ... 1815–1860* (Glasgow, 1946).

Crosthwaite, Sir C., *The Pacification of Burma* (London, 1912).

Crowder, M., *Revolt in Bussa* (London, 1973).

Crowe, Brig. J.H.V., *General Smuts' Campaign in East Africa* (London, 1918).

*Cubitt, D.J., *Lord Cochrane and the Chilean Navy, 1818–1823* (Ph.D. Thesis, Edinburgh Univ., 1974).

Cunninghame Graham, R.B., *José Antonio Páez* (London, 1929).

Dalhousie, Private Letters of the Marquess of, ed., J.G.A.Baird (Edinburgh, 1910).

Daly, Memoirs of General Sir Henry Dermot (London, 1905).

Daniell, D.S., *Cap of Honour. The Story of the Gloucestershire Regiment (the 28th/61st Foot) 1694–1950* (London, 1951).

Davidson, Basil, *The Liberation of Guiné* (Harmondsworth, 1969).

Davidson, Basil, *In the Eye of the Storm. Angola's People* (London, 1972).

Davies, R., *The Camel's Back. Service in the Rural Sudan* (London, 1957).

Davis, S.P., *Reservoirs of Men. A History of the Black Troops of French Africa* (Chambéry, 1934).

*Dawes, M.: Diaries, 1830–42 (NAM).

Denison, Lt-Col. G.T., *Soldiering in Canada. Recollections and Experiences* (London, 1900).

*Dickinson, A.H.: Papers relating to the Singapore mutiny, 1915 (IWM).

Dilks, D., *Curzon in India*, vol.2 (London, 1970).

Dilks, D., and Bridge, R., 'The Great Game' (no.48 of BBC series, 'The British Empire', 1972).

Diösy, A., *The New Far East* (London, 1898).

Dolbey, Capt. R.V., *Sketches of the East Africa Campaign* (London, 1918).

Donghi, T.H., 'Revolutionary Militarization in Buenos Aires 1806–1815' (*Past and Present*, no.40, 1968).

Doveton, Capt. F.B., *Reminiscences of the Burmese War, in 1824–5–6* (London, 1852).

Downes, Capt. W.D., *With the Nigerians in German East Africa* (London, 1919).

Downey, F., *Indian Wars of the U.S. Army (1776–1865)* (1962; 1964 edn, Derby, Connecticut).

Dunn, J.P., *Massacres of the Mountains. A History of the Indian Wars of the Far West 1815–1875* (1886; reprint, London, 1963).

Dunsterville, Gen. L.C., *The Adventures of Dunsterforce* (1920; London edn, 1932).

Durand, Col. A., *The Making of a Frontier* (1899; London edn, 1908).

*Duthie, J.L., *British Central Asian Policy 1856–1881* (Ph.D.Thesis, Glasgow Univ., 1976).

Emery, F., *The Red Soldier. Letters from the Zulu War, 1879* (London, 1977).

Engels, Frederick, 'The Moorish War, 1859–60' (in *Revolution in Spain*, collected articles by Marx and Engels, London, 1939).

Enloe, Cynthia H., *Ethnic Soldiers. State Security in Divided Societies* (Harmondsworth, 1980).

*Ewart, Maj.-Gen. Sir Richard: Papers (IWM).

Fanon, Franz, *A Dying Colonialism* (1959; English edn, New York, 1967).

Fein, Helen, *Imperial Crime and Punishment. The Massacre at Jallianwala Bagh and British Judgment, 1919–1920* (Honolulu, 1977).

Fenwick, K., ed., *Voice from the Ranks* (narrative of Timothy Gowing; London, 1954).

Ferrier, J.P., *Caravan Journeys and Wanderings in Persia, Afghanistan, Turkistan, and Beloochistan* (English translation, ed., H.D.Seymour, London, 1857; reprint, Karachi, 1976).

'Flaneur') Ten Years of Imperialism in France (Impressions of a (Edinburgh, 1862).

Firth, Raymond, *Human Types* (1938; revised edn, London, 1975).

Fitzmaurice, Lord Edmond, *The Life of Granville George Leveson Gower, Second Earl Granville* (3rd edn, London, 1905).

Fleming, P., *Bayonets to Lhasa* (London, 1961).

*Fleming, William: Letters (NAM).

Foner, P.S., *A History of Cuba and its relations with the United States*, vol.2, 1845–95 (New York, 1963).

Foot, M.R.D., ed., *War and Society* (London, 1973).

Forbes, Archibald, *Memories and Studies of War and Peace* (1895; London edn, 1896).

Forde, D., and Kaberry, P.M., eds., *West African Kingdoms in the Nineteenth Century* (London, 1967).

*Foster, Pte Edward: Diary, 1803–25 (NAM).

Fraser-Tytler, W.K., *Afghanistan. A Study of Political Developments in Central and Southern Asia* (1950; 3rd edn, revised by M.C.Gillett, London, 1967).

Galbraith, J.S., *Crown and Charter. The Early Years of the British South Africa Company* (Berkeley, 1974).

Gardner, B., *Mafeking. A Victorian Legend* (1966; London edn, 1968).

Garratt, G.T., *Mussolini's Roman Empire* (Harmondsworth, 1938).

Geary, G., *Burma after the Conquest* (London, 1886).

Gellhorn, Martha, *The Face of War, from Spain (1937) to Vietnam (1966)* (London edn, 1967).

German Colonial Office, *The Treatment of Native and Other Populations ... Answer to the English Blue Book of Aug. 1918* (Berlin, 1919).

German Colonial Office, *How Natives are Treated in German and in French Colonies ... A Reply to ... the Journal Officiel de la République Française ...* (Berlin, 1919).

Gettleman, M.E., ed., *Vietnam. History, Documents, and Opinions on a Major World Crisis* (1965; Harmondsworth edn, 1966).

Gibbs, Maj. H.R.K., *The Gurkha Soldier* (Calcutta, 1914).

Gilbert, M., *Servant of India ... Sir James Dunlop Smith* (London, 1966).

Gillard, D., *The Struggle for Asia 1828–1914. A Study in British Imperialism* (London, 1977).

Gopal, S., *Jawaharlal Nehru. A Biography*, vol.2 (London, 1979).

Gorce, P.-M. de la, *The French Army. A Military-Political History* (English edn, London, 1963).

Gordon, Sir A.H., *Letters and Notes written during the Disturbances in ... Fiji, 1876* (privately printed, Edinburgh, 1879).

Goschen, *The Diary of Edward* (1900–1914; ed., C.H.D.Howard, London, 1980).

Gupta, A., *Reporting Africa* (Delhi, 1969).

Gwynn, Maj.-Gen. Sir C.W., *Imperial Policing* (London, 1934).

Haggard, H.Rider, *Allan Quartermain* (London, 1887).

Hall, D.G.E., *A History of South-East Asia* (London, 1955).

Halliday, F., *Mercenaries: 'Counter-Insurgency' in the Gulf* (Nottingham, 1977).

Hamer, W.S., *The British Army. Civil-Military Relations 1885–1905* (Oxford, 1970).

Hamond, R.J., *Portugal in Africa 1815–1910* (Stanford, 1966).

Hanham, H.J., 'Religion and Nationality in the Mid-Victorian Army', in Foot, *War and Society*.

Hardie, F., *The Political Influence of the British Monarchy 1868–1952* (London, 1970).

Hardman, F., *The Spanish Campaign in Morocco* (Edinburgh, 1860).

*Hardy, John Brathwaite (and family): Papers (NAM).

Harries-Jenkins, G., *The Army in Victorian Society* (London, 1977).

Harrison, B., *South-East Asia. A Short History* (London, 1954).

Harvey, C., *The Lights of Liberalism . . . 1860–86* (London, 1877).

Hauner, M., ' . . . National Socialist Foreign Policy: Revolution and Subversion in the Islamic and Indian world', in Hirschfeld, G., and Kettenacker, L., eds., *"The Führer State": Myth and Reality* (Stuttgart, 1981).

Henderson, Col. G.F.R., *The Science of War* (London, 1905).

*Henderson, Lt-Col. K.H.: Papers (IWM).

Hermassi, E., 'Impérialisme et décadence politique au Maghreb', in A. Abdel-Malek, ed., *Sociologie de l'impérialisme* (Paris, 1971).

Herold, J.C., *Bonaparte in Egypt* (London, 1962).

Hibbert, C.R., *Wolfe at Quebec* (London, 1959).

Hibbert, C.R., *The Great Mutiny, India 1857* (1978; Harmondsworth edn, 1980).

Hobsbawm, E.J., *Bandits* (1969; Harmondsworth edn, 1972).

Hodgkin, T., *Vietnam: The Revolutionary Path* (London, 1981).

Holt, E., *The Strangest War. The Story of the Maori Wars 1860–1872* (London, 1962).

Hunter, Sir W.W., *Annals of Rural Bengal* (1868; 7th edn, London, 1897).

Iglesias y Barcones, T., 'Carta pastoral al ejército y armada' (Madrid, 1860).

Ikime, Obaro, *The Fall of Nigeria. The British Conquest* (London, 1977).

Indian Army H.Q., *The Third Afghan War 1919. Official Account* (Calcutta, 1926).

Ingold, Commandant F., *Les troupes noires au combat* (Paris, 1940).

*Ivelaw-Chapman, Air Chief Marshal Sir R.: Extracts from memoirs (IWM).

*Ironside, Lord: Papers (IWM).

James, D., *Lord Roberts* (London, 1954).

Jardine, D., *The Mad Mullah of Somaliland* (London, 1923).

Jemolo, A.C., *Church and State in Italy 1850–1950* (English edn, Oxford, 1960).

Johnstone, Capt. H.M., *A History of Tactics* (London, 1906).

Joshi, P.C., ed., *Rebellion 1857, a symposium* (Delhi, 1957).

Kanya-Forstner, A.S., *The Conquest of the Western Sudan. A Study in French Military Imperialism* (Cambridge, 1969).

Kawaguchi, Ekai, *Three Years in Thibet* (Madras, 1909).

Kaye, Sir J.W., *The Life and Correspondence of Maj.-Gen. Sir John Malcolm*, vol.1 (London, 1856).

Kaye, Sir J.W., *History of the Sepoy War in India* (London, 1965).

Keay, J., *The Gilgit Game. The Explorers of the Western Himalayas 1865–95* (Hamden, Connecticut, 1979).

*Kell, Maj.-Gen. Sir Vernon: Papers (IWM).

*Kellie, Lt-Col. G.J.D.: Papers (IWM).

Keltie, J.S., *The Partition of Africa* (London, 1893).

Kiernan, V.G., 'Colonial Africa and its Armies', in Bond, B., and Roy, I., eds., *War and Society*, vol.2 (London, 1977).

Kincaid, D., *British Social Life in India, 1608–1937* (1938; 2nd edn, London, 1973).

King, Capt. W.R., *Campaigning in Kaffirland ... 1851–2* (London, 1853).

Kipling, Rudyard, *Kim* (1901; London edn, 1944).

Knight, E.F., *Where Three Empires Meet* (London, 1895).

Knox, Maj.-Gen. Sir A., *With the Russian Army 1914–1917* (London, 1921).

Koinange, Mbiyu, *The People of Kenya Speak for Themselves* (Detroit, 1955).

Kolarz, W., *Russia and her Colonies* (London, 1952).

Krausse, A., *Russia in Central Asia 1858–1899* (London, 1899).

Kunene, Mazisi (translator), *Emperor Shaka the Great. A Zulu Epic* (Unesco, 1979).

Lamb, A., *Britain and Chinese Central Asia. The Road to Lhasa 1767 to 1905* (London, 1960).

Lambrick, H.T., *John Jacob of Jacobabad* (London, 1960).

Lanessan, J.L. de, *L'expansion coloniale de la France* (Paris, 1886).

*Latre, Col. de: Notebook in Ceylon, 1817–18 (NAM).

Laurie, W.F.B., *The Second Burmese War. A Narrative of the Operations at Rangoon in 1852* (London, 1853).

Laurie, W.F.B., *Our Burmese Wars and Relations with Burma* (London, 1880).

Law, R., 'Horses, Firearms, and Political Power in Pre-Colonial West Africa' (*Past and Present*, no.72, 1976).

Lehmann, J.H., *All Sir Garnet. A Life of Field-Marshal Lord Wolseley* (London, 1964).

Lehmann, J.H., *Remember You Are An Englishman. A Biography of Sir Harry Smith* (London, 1977).

Lermontov, Mikhail, *Selected Works* (Moscow, 1976).

Lettow-Vorbeck, Gen. P.E. von, *My Reminiscences of East Africa* (London, 1920).

*Lewis, Maj.-Gen. H.V.: Papers (IWM).

Lewis, I.M., *The Modern History of Somaliland. From Nation to State* (London, 1965).

Lewis, M., *The Navy of Britain. A Historical Portrait* (London, 1948).

Livingstone's Missionary Correspondence 1841–1856, ed., I. Schapera (London, 1961).

Lloyd-Jones, W., *KAR ... the origin and activities of the King's African Rifles* (London, 1926).

Loney, M., *Rhodesia. White Racism and Imperial Response* (Harmondsworth, 1975).

Ludowyk, E.F.C., *The Modern History of Ceylon* (London, 1966).

Lyall, Sir Alfred, *The Rise and Expansion of the British Dominion in India* (1894; 5th edn, London, 1910).

MacBeth, R.G., *The Making of the Canadian West* (1898; 2nd edn, Toronto, 1905).

*Mackie, Lt Donald McDonald: Papers (IWM).

McNeill, W.H., *Plagues and Peoples* (Oxford, 1977).

Magnus, P., *Kitchener. Portrait of an Imperialist* (1958; Harmondsworth edn, 1968).

Majumdar, R.C., *The Sepoy Mutiny and the Revolt of 1857* (2nd edn, Calcutta, 1963).

Malcolm, Maj.-Gen. Sir John, *The Political History of India from 1784 to 1823*, vol.2 (London, 1826).

Malgeri, F., *La Guerra Libica (1911–1912)* (Rome, 1970).

Malleson, Col. G.B., *The Indian Mutiny of 1857* (4th edn, London, 1892).

Mansfield, P., *The British in Egypt* (London, 1971).

Marcus, H.G., *The Life and Times of Menelik II. Ethiopia 1844–1933* (Oxford, 1975).

Margesson, Lt-Col. J., *A Short History of the Royal Regiments of Wales (24th/41st Foot)* (Cardiff, 1977).

Marshall, H., *Military Miscellany* (London, 1846).

Martin, R.G., *Lady Randolph Churchill. A Biography* (London, 1969–72).

Marvin, C., *The Russians at Merv and Herat, and their Power of Invading India* (London, 1883).

Marx, Karl, *The Eastern Question* (articles of 1853–56, ed., E.M. and E. Aveling, London, 1897).

Marx and Engels, *The First Indian War of Independence 1857–1859* (collected articles, Moscow, 1959).

Marx and Engels, *On Colonialism* (collected articles, Moscow, 1960).

Mason, Philip, *A Matter of Honour. An Account of the Indian Army* (1974; Harmondsworth edn, 1976).

Maude, A., *The Life of Tolstoy*, vol.1 (London, 1908).

Maxwell, Sir P.B., *Our Malay Conquests* (London, 1878).

*Maxwell-Smith, C.: Papers (IWM).

Mercer, C., *The Foreign Legion* (1964; London edn, 1966).

Miller, F.A., *Dmitree Miliutin and the Reform Era in Russia* (Vanderbilt Univ. Press, 1968).

*Mills, Surgeon John: Diaries, 1846-59 (NAM).

Milne, J., *The Romance of a Pro-Consul . . . Sir George Grey, K.C.B.* (1899; London edn, n.d. [1908]).

Milne, J., *The Epistles of Atkins* (London, n.d. [1902]).

Milner, Viscount, *Questions of the Hour* (London, 1923).

Miners, N.J., *The Nigerian Army 1956–1966* (London, 1971).

Morgan, J.H., ed. and trans., *'The German War Book. Being the Usages of War on Land' issued by the Great General Staff of the German Army* (London, 1915).

*Morgan, Lt-Col. M.H.L., 'The Truth about Amritsar' (IWM).

Morton, D., *The Last War Drum. The North West Campaign of 1885* (Toronto, 1972).

Moyse-Bartlett, Lt-Col. H., *The King's African Rifles* (Aldershot, 1956).

Moyse-Bartlett, Lt-Col. H., *Louis Edward Nolan and his influence on the British Cavalry* (London, 1971).

Narain, Prem, *Press and Politics in India 1885–1905* (Delhi, 1970).

Nehru, Jawaharlal, *An Autobiography* (London, 1936).

*Nicholson, Private J.: Letters, 1845–49 (NAM).

Nicolson, N., *Alex. The life of Field Marshal Earl Alexander of Tunis* (1973; London edn, 1976).

Nigam, N.K., *Delhi in 1857* (Delhi, 1957).

Norman, C.B., *Tonkin, France in the Far East* (London, 1884).

*Northey, Brig.-Gen. E.: Papers (IWM).

O'Ballance, E., *The Algerian Insurrection, 1954–62* (London, 1967).

O'Dwyer, Sir Michael, *India as I Knew It 1885–1925* (London, 1925).

Osborn, Capt. S., *The Past and Future of British Relations in China* (Edinburgh, 1860).

Osburn, Lt-Col. A., *Must England Lose India? (The Nemesis of Empire)* (London, 1930).

Parliamentary Papers, 1900, China No.3 (Cmd 257), *Correspondence Respecting the Insurrectionary Movement in China*.

Parry, J.H., *The Spanish Seaborne Empire* (London, 1966).

Pasley, Capt. C.W., *Essay on the Military Policy and Institutions of the British Empire* (3rd edn, London, 1811).

Payne, S.G., *Politics and the Military in Modern Spain* (Stanford, 1967).

Pearman's Memoirs, Sergeant, ed., Marquess of Anglesey (London, 1968).

*Pearson, Gen. T.T.H.: Papers (NAM).

*Pennycuick, Lt-Col. J.: Papers (NAM).

*Pine, Surgeon C.: Diaries (NAM).

Plaatje, The Boer War Diary of Sol. T. An African at Mafeking, ed., J.L. Comaroff (1973; London edn, 1976).

*Pollard, Charles: Papers (Institute of South Asian Studies, Cambridge).

Pollock, S., *Mutiny for the Cause* (London, 1969).

Pomeroy, W.J., *American Neo-Colonialism. Its Emergence in the Philippines and Asia* (New York, 1970).

Ponte, Bruno da, *The Last to Leave. Portuguese Colonialism in Africa* (London, 1974).

'Pousse Cailloux' (foot-slogger, infantryman), 'A Footnote' (Tibet, 1904), in 'Blackwood' Tales from the Outposts, vol.1 (Edinburgh, 1932).

Powell, G., *The Kandyan Wars. The British Army in Ceylon 1803–1818* (London, 1973).

Prendergast, Brig. J., *Prender's Progress. A Soldier in India, 1931–47* (London, 1979).

*Pughe, Maj.-Gen. J.R.: Autobiography, ed., Lt-Gen. Sir A.A. Bingley (NAM).

Purcell, V., *The Boxer Uprising. A Background Study* (Cambridge, 1963).

Ransford, O., *The Great Trek* (1972; London edn, 1974).

Rawlinson, Maj.-Gen. Sir H.C., *England and Russia in the East* (2nd edn, London, 1875).

*Riddell, J.W., 'The Army Life of an NCO in the Rifle Brigade 1907–1933' (IWM).

Riesen, R., *Le silence du ciel* (Paris, 1956).

Roberts, F. (later Lord), *Letters Written during the Indian Mutiny* (London, 1924).

Robertson, E.M., *Mussolini as Empire-Builder. Europe and Africa 1932–36* (London, 1977).

Ross, J.D., *Sixty Years: Life and Adventures in the Far East* (London, 1911).

Ross, O.C.D., *Spain and the War with Morocco* (London, 1860).

Rothwell, V., 'The British Government and Japanese Military Assistance 1914–18' (*History*, Feb. 1971).

Roy, J.-J.-E., ed., *Quinze ans de séjour à Java ... Souvenirs d'un ancien officier* (Tours, 1861).

Rudin, H.R., *Germans in the Cameroons 1884–1914. A Case Study in Modern Imperialism* (London, 1938).

*Russell, Maj. A.B.: Extracts from memoirs (IWM).

(Ryder, Corp. J.), *Four Years' Service in India. By a Private Soldier* (Leicester, 1853).

Sale, Lady (Florentia), *A Journal of the Disasters in Affghanistan, 1841–2* (London, 1843).

Sanderson, E., *Africa in the Nineteenth Century* (London, 1898).

Sardesai, D.R., *British Trade Expansion in Southeast Asia 1830–1914* (Delhi, 1977).

Sarmiento, D.F., *Viajes por Europa, Africa i América 1845–1847* (1849; *Obras*, vol.5, Paris, 1909).

Scholl-Latour, P., *Death in the Ricefields. Thirty Years of War in Indochina* (1979; English edn, London, 1981).

Schreiner, Olive, *Trooper Peter Halkett of Mashonaland* (London, 1897).

Schuyler, E., *Turkistan* (London, 1876).

Scott, D., *Ask That Mountain. The Story of Parihaka* (Auckland, 1975).

Scott, J.G., 'The Chinese Brave' (*Asiatic Quarterly*, 1886).

Ségur, Comte Philippe de, *La Campagne de Russie* (1824; Nelson edn, Paris, n.d.).

Ségur, Comte Philippe de, *Un Aide de Camp de Napoléon. De 1800 à 1812* (1873; Nelson edn, Paris, n.d.).

Shaplen, R., *Time out of Hand. Revolution and Reaction in Southeast Asia* (London, 1969).

Sherer, J.W., *Havelock's March on Cawnpore 1857. A Civilian's Notes* (collected articles, London, 1910).

Shibeika, Mekki, *British Policy in the Sudan 1882–1902* (Oxford, 1952).

Sibeko, A., 'An Epic of African Resistance' (Isandhlwana; *The African Communist*, no.76, London, 1979).

Sibley, Maj. J.R., *Tanganyika Guerrilla: East African Campaign 1914–18* (London, 1973).

Silva, K.M.de, 'The Kandyan Kingdom and the British – The Last Phase, 1796 to 1818', in Univ. of Ceylon, *History of Ceylon*, vol.3 (Peradeniya, 1973).

*Simmons, Flight-Lt A.: Diaries (IWM).

Sinclair, K., 'The Maori Challenge' (no.25 of BBC series, 'The British Empire', 1972).

Sinclair, K., *The Pelican History of New Zealand* (Harmondsworth, revised edn, 1980).

Singh, Hira Lal, *Problems and Policies of the British in India 1885–1898* (Bombay, 1963).

Singhal, D.P., *India and Afghanistan 1876–1907* (Univ. of Queensland Press, 1963).

Sita Ram, *From Sepoy to Subedar* (1873; ed., J. Lunt, London, 1970).

*Skoulding, Air Commodore F.A.: Papers (IWM).

Sleeman, Maj.-Gen. Sir W.H., *Journey through the Kingdom of Oude in 1849–50* (London, 1858).

Smailes, Helen, *Scottish Empire* (Edinburgh, 1981).

Smith, I.R., *The Emin Pasha Relief Expedition 1886–1890* (Oxford, 1972).

Smuts, J.C., *Jan Christian Smuts* (London, 1952).

*Spencer, Brig. F.E.: Papers (IWM).

Spiers, E.M., 'The Use of the Dum Dum Bullet in Colonial Warfare' (*Journal of Imperial and Commonwealth History*, 1975).

Spiers, E.M., *The Army and Society 1815–1914* (London, 1980).

Spiers, E.M., *Haldane: An Army Reformer* (Edinburgh, 1980).

*Stamp, C.A.: Papers (IWM).

Steevens, G.W., *In India* (London, 1899).

Steiger, G.N., *China and the Occident. The Origin and Development of the Boxer Movement* (Yale Univ. Press, 1927).

Stevenson, Lloyd George. A Diary by Frances, ed., A.J.P. Taylor (London, 1971).

Stevenson, Robert Louis, *Vailima Letters*, ed., S. Colvin (London, 1895).

Stewart, A.T.Q., *The Pagoda War. Lord Dufferin and the Fall of the Kingdom of Ava 1885–6* (London, 1972).

Stewart, Maj.-Gen. Sir N., *My Service Days. India, Afghanistan, Suakim '85, and China* (London, 1908).

*Strickland, Gen. Sir Peter: Diaries (IWM).

*Strong, Capt. F.E.K., R.N.: Papers (IWM).

Stuart, Col. W.K., *Reminiscences of a Soldier* (London, 1874).

Subaltern, Leaves from the Journal of a, during the Campaign in Punjaub Sept. 1848 to March 1849 (by D.A. Sandford; Edinburgh, 1849).

*Swindlehurst, Private J.P.: Diary, 1919–21 (IWM).

Tarling, N., *Sulu and Sabah* (Kuala Lumpur, 1978).

Templewood, Lord (Sir Samuel Hoare), *Ambassador on Special Mission* (London, 1946).

Theobald, M.D., *The Mahdiya. A History of the Anglo-Egyptian Sudan, 1881–1899* (London, 1951).

Theobald, M.D., *Ali Dinar, Last Sultan of Darfur 1898-1916* (London, 1965).

Thompson, V., and Adloff, R., *French West Africa* (London, 1958).

Thorburn, S.S., *Bannu; or Our Afghan Frontier* (London, 1876).

Tolstoy, Leo, *The Cossacks* (1863; English edn, Harmondsworth, 1960).

*Townson, Wing-Commander R.: Memoirs (IWM).

Trench, C. Chevenix, *Charley Gordon: An Eminent Victorian Reassessed* (London, 1978).

Trend, J.B., *Bolívar and the Independence of Spanish America* (London, 1946).

Trevelyan, G.O., *The Competition Wallah* (2nd edn, London, 1866).

Trotter, Capt. L.J., *The Life of Hodson of Hodson's Horse* (1901; London edn, 1906).

Trotter, Capt. L.J., *The Bayard of India: A Life of General Sir James Outram* (1903; London edn, 1909).

Turney-High, H.H., *Primitive War* (Univ. of S. Carolina Press, 1949).

Underhill, E.B., *The Tragedy of Morant Bay. A Narrative of the Disturbances in the Island of Jamaica in 1865* (London, 1895).

Underwood, F.M., *United Italy* (London, 1912).

Upton, Maj.-Gen. E., *The Armies of Asia and Europe* (New York, 1878).

Vámbéry, A., *History of Bokhara* (London, 1873).

Vlekke, B.H.M., *Nusantara. A History of the East Indian Archipelago* (Harvard Univ. Press, 1945).

*Waddington, Major Charles: Account of the battle of Meeanie (NAM).

Wakeman, F., *Strangers at the Gate. Social Disorder in South China, 1839–1861* (Univ. of California Press, 1966).

Wale, H.J., *Sword and Surplice; or, Thirty Years' Reminiscences of the Army and the Church* (London, 1880).

Walmsley, H.M., *Sketches of Algeria during the Kabyle War* (London, 1858).

*Wan Chi-hung, *Patriotism or Conciliation in Sino-British Relations, 1839–1848: Lin Tse-hsü and Ch'i Ying* (Ph.D. Thesis, Edinburgh Univ., 1978).

*War Office, 'Cost of Principal British Wars, 1857–1899' (Confidential print, 1902; copy in NAM).

War Office, *Handbook of the French Army* (1914 edn).

War Office, *Manual of Field Works (All Arms)* (1921).

War Office, *Military Report on British Somaliland*, vol.1 (1925).

Warbey, W., MP, *Vietnam: the Truth* (London, 1965).

Waterfield, The Memoirs of Private, ed., Swinson, A., and Scott, D. (London, 1968).

*Wedgwood, J.C. (Lord Barlaston): Papers (IWM).

Wells, H.G., *War and the Future. Italy, France and Britain at War* (London, 1917).

*Wetherall, Lt-Gen. F.A.: Memorial to H.M. Treasury, 1828 (NAM).

Wills, W.A., and Collingridge, L.T., eds., *The Downfall of Lobengula* (London, 1894).

Wilson, C.J., *The Story of the East African Mounted Rifles* (Nairobi, ?1938).

Wintringham, Tom, *Weapons and Tactics* (London, 1943).

Wolf, E.R., *Peasant Wars of the Twentieth Century* (1969; London edn, 1973).

Wong, J.W., *Yeh Ming-ch'en, Viceroy of Liang Kuang 1852–8* (Cambridge, 1976).

Woodham-Smith, C., *Florence Nightingale 1820–1910* (1951; Harmondsworth edn, 1955).

Wu Yung, *The Flight of an Empress*, ed., I. Pruitt (Yale Univ. Press, 1936).

Yapp, M.E., *Strategies of British India. Britain, Iran and Afghanistan 1798–1850* (Oxford, 1980).

Yeats-Brown, F., *Martial India* (London, 1945).

*Young, Maj. C.W.: Papers, China 1843 (NAM).

Younghusband, Sir F., *India and Thibet* (London, 1910).

Zetland, *'Essayez': the Memoirs of Lawrence, Second Marquess of* (London, 1956).

Addenda to the Booklist

Ellis, John, *The Social History of the Machine Gun* (London, 1975).
Featherstone, Donald, *Colonial Small Wars* (Newton Abbot, 1973).
'Loti, Pierre', *Le roman d'un Spahi* (Paris, 1881).

INDEX